Sex and Politics in South Africa

Sex and Politics in South Africa

edited by Neville Hoad, Karen Martin and Graeme Reid

DOUBLE
STOREY
a juta company

Contents

7   Foreword **Ruth Mompati**
8   The Editors and Contributors

14   Introduction **Neville Hoad**

PART 1: Sexuality and the liberation struggle

28   Fragments from the archives I **Graeme Reid**
34   ESSAY: Solidarity – with whom? The international gay and lesbian rights movement and apartheid **Jens Rydström**
50   PERSONAL TESTIMONY: A lesson well worth learning **Kevan Botha**
54   ARCHIVE: Notes for a speech at the 1986 ILGA world conference **Alfred Machela**
58   PERSONAL TESTIMONY: Where was I in the eighties? **Ann Smith**
64   ARCHIVE: Because I'm gay and I believe **Paul Mokgethi**
68   ARCHIVE: My life underground **Paddy Nhlapo**
72   INTERVIEW: If we can't dance to it, it's not our revolution **Julia Nicol**
86   ARCHIVE: Call for action, Rand Gay Organisation
88   ARCHIVE: Pamphlet, End Conscription Campaign
90   ARCHIVE: Published letters **Glen Shelton, Simon Nkoli**
92   ARCHIVE: Private letters **Ivan Toms, Edwin Cameron**
96   ARCHIVE: Photograph of Simon Nkoli and Ivan Toms
98   ESSAY: Cape Town activists remember sexuality struggles **Mikki van Zyl**
118   ESSAY: Homosexuality and the South African left: The ambiguities of exile **Gerald Kraak**
136   REBUTTAL: Mystifying history: The thing that goes bump in the night **Tim Trengove Jones**
140   ESSAY: The moment the ANC embraced gay rights **Peter Tatchell**
148   ARCHIVE: 'ANC dashes hopes for gay rights in SA' **Peter Tatchell**
149   ARCHIVE: Telex **Thabo Mbeki**
150   ARCHIVE: Address at Simon Nkoli's memorial service **Mosiuoa 'Terror' Lekota**

154   ARCHIVE: Letters from prison **Simon Nkoli**

158   ARCHIVE: Letter to Kevan Botha **Caroline Heaton-Nicholls**

164   ARCHIVE: Photographs of GLOW meeting

165   ARCHIVE: Photographs of Simon Nkoli's release-from-prison party

166   ARCHIVE: Address at Simon Nkoli's memorial service **Kevan Botha**

168   ARCHIVE: Simon Nkoli obituary **Zackie Achmat**

170   ARCHIVE: Cartoon, ''n Poefadder het my gepik'

Part 2: The Constitution

174   Fragments from the archives II **Graeme Reid**

178   ARCHIVE: Presentation to GLOW Action Committee and SHOC workshop
       Edwin Cameron

188   ESSAY: Engendering gay and lesbian rights: The Equality Clause in the
       South African Constitution **Jacklyn Cock**

210   ARCHIVE: Submission to the Convention for a Democratic South Africa
       The Equality Foundation

212   ARCHIVE: 'We must claim our citizenship' National Coalition for Gay
       and Lesbian Equality

222   ARCHIVE: Letter to the Constitutional Assembly **Archbishop Desmond Tutu**

223   The Equality Clause

224   Afterword **Bafana Mhlanga**

Part 3: Guide to GALA resources

228   Guide to the Gay and Lesbian Archives of South Africa **Anthony Manion**

253   List of Acronyms

254   Index

256   Acknowledgements

First published 2005 by Double Storey Books,
a division of Juta & Co. Ltd,
Mercury Crescent, Wetton, Cape Town

ISBN 1-77013-015-2

Edited by Helen Laurenson
Text design and layout by Jenny Sandler
Cover design by Michiel Botha
Cover photo by John Hogg
Printed by Paarl Print, Paarl

Foreword

In August 1987 I was interviewed by a British journalist, Peter Tatchell, in
the London offices of the African National Congress. It was an interview that
became unexpectedly controversial and placed me at the centre of a row over
the ANC's stance on sexual orientation. This was a much unexpected outcome
from my point of view. The occasion was South African Women's Day and the
interview revolved around the contribution of women to the ongoing liberation
struggle in South Africa. At that stage the ANC was banned in South Africa and
operating in exile.

At the end of the interview, as I was standing up to leave, the journalist unexpectedly asked me about the ANC's attitude to gays. I said that it was not a
problem in the organisation. Pressed to give an answer, I reiterated that the
ANC had no stand on the matter as it was not a problem within our organisation. I did not even know that it happened very often. I thought that it was a
European problem. And I must admit that I belong to the old school. I grew up
in a time when you did not interfere in the private lives of other people. Even in
the older days, when people chose that way of life it was their concern.

But times change and attitudes change. In 1992 the ANC adopted a Bill of
Rights which included 'sexual orientation' as a form of gender discrimination
which would not be tolerated in the new South Africa. This was enshrined in
South Africa's Constitution in 1996.

This book charts the history of that period. Looking back, I like to think that
the debate that was sparked by that interview had a positive outcome.

Dr RS Mompati
Office of the Mayor, Naledi Local Municipality
Vryburg, March 2005

The Editors and Contributors

EDITORS

Hoad **Neville**

Neville Hoad is an assistant professor of English at the University of Texas. He received a PhD in English and comparative literature from Columbia University, and has held post-doctoral fellowships at the University of Chicago. He has published articles on lesbian and gay politics in South Africa in *Development Update, Public Culture* and *GLQ: A Journal of Lesbian and Gay Studies*, and articles on the relationship of sexual identity politics to globalising neoliberalism in *Postcolonial Studies, Cultural Critique* and in edited anthologies. He is completing a book manuscript entitled *African Intimacies: Race, Homosexuality and Globalization in African Literature and History.*

Martin **Karen**

Karen Martin is a professional editor. She also does archival research from time to time, and was the archivist at the Gay and Lesbian Archives of South Africa (GALA) in its early days. She is the co-editor with Joanne Bloch of *Balancing Act: South African Gay and Lesbian Youth Speak Out* (2005), a collection of interviews. She has an honours degree in linguistics and a post-graduate diploma in African studies from the University of Cape Town.

Reid **Graeme**

Graeme Reid is a researcher in the Cultures of Sexuality and Power programme at the Wits Institute for Social and Economic Research (WISER), Johannesburg. He has an MA in social anthropology and is currently registered for a PhD at the Amsterdam School for Social Science Research, University of Amsterdam. His research proposes to understand the elaboration of gay lifestyles and their reception in South Africa in the context of broader debates about sexuality, culture and race. He has published articles and co-directed a video documentary on gay cultural identities in South Africa. He is one of the editors of *Refiguring the Archive* (2002), a co-author with Liz Walker of *Waiting to Happen: HIV/AIDS in South Africa* (2004) and co-editor with Liz Walker of *Men Behaving Differently: South African Men Since 1994* (2005).

CONTRIBUTORS

Achmat **Zackie**

Born in Johannesburg, Zackie Achmat was raised in a Muslim community in Cape Town. He was one of the leaders of the 1976 anti-apartheid school boycotts, and between 1976 and 1980 he was arrested and detained by the security police several times. After his release from prison in 1980 he worked underground for the banned African National Congress (ANC) to promote the ANC at a mass level. In 1994, Achmat initiated the National Coalition for Gay and Lesbian Equality and, as the chair of the Interim Executive Committee, saw it through its campaigns to ensure the retention of the Equality Clause in the Constitution. In 1990, Achmat discovered he was HIV-positive and began working with voluntary community organisations concerned with the growing AIDS crisis. In 1998, he co-founded the Treatment Action Campaign (TAC), an HIV/AIDS pressure group. He took a public stance of not taking anti-retroviral medication until it became available at an affordable price. He is currently chairperson of the TAC. His HIV/AIDS work has earned him several international awards and honorary degrees from South African universities. Achmat has also researched and directed a number of documentary films, including *Apostles of Civilised Vice*, a history of South African homosexuality, which was released in 1999.

Botha **Kevan**

Kevan Botha has been active in gay and lesbian politics in South Africa since the early 1980s, when he was a member of the Gay Association of South Africa (GASA). A lawyer by profession, Botha represented the Equality Foundation, a trust established to promote legal equality for lesbians and gay men in South Africa, at the Convention for Democracy in South Africa (CODESA), where he was responsible for making submissions in the interests of lesbian and gay equality. He then acted as parliamentary lobbyist for the National Coalition for Gay and Lesbian Equality (NCGLE).

Cameron **Edwin**

Edwin Cameron is a respected advocate of human rights. As professor of law at the University of the

8

Witwatersrand he helped to establish the AIDS Law Project in the Centre for Applied Legal Studies in 1991, was founding convenor of the non-governmental network, the AIDS Consortium, in 1992, and a leading figure in the National AIDS Convention of South Africa (NACOSA). He helped draft a charter of rights on HIV/AIDS. Cameron was influential in securing the inclusion of 'sexual orientation' in the Equality Clause of the Bill of Rights in South Africa's Constitution. He is the co-editor, with Mark Gevisser, of *Defiant Desire* (1994), a foundational academic text on gay and lesbian lives in South Africa. Cameron was appointed a judge of the High Court in 1995. He was elected chair of the Council of the University of the Witwatersrand in 1998. In 1999, prior to his appointment as Acting Justice to the Constitutional Court, Cameron publicly disclosed that he was living with AIDS. In 2000 he was appointed a Judge of Appeal in the Supreme Court of Appeal.

CAPITAL GAY

Jointly established by Graham McKerrow and Michael Mason, the weekly London newspaper *Capital Gay* was first published in 1981 and went on to become Britain's longest-running free gay newspaper. By the time it closed in 1995, it had a circulation of about 20,000 in London and Brighton. It is credited by the Oxford English Dictionary as the first publication in the world to use the term HIV.

COCK Jacklyn

Jacklyn Cock is professor of sociology at the University of the Witwatersrand. She has published widely in her areas of specialist interest, which include violence and inequality in South African society, and demilitarisation and the proliferation of light weapons in the Southern African region.

COHEN Steven

Pioneering artist Steven Cohen is best known for his controversial live performances, which confront issues of identity, in particular in relation to Jewishness, homosexuality and race. Gaining increasing recognition as one of South Africa's most innovative artists, Cohen won the First National Bank Vita National Art Award, South Africa's leading art prize, in 1998. Cohen works in close collaboration with his partner, Elu.

END CONSCRIPTION CAMPAIGN

Formed in 1983 in protest against compulsory military service, the ECC mobilised support for its campaigns, proposed service alternatives, supported conscientious objectors, and provided a forum for the public with information and education on conscription and the alternatives. Banned in August 1988, it was officially unbanned with other anti-apartheid organisations at the beginning of 1990. Conscription in South Africa continued until the new government came into power in April 1994.

EQUALITY FOUNDATION

The Equality Foundation was established using funds raised for a prior initiative, the National Law Reform Fund (NLRF). The NLRF was set up in 1986 to facilitate submissions to a proposed government review of existing legislation on homosexuality. The review never took place and the funds were transferred to a trust. In 1993 these funds (which had accrued significantly) were transferred to the Equality Foundation for lobbying for the inclusion of 'sexual orientation' in the Equality Clause in South Africa's new Constitution. The Equality Foundation also made funds available for the establishment of the National Coalition for Gay and Lesbian Equality (NCGLE) in 1994.

EXIT

Exit has been South Africa's principal gay and lesbian publication since its establishment in 1985 when it replaced the GASA newsletter *Link/Skakel,* which had been in circulation since 1982. It is a Johannesburg-based monthly and online (www.exit.co.za) newspaper.

HEATON-NICHOLLS Caroline

Caroline Heaton-Nicholls spent the first seven years of her career working with renowned human rights lawyer Priscilla Jana at her Johannesburg practice, starting as an articled clerk. During this time she formed part of the defence team in several treason trials, including the Delmas Treason Trial. In 1988 she married Delmas Treason trialist Gcina Malindi on the eve of his five-year imprisonment on Robben Island. She is a partner in the law firm Nicholls, Cambanis and Associates, which has acted on a number of landmark cases for the NCGLE and the Lesbian and Gay Equality Project.

9

INTERNATIONAL LESBIAN AND GAY ASSOCIATION

Founded in 1978, the International Lesbian and Gay Association (ILGA) is an international network of national and local lesbian, gay, bisexual and transgendered (LGBT) rights activist groups. At present it has more than 400 member organisations. ILGA focuses public and government attention on discrimination against LGBT people by supporting programmes and protest actions, applying diplomatic pressure, providing information and working with international organisations and the international media. Every one or two years, members of ILGA gather at a world conference to review and plan ILGA's work.

KRAAK Gerald

Gerald Kraak is the director of Atlantic Philanthropies, a donor agency working in the South African development sector. He is the author of *Breaking the Chains: Labour in South Africa in the 1970s and 1980s* (1994) and co-author, with Gavin Cawthra and Gerald O'Sullivan, of *War and Resistance* (1993), a study of the South African war resistance movement.

LEKOTA Mosiuoa 'Terror'

Mosiuoa 'Terror' Lekota was born in Kroonstad in 1948. In 1972 he was prevented from pursuing a social sciences degree when he was expelled from the University of the North for student political activities. Thereafter he became an organiser for the South African Students Organisation. In 1974 he was arrested, and in the subsequent trial sentenced to six years' imprisonment on Robben Island. Released in 1982, he was elected national publicity secretary at the launch of the United Democratic Front in 1983. His involvement in the Vaal Triangle rent boycott led to his re-arrest in 1985 when he and 21 others were charged with high treason in the Delmas Treason Trial. In 1988, Lekota was one of four of the accused found guilty and he was sentenced to 12 years. However, all four were acquitted on appeal in 1989. After the unbanning of the African National Congress, Lekota was elected onto the National Executive Committee in 1991. He served as premier of the Free State province from 1994 to 1996, and was the first chairperson of the new National Council of Provinces when it convened in February 1997. He was appointed Minister of Defence after South Africa's second democratic elections in 1999. His nickname 'Terror' originated on the soccer field.

MACHELA Alfred

Alfred Machela established the Rand Gay Organisation (RGO) in 1986 and served as its chairperson. He represented the RGO at the 1988 ILGA conference in Oslo where he drew international attention to the need for effective measures to combat the growing HIV/AIDS epidemic in South Africa. He was instrumental in facilitating the initial grant from the Norwegian government which led to the establishment of the Soweto-based Township AIDS Project in 1989. In the same year he left South Africa to take up permanent residence in Stockholm.

MANION Anthony

Anthony Manion was born in East London and educated at the University of Cape Town, before moving to Johannesburg in 2001 to work as the archivist for the Gay and Lesbian Archives of South Africa (GALA).

MBEKI Thabo

Thabo Mbeki was born in Transkei in 1942. Both his parents were activists, and his father was a leading figure in the African National Congress (ANC) in the Eastern Cape. Mbeki joined the ANC Youth League at the age of 14 and became active in student politics. He left South Africa for Tanzania in 1962 under orders from the ANC, and from there he moved to the UK where he completed a Master's degree in economics at Sussex University in 1966, playing a prominent role in building the youth and student sections of the ANC in exile. He worked at the ANC's London office before being sent to the Soviet Union for military training in 1970. From 1971, Mbeki worked with the ANC in exile in Zambia. He travelled throughout Africa for the ANC and became political secretary to its president, Oliver Tambo, in 1978. In the 1980s, Mbeki was the ANC's director of information, becoming its director of international affairs in 1989. After South Africa's ban against the ANC was lifted in 1990, Mbeki was a key ANC negotiator in the talks that led to the end of apartheid. He was named chairman of the ANC in 1993 and, after the 1994 elections, became South Africa's deputy president. At the ANC's 50th national conference in December 1997, Mbeki was elected ANC president. He was elected president of South Africa in June 1999, and re-elected in 2004.

Mhlanga **Bafana**

Bafana Mhlanga was born in Sakhile township, Standerton, in 1971. He was a founder member of the Gay and Lesbian Organisation of Sakhile (GLOS), formed in 1995, and chairperson until he relocated to Ermelo in 2000. Aside from working as a receptionist for the provincial health department, Mhlanga continues to organise workshops and functions under the auspices of Gays and Lesbians of Mpumalanga (GLOM).

Mokgethi **Paul**

Paul Kefiloe Boas Mokgethi was born in Soweto in 1967. He was one of the founding members of the Gay and Lesbian Organisation (GLOW) of the Witwatersrand, in 1988. His deeply religious Anglican roots led him to participate in a Bible study and prayer group of like-minded gay and lesbian Christians in 1993. This group constituted itself as a formal congregation the following year, when the Hope and Unity Metropolitan Community Church was established. In 1998 Mokgethi led a tour of the HUMCC choir to the Gay Games in Amsterdam. He was ordained as a member of the Universal Fellowship of Metropolitan Community Churches in Los Angeles in 1999. He is an active member of the African Network of Religious Leaders Living with or Personally Affected by HIV and AIDS (ANERELA+) and is vice-chair of the board of Behind the Mask, a website devoted to LGBTI rights and issues throughout Africa. He currently works at GALA where he is involved in an initiative to document the lives of lesbian and gay people living with HIV/AIDS.

Mompati **Ruth**

Ruth Mompati was born in 1925 in Ganyesa, in the Vryburg district, and grew up there. From 1953 to 1961 she worked as a legal secretary to Nelson Mandela and Oliver Tambo in their law practice. She officially joined the African National Congress (ANC) in 1953, and became a member of the National Executive Committee of the ANC Women's League in 1954. Mompati was one of the leaders of the famous 9 August 1956 women's march. She went into exile in 1962, and underwent military training in the Soviet Union until 1964. In 1965 in Tanzania, Mompati was made secretary to the president of the ANC and became head of the women's section. From 1966 to 1973, Mompati was an elected member of the ANC's National Executive Committee. Throughout

the 1970s much of her work was to inform the international community about South Africa and about the ANC. Between 1981 and 1984, Mompati served as the chief representative of the ANC in the UK. She became part of the delegation that opened talks with the South African government in 1990. She returned to South Africa permanently in 1991. In 1994, she was elected a Member of Parliament. She was ambassador to Switzerland from 1996 to 2000. She is currently the mayor of her hometown, Vryburg.

National Coalition for Gay and Lesbian Equality

The National Coalition for Gay and Lesbian Equality (NCGLE) was launched at the end of 1994. Its initial purpose was to fight for the retention of sexual orientation in the Equality Clause of South Africa's new Constitution. At its national conference in 1995, the four major aims of the organisation were defined as follows: to retain the Equality Clause in the final Constitution; to scrap unjust laws; to challenge discrimination through constitutional litigation; and to train representative and effective lesbian and gay leadership. The NCGLE was a national umbrella organisation that was set up by a small group of lesbian and gay activists who saw the formation of the coalition as politically imperative and strategically necessary. At its peak the NCGLE claimed a membership of 78 affiliate organisations. The affairs of the NCGLE were managed by an Interim Executive Committee drawn from all provinces within South Africa where there were active lesbian and gay structures. After the Constitution was adopted, the NCGLE lobbied government for related changes in legislation, often going to the Constitutional Court. Having achieved its primary objective, the NCGLE disbanded in 1999 and was replaced by the Lesbian and Gay Equality Project, which continued the legal reform and advocacy work initiated by the NCGLE.

Nhlapo **Sipho Paddy**

Paddy Nhlapo was born in KwaThema township, on the outskirts of Springs, in 1970. He involved himself in underground political activities during the turbulent decade of the 1980s. During the period of political transition he worked for the African National Congress and subsequently for ANC MP Chris Dlamini in Parliament. He then volunteered for the National Coalition for Gay and Lesbian Equality. He soon became the national organiser, and worked intensively in mobilising gay and lesbian youth. He was diagnosed as HIV-positive in 1992, and in 1997 decided to disclose his status publicly. He has worked in media and HIV/AIDS education including as a talk-show host in the educational television documentary *Beat It*, and to his current work in the National Association of People Living with HIV/AIDS. He is currently an Account Executive at Ochre Media in Johannesburg.

Nicol **Julia**

Julia Nicol was born in Johannesburg in 1956. She was educated at the University of Cape Town, and worked as a librarian until ill-health necessitated her retirement in 1997. She was a founder member of the Cape Town organisations Lilacs, Lesbians and Gays Against Oppression (LAGO), and the Organisation of Lesbian and Gay Activists (OLGA).

Nkoli **Simon**

Simon Tseko Nkoli was born in 1957 in Soweto. Nkoli became a youth activist with the Congress of South African Students and the United Democratic Front. In 1983 he joined the mainly white Gay Association of South Africa (GASA), and after coming out in an interview with *City Press*, he formed the Saturday Group, the first black gay group in Africa. In 1984, after speaking at rallies in support of rent boycotters in the Vaal Triangle townships, he was arrested and faced the death penalty for treason with 21 other political leaders in the Delmas Treason Trial. By coming out while a prisoner, Nkoli challenged the attitude of the African National Congress to gay rights. He was acquitted and released from prison in 1988. That year Nkoli founded the Gay and Lesbian Organisation of the Witwatersrand. He began travelling widely and was given several human rights awards in Europe and the US. He was a member of the International Lesbian and Gay Association board, representing the African region. Nkoli was one of the first gay activists to meet with Nelson Mandela in 1994. He was one of the leading personalities in the National Coalition for Gay and Lesbian Equality, and helped establish Soweto's Township AIDS Project in 1990, working there on community education campaigns until 1996. After becoming one of the first publicly HIV-positive African gay men, he initiated the Johannesburg-based group Positive African Men's Project (PAMP). In the months before his death, supported by his British partner Roderick Sharp, Nkoli was writing his mem-

oirs, and was concerned with the anti-homosexual campaigns in neighbouring Zimbabwe, Namibia, Swaziland, Botswana and Zambia. Nkoli died in hospital in Johannesburg on the eve of World AIDS Day, on 30 November 1998. Memorial services were held for him in the Anglican cathedrals in Johannesburg and Cape Town. The September 1999 Gay and Lesbian Pride Parade in Johannesburg was dedicated to his memory, and a downtown street corner was named in his honour.

Rand Gay Organisation

The RGO was founded in 1986 by Alfred Machela and other former members of the Gay Association of South Africa, notably Roy Shepherd and Trevor Payne. A small group, with a predominantly black membership base, it lasted for only a year.

Rydström **Jens**

Jens Rydström, assistant professor at Stockholm University's Centre for Gender Studies, is a former activist of the International Lesbian and Gay Association (ILGA). He is the author of *Sinners and Citizens: Bestiality and Homosexuality in Sweden 1880–1950* (2003). He is currently working on a project about the history of the law governing civil unions for gays and lesbians in Sweden.

Smith **Ann**

Ann Smith is an independent educational consultant after having been in the department of English at the University of the Witwatersrand for 23 years. She is a part-time lecturer at the Wits Business School, does contract work for the University of South Africa and runs a literary theory course for English honours students at the University of Pretoria. Her principal research areas are feminism, gender studies, gay and lesbian studies and queer theory, particularly as they relate to pedagogy and classroom practice. Her most recent academic publications reflect this interest, as does her extensive materials development work.

Tatchell **Peter**

Peter Tatchell is a British-based writer and human rights activist. He began campaigning for gay and lesbian rights in 1969, aged 17. Prominent in the London Gay Liberation Front in the early 1970s, he helped organise protests against police harassment and the medical classification of homosexuality as an illness. Two years later, in East Berlin, he was arrested and interrogated by the secret police after staging the first ever gay rights protest in a communist country. In 1999, in London, he ambushed the motorcade of the president of Zimbabwe, Robert Mugabe, and made a citizen's arrest of the president on charges of torture and other human rights abuses. He is the author of *We Don't Want to March Straight: Masculinity, Queers and the Military* (1995).

Toms Ivan

Ivan Toms is a medical doctor and founded the Empilisweni South African Christian Leadership Assembly clinic in Crossroads, Cape Town, in 1980. Having previously served in the South African Defence Force as a conscript, Toms became a conscientious objector when conscripted to serve in a one-month military camp ten years later. Toms was a leading public figure in the End Conscription Campaign. In 1988 he was sentenced to 640 days' imprisonment for refusing to serve in the South African Defence Force. He spent nine months in Pollsmoor prison before being released. His three-week hunger strike protest against troops in the township in 1985 is well known. He remained involved in non-governmental primary health care work until 1996, when he joined the Cape Metropolitan Council. In 1999 he was appointed Medical Officer of Health for Cape Town and in 2002 Director of City Health for Cape Town.

Trengove Jones Tim

Tim Trengove Jones lectures in English literature and media studies at the University of the Witwatersrand. He has written widely on gay cultural matters in academic publications and the gay and mainstream media. He has also written extensively on the politics of HIV/AIDS in South Africa.

Tutu Desmond

Archbishop Desmond Tutu was born in Klerksdorp, near Johannesburg, in 1931. After leaving school he trained as a teacher, and in 1954 he graduated from the University of South Africa. After three years as a high school teacher, he decided to enter the ministry. He was ordained to the priesthood in Johannesburg three years later. Following further theological studies in London, Tutu held several positions in teaching and theological work in South and Southern Africa. In 1975 he was appointed Dean of St Mary's Cathedral in Johannesburg, the first black person to hold that position. Then, in 1978, he was persuaded to leave

his job as Bishop of Lesotho to become the new general secretary of the South African Council of Churches (SACC). It was in this position, which he held until 1985, that Tutu became a national and international figure. As chairperson of the SACC, Tutu led a formidable crusade for justice and racial conciliation in South Africa. His work was recognised in 1984, when he was awarded the Nobel Peace Prize. Then, following a short stint as the Bishop of Johannesburg, Tutu was elected Archbishop of Cape Town in 1986, an office he held until his retirement in 1996. In 1996, he was appointed by President Nelson Mandela to chair the Truth and Reconciliation Commission, the body set up to probe gross human rights violations during apartheid. Following the presentation of the commission's report to the president in October 1998, Tutu has been visiting professor at several universities abroad, and has also published several books.

Van Zyl Mikki

Mikki van Zyl was active in the anti-apartheid struggle from the late 1970s. Since 1993 she has run her own research business, which is an associate of iNCUDISA (the Institute for Intercultural and Diversity Studies of Southern Africa) at the University of Cape Town. Van Zyl's academic foundation is gender studies, and she has degrees in communication and media studies and an M.Phil. in sociology. She has done extensive qualitative research on topics such as gender-based violence, the human rights of gays and lesbians, land reform and gender, exiles in the anti-apartheid struggle, identity-based gender social movements, and institutional culture. She has lectured in media studies, sociology, criminology and diversity studies, and for the last fifteen years has worked as a trainer, writer and consultant in gender and development and participatory research methodologies.

SOURCES

The following sources were consulted in compiling these biographies: *Steven Cohen* (TaxiArt, 2003); The Kairos Collection, Department of Historical Papers, the University of the Witwatersrand; Kathryn Mathers article on www.objector.org; R Aldrich and G Wotherspoon, *Who's Who in Contemporary Gay and Lesbian History* (Routledge, 2001); *Guide to the Resources of the Gay and Lesbian Archives of South Africa*.

13

Introduction

Neville Hoad

This anthology brings together a number of academic essays, activist inter-views, and primary historical documents from the Gay and Lesbian Archives of South Africa in Johannesburg, with the aim of assembling a dossier on the relationship between lesbian and gay organising and the South African national liberation struggle. We hope to suggest that this relationship was multi-faceted: strategic, principled, institutional, mutually determining, contested, structural and personal. This collection is not exhaustive, and the idea of a dossier, rather than an account or a narrative, is critical.

The inclusion of a clause prohibiting discrimination on the grounds of sexual orientation in the South African Constitution of 1996 was a world-historical event. The collection that we have assembled provides material for a series of speculations into the key circumstances, personnel, issues and conflicts around this constitutional clause.

We hope the collection will be of interest to a wide readership beyond South African specialists. The various essays address the relation of emergent social movements to a newly democratic state; the relation of sexual identity to other social variables such as race, class, gender, nation; the role of international activism in effecting national change; the place of sexuality within liberal multi-cultural debates, *inter alia*.

The wider South African liberation struggle elicited a massive response from the international community in terms of both national and transnational anti-apartheid movements, which – along with the exiled and local political group-ings – had varying and often conflicting positions on sexuality as a variable, in the attempt to imagine and institute a democratic regime in South Africa. The South African case is both typical and exceptional in thinking through the place of sexual politics in the shift from a Cold War era to neoliberal globalisation.

The place of the most recent generation of human rights – those based on a category called sexual orientation being prominent amongst them – in an era of globalisation is a complicated one. Tolerance of homosexuality is, amongst other things, often seen as a marker of civilised sexual values, obliquely invoked by states like Israel (Fink and Press, 1999), Taiwan (Patton, 2002) and, more recently, Romania (Stychin, 2002). These states use their anti-discrimination against homosexuals laws in processes of global exclusion and differentiation, or as a means of deflecting attention from other human rights abuses within their borders; and in the Romanian instance, to strengthen its case for entry into the European Union. Tolerance of homosexuality becomes an indicator of civilised modernity, but in the African context, and perhaps also in a more generalised postcolonial one, the bourgeois nuclear family is often seen as the proper intimate form of modernity.

Much of the often excellent new scholarship on the global aspects of sexual minority politics tends to be short on history. We imagine our collection to engage this emergent scholarship methodologically, as well as to contribute to ongoing contestations in South Africa around the place of sexual citizens in a national and transnational context (Hawley, 2002, Cruz-Malave and Manalansan, 2002, Drucker, 2000, Cameron and Gevisser, 1995, Altman 2000). The collection brings academics, archivists and activists into conversation with each other in the interests of fostering both a scholarly and public discussion on sexuality, democracy, cultural identity and political economy.

A brief chronology of legal and social restrictions around sexuality in South African history can provide an important informing context for the fragmented but lively activism around sexuality issues in the 1980s, which led into the anti-discrimination clause in the provisional Constitution, and the subsequent establishment of the National Coalition for Gay and Lesbian Equality (NCGLE).[1] This organisation was initially established to ensure the retention of the clause in the new Constitution of the post-apartheid state.

Given the imperative of creating, maintaining and reproducing distinct racial groupings, the ideology of the apartheid era state was deeply if incoherently

15

---

1. See Edwin Cameron in Cameron and Gevisser, 1995, for a more detailed background on the shifting legal status of lesbians and gay men in South Africa.

invested in questions of reproductive heterosexual sexuality. Sexual conduct between members of different racial groupings has a long history of criminalisation. The 1927 Immorality Act criminalised sexual activity between whites and Africans. One of the first pieces of legislation enacted by the new National Party government, which came to power in 1948, was the Prohibition of Mixed Marriages Act of 1949, which criminalised sexual conduct outside of marriage as well as sex between whites and coloureds, and whites and Asians. The Mixed Marriages Act of 1950 banned marriages between members of different racial classifications.

As these laws indicate, the state imagined sexual control as central to the effective implementation and sustaining of apartheid policies. This legislative attempt to control the sexual behaviour of all South Africans extended beyond laws with explicit racial content. The amended Immorality Act of 1957 explicitly criminalised prostitution, 'unlawful carnal intercourse and other acts in relation thereto'. While the Act did not explicitly mention homosexual sex acts, common law provisions inherited from South Africa's British colonial history still pertained, though they were not extensively deployed. Nevertheless, the 1957 Act laid the cornerstone for the legislative extension of interracial sexual interdictions to what we might now recognise as gay men.

Within the effective shutdown of political civil society following the Sharpeville massacre of 1960 and the banning of the African National Congress and exile or imprisonment of its leaders in the early 1960s, the South African government increasingly acquired the attributes of a puritan police state. A media scandal around a gay party in Forest Town, an affluent white suburb of Johannesburg, in January 1966 was the impetus for further draconian legislation around sexuality; but in neat, almost Foucauldian reverse discourse fashion, it prompted the first modest legal reform movement by white middle-class gay men. Police raided a large party with approximately 350 men in attendance. Since this was a social gathering in a private house, and few men were caught in the act of sex itself, it was difficult to prosecute under the provisions of common law anti-sodomy laws or public indecency laws. Among those arrested were nine men detained for 'masquerading as women', and one held for 'indecent assault on a minor'. The 1957 Immorality Act covered public offences only, and therefore could also not be mobilised against the party-goers.

The apartheid state's desire to bring this emergent gay subculture into the purview of criminal law required new legislation. The new proposed legislation 'sought to make male and female homosexuality an offence punishable by compulsory imprisonment of up to three years' (Gevisser, 1995). The law would have been innovative in relation to the common law by criminalising lesbians and by shifting the grounds for prosecution from sexual acts to minority sexual identities. A parliamentary committee was formed to investigate the possibility of amending the existing Immorality Acts, and gay men and lesbians affected began to organise to prevent their further criminalisation.[2] While not as comprehensive as first feared, the 1969 amendment to the Immorality Act seemed deliberately designed to combat the emergence of gay subculture, in terms that now appear almost farcical. The following were criminalised: 'any act by a male person ... with another male person at a party ... which is calculated to stimulate sexual passion or to give sexual gratification'. Perhaps learning from the language of banning and restraining orders applied to political opponents of apartheid, a 'party' was defined as 'any occasion where more than two persons are present'. The only requirement for arresting persons participating in such activities as kissing, hugging, dancing and stripping was that more than two people be present. The amendment also prohibited 'the manufacture or distribution of any article intended to be used to perform an unnatural sexual act' (Gevisser, 1995, 30–31).

The state thus legally connects race and sex in ways that subsequent lesbian and gay organisations will have to respond to. Effectively criminalised by the apartheid regime, white gay men had the nascent possibility of making common cause with South Africa's disenfranchised and criminalised racial majority, but the cleavages of massive class and racial privilege would have to be bridged. It took until the 1980s to see the emergence of multiracial lesbian and gay organisations that attempted to cross these divides and affiliate with the wider liberation struggle. The affiliation of both the Organisation of Lesbian

17

2. The Gay and Lesbian Archives of South Africa (GALA) has all the depositions as well as the private papers of Joe Garmeson, a key player in the law reform movement.

and Gay Activists (OLGA) in Cape Town and the Gay and Lesbian Organisation of the Witwatersrand (GLOW) in Johannesburg with the United Democratic Front (UDF) in the late 1980s marks a seismic shift in the history of lesbian and gay politics in South Africa. It is the aspiration of this anthology to invite the telling of this story – heroic, shameful, complicit and resistant as it may be.

We believe that there is now sufficient distance to attempt to write a history of the tumultuous eighties, to contribute to an ongoing scholarly and public discussion about the place of criminalised sexuality in the wider liberation struggle, to attempt to account for the inclusion of the path-breaking constitutional clause, to work through the ways the history of these individuals and organisations supplements, contradicts and differentially embodies the main thrusts of the South African national liberation struggle.

Coincidental with the history of the individuals and organisations chronicled in this anthology is the anticipatory dismantling of the legal cornerstones of the apartheid state. As Johnson, 1997, notes: 'President PW Botha decriminalised interracial sex in 1985 and the Immorality Amendment Act 2 of 1988 was passed to codify the change in the law. However, a committee was subsequently formed to investigate the Immorality Act. Among its other findings, the committee recommended that Parliament further investigate criminalising same-sex activity between women, expressing abhorrence to homosexuality, and creating rehabilitation programmes or other desirable forms of punishment for gays and lesbians prosecuted under the Act.' The post-apartheid state's rearticulation of race and sexuality has relied less on law and more on the rhetoric of familialist nationalism.

Obviously, this is an overdetermined history, where one narrative line, such as the brief national legal one above, will not suffice; and the documents, analyses and testimonials from the recent archiving of the history of lesbian and gay organising stand in various relations to the emergent historiographies of what is variously termed the post-apartheid state and civil society, or South Africa in an era of internally led structural adjustment. We present this story of laws in the introduction both as a backdrop to what follows, but also as a salutary caveat to constitutionalist triumphalism. Apartheid may have been underwritten by a legal edifice, but its vectors of oppression were as much economic and social, and, given the failure of the new regime to respond effectively to the HIV/AIDS pandemic, it is clear that a constitution guaranteeing freedom from discrimination on the grounds of gender, race and sexual orientation, *inter alia*, is far from sufficient in creating a sexually free and empowered citizenry.

Letties, moffies, stabanes, skesanas, injongas ... make their own history but under conditions that are not of their making.[3] Our list of identifying terms is far from comprehensive and each item on that list indicates a different configuration of identity, desire, practice, possibility, held together by the phrase 'sexual orientation' in the South African Constitution – the meaning of which is continually being revised by the South African courts. In the arena of employment benefit rights, the Pretoria High Court ruled against the police medical aid, Polmed, for refusing to allow a lesbian police office to register her partner as a dependant.[4] In April 1998, the Johannesburg High Court overturned a previous court order allowing a welfare agency to remove a child from its lesbian mother and placing it in the care of its grandparents.[5] Also in April 1998, six gay and lesbian couples, with the support of the NCGLE, lodged urgent applications to overturn home affairs minister Mangosuthu Buthelezi's decision not to allow permanent residence rights to the foreign-born partners of gay men and lesbians. The petitioners were successful in a ruling that overturned the Aliens Act in February 1999.[6] In addition to these court decisions, significant legislative victories have been won. The Basic Conditions of Employment Act of 1997 and the Employment Equity Act of 1998 outlaw any workplace discrimination, while the National Defence Act of 2001 prohibits discrimination on the basis of sexual orientation in the military. These are noteworthy achievements for any national lesbian and gay movement.[7]

We have organised the material into two clusters. The first provides material around sexuality and the national liberation struggle locally and internationally. Apartheid and the struggle against it mobilised a transnational constituency risking a solidarity tourism at worst, invoking a global and universalist commitment to human rights and social justice at best. The controversy around the

19

3. I riff here on Marx's famous axiom on human historical agency in The Eighteenth Brumaire of Louis Napoleon.
4. See: http://mg.co.za/mg/za/archive/98feb/04-news.html
5. See: http://mg.co.za/mg/za/archive/98apr/21-news.html
6. See: http://mg.co.za/mg/za/archive/98apr/28-news.html and http://mg.co.za/mg/za/archive/99feb/14-news.html
7. For a more comprehensive list of the legal protections extended to South African lesbian and gay citizens, see http://www.equality.org.za/archive/2002/achievedsa.php

Gay Association of South Africa's (GASA's) membership of the International Lesbian and Gay Association (ILGA) seems emblematic here, restaging the drama around the apartheid state's place in the international community that was evident in the cultural, sports and academic boycotts and the divestment campaigns more generally. This controversy intersects powerfully with events more easily contained within the sphere of the national in the person and fig-ure of Simon Nkoli, gay activist and freedom fighter accused in the travesty of justice that was the Delmas Treason Trial. The treason trial attempted, *inter alia*, to convict a crowd of people for an act of murder under the doctrine of common purpose, and common purpose was attributed on the basis of mem-bership in the anti-apartheid coalition, the UDF. Three of the accused were already in police custody at the time of the murder.

The second cluster engages attempts to account for the inclusion in the new Constitution of an Equality Clause which included sexual orientation, as well as to assess the role of backroom negotiations by key players in the drafting process, and the question of timing in terms of wider global political changes. The lateness of South Africa in the postcolonial moment is significant. In the drafting of the South African Constitution, an attempt was self-consciously made to learn from the failures of prior liberation movements across the globe. The ANC's Women's League was adamant that their national liberation move-ment was not going to repeat the sexist failings of decolonisation. The ANC's commitment to reserving 30 per cent of all its parliamentary positions for women was one result. The Constitution was to be the most inclusive and most progressive. Given the illegitimacy of the regime being replaced and the imperative to incorporate the most recent, 'advanced' form of human rights, the timing of the South African Constitution in the history of postcolonialism facilitated the entrenchment of lesbian and gay human rights. Ironically, this same timing in the moment of globalisation has severely hampered South Africa's first democratically elected government in the mounting of programmes of national reconstruction and distributive justice. Moreover, with the formation of the NCGLE after the appearance of the clause in the provisional Constitution, we see an attempt to create a national movement from above, and evidence that grassroots activity responds to rather than produces legal change (De Vos, 2000). Mark Gevisser argues for a combination of local and international factors in the passage of the Equality Clause:

> The primary reason why the notion of gay equality passed so smoothly in the Constitution is most likely that the ANC elite has a utopian social progressive ideology, influenced largely by the social-democratic movements in the countries that supported it during its struggle: Sweden, Holland, Britain, Canada, Australia (Gevisser, 2000, 118).

He argues for the absence of a homophobic church, the entrenchment of human rights ideals within the liberation movement, and the 'coming out' of prominent activist, Simon Nkoli, during the Delmas Treason Trial as other significant contributing factors (Gevisser, 2000, 118–19).

To move forward into the present and to elaborate on the limits and achievements of the South African national liberation struggle, with specific reference to the politics of sexual identity in a global frame, remains a challenge for future work. As Glen Elder has powerfully argued, the return of South Africa to the global 'gay' community and marketplace has been a mixed blessing for same-sex erotically inclined South Africans, with costs and benefits still lining up in terms of old apartheid dichotomies (Elder, 2005). The emergence of the HIV/AIDS pandemic as a major public health and security crisis in the sub-continent marks another powerful limit. While much of the activism around HIV/AIDS has been spearheaded by activists with connections to lesbian and gay organising in South Africa, the frame of the politics of sexual identity cannot remotely contain the various narrative and analytic strategies for beginning to make sense of the pandemic. Phaswane Mpe's marvellous novel, *Welcome to Our Hillbrow*, marks an important and self-consciously articulated attempt to show the impact of the HIV/AIDS pandemic on the sexual and social lives of 'the educated, the respectable, the normal'.[8] We imagine the materials in this anthology as allowing for the possibility of historical depth in the increasingly urgent analyses of questions of race, political economy and sexuality in the context of the HIV/AIDS pandemic.

21

---

8. 'I was interested in looking at that part of sexuality that people don't stigmatise, the sexuality of people who are supposed to be educated and respectable,' (Phaswane Mpe, quoted in Tait, 2001).

We provide this mix of analysis, testimonial and archival material in the interest of encouraging further scholarship, as a way of acknowledging the multiplicity of the possible stories that can and should be told about this time, and as a gesture to the deeply felt and ethically charged atmosphere in which these events occurred. We want these various voices, positions, genres and passions to compete for the reader's attention. While this commitment to polyphony, multiplicity and even contradiction may risk an abdication of political, scholarly and editorial responsibility, we hope the anthology will function more as an invitation to the voices, positions and experiences not represented to respond. Let the inevitable gaps function as opportunities for insurgency rather than occasions for further exclusion.

The effort of the Truth and Reconciliation Commission to create a powerful public conversation about justice and forgiveness in the light of the appalling history of apartheid reveals an investment in the question of group and private memory that is salutary for the endeavours of this anthology. The embedding of the personal and the political is something we hope the juxtaposition of the testimonies with the archival material will vivify – the personal connections that allow for historical change and the historical circumstances that allow for new forms of personal intimacies and associations. Readers are encouraged to read with sympathy both Caroline Heaton-Nicholls's righteously indignant letter to Kevan Botha regarding his use of the Delmas Treason Trial at ILGA meetings in 1986, and Botha's moving account of his subsequent shifting political awareness in his speech at Simon Nkoli's memorial service in 1998. These texts, while deeply personal, are highly suggestive of the wider emotional tenor of their times – 1986 and 1998, respectively. It is the implied argument of Greta Schiller's 1998 film, *The Man Who Drove with Mandela*, that the close personal friendship between Cecil Williams and the ANC leadership in the early sixties is a significant factor in the ANC's subsequent pro-homosexual position. Nelson Mandela, in hiding, is impersonating Williams's chauffeur when arrested. Williams subsequently hides from the police in a Johannesburg bath-house before going into exile himself in England. Materials in the anthology also acknowledge both the resilience and frailty of similar personal connections under often very difficult political conditions, and may allow for speculations on the significance of questions of affect in historical narratives of change. We also hope that the juxtaposition of testimony, archival materials and academic historical argument will both demystify and problematise the way scholars write this recent history, inviting readers to ponder the ways in which personal experience may be unassimilable to more formal kinds of history-writing, along with the ways in which archived materials, while ostensibly about the past, continue to offer an invitation to future readers and writers. The various essays, including this introduction, attempt to order and to frame the fragments of historical experience encapsulated in the archival materials, but these materials may have a resistant integrity that reminds us that history is paradoxically always that which comes after the event, even determines what nuggets of experience get to be an event.

As my riff on Marx's axiom in *The Eighteenth Brumaire of Louis Napoleon* earlier suggested, we see the major theoretical problem of the anthology as the question of agency – structural, personal, transpersonal, overdetermined. Arguably, apartheid placed the question of sex as central to national and social as well as racial definition. Liberal rhetorics would confine sex to the realm of the private. The problem becomes not one of getting the state out of our bedrooms, off our bodies, but one of how to mobilise the state and various other representative forms of collectivity and power in the interest of diversely desiring bodies. How did the significant changes in the legal position of same-sex loving South Africans come about? How useful is it to give credit and attribute shame? How might the ideas and impetuses of these late apartheid era individuals and organisations be used in continuing struggles for social and sexual justice in contemporary South Africa? How might alliances with international institutions and audiences be most effectively employed? Was it possible to build cross-class multiracial lesbian and gay organisations in the fight against apartheid? Was this aspiration/attempt effective or even desirable? These are some of the key questions we hope this anthology can begin to address.

Works Cited

Altman, Dennis (2000). *Global Sex*. Chicago: University of Chicago Press.

Cameron, Edwin and Gevisser, Mark (1995). 'Defiant desire' in Cameron, Edwin and Gevisser, Mark (eds). *Defiant Desire: Gay and Lesbian Lives in South Africa*. New York: Routledge.

Cruz-Malave, Arnaldo and Manalansan, Martin (eds) (2002). *Queer Globalizations: Citizenship and the Afterlife of Colonialism*. New York: New York University Press.

De Vos, Pierre (2000). 'The Constitution made us queer: the sexual orientation clause in the South African Constitution and the emergence of gay and lesbian identity' in Herman, Didi and Stychin, Carl (eds). *Sexuality in the Legal Arena*. London: Athlone.

Drucker, Peter (ed.) (2000). *Different Rainbows*. London: Gay Men's Press.

Elder, Glen (2004). 'Somewhere over the rainbow: Cape Town South Africa as a gay destination' in Ouzgane, Lahoucine and Morrell, Robert (eds). *African Masculinities*. London: Palgrave Macmillan and Pietermaritzburg: University of Natal Press.

Fink, Sumaka'i Amir and Press, Jacob (eds) (1999). *Independence Park: The Lives of Gay Men in Israel*. Stanford, CA: Stanford University Press.

Gevisser, Mark (1995). 'A different fight for freedom' in Cameron, Edwin and Gevisser, Mark (eds). *Defiant Desire: Gay and Lesbian Lives in South Africa*. New York: Routledge.

Gevisser, Mark (2000). 'Mandela's stepchildren: homosexual identity in post-apartheid South Africa' in Drucker, Peter (ed). *Different Rainbows*. London: GMP.

Hawley, John (ed.) (2002). *Postcolonial/Queer*. Albany, NY: State University of New York Press.

Johnson, Voris E (1997). 'Making words on a page become everyday life: a strategy for helping gay men and lesbians achieve full equality under South Africa's Constitution.' http://www.law.emory.edu/EILR/volumes/fall97/johnson.html.

Mpe, Phaswane (2002). *Welcome to Our Hillbrow*. Pietermaritzburg: University of Natal Press.

Patton, Cindy (2002). 'Stealth bombers of desire: the globalization of "alterity" in emerging democracies' in Cruz-Malave, Arnaldo and Manalansan, Martin (eds). *Queer Globalizations: Citizenship and the Afterlife of Colonialism.* New York: New York University Press.

Schiller, Greta (1998). *The Man Who Drove with Mandela.* New York: Cinema Guild.

Stychin, Carl (2002). 'From integration to civilisation: reflections on sexual citizenship in a European legal order.' Conference paper given at Gender, Sexuality and Law II, Keele University, June 2002.

Tait, Lawrence (2001). 'Welcome to our literature' in *Sunday Times*, Lifestyle Section, 16 September 2001.

Part 1

Sexuality and the liberation struggle

Fragments from the archives I **Graeme Reid**

ESSAY: Solidarity – with whom? The international gay and lesbian rights movement and apartheid **Jens Rydström**

PERSONAL TESTIMONY: A lesson well worth learning **Kevan Botha**

ARCHIVE: Notes for a speech at the 1986 ILGA world conference **Alfred Machela**

PERSONAL TESTIMONY: Where was I in the eighties? **Ann Smith**

ARCHIVE: Because I'm gay and I believe **Paul Mokgethi**

ARCHIVE: My life underground **Paddy Nhlapo**

INTERVIEW: If we can't dance to it, it's not our revolution **Julia Nicol**

ARCHIVE: Call for action, **Rand Gay Organisation**

ARCHIVE: Pamphlet, **End Conscription Campaign**

ARCHIVE: ANC dashes hopes for gay rights in SA **Peter Tatchell**

ARCHIVE: Published letters **Glen Shelton, Simon Nkoli**

ARCHIVE: Private letters **Ivan Toms, Edwin Cameron**

ARCHIVE: Photograph of Simon Nkoli and Ivan Toms

ESSAY: Cape Town activists remember sexuality struggles **Mikki van Zyl**

ESSAY: Homosexuality and the South African left: The ambiguities of exile
Gerald Kraak

REBUTTAL: Mystifying history: The thing that goes bump in the night
Tim Trengove Jones

ESSAY: The moment the ANC embraced gay rights **Peter Tatchell**

ARCHIVE: Telex **Thabo Mbeki**

ARCHIVE: Address at Simon Nkoli's memorial service **Mosiuoa 'Terror' Lekota**

ARCHIVE: Letters from prison **Simon Nkoli**

ARCHIVE: Letter to Kevan Botha **Caroline Heaton-Nicholls**

ARCHIVE: Photographs of GLOW meeting

ARCHIVE: Photographs of Simon Nkoli's release-from-prison party

ARCHIVE: Address at Simon Nkoli's memorial service **Kevan Botha**

ARCHIVE: Simon Nkoli obituary **Zackie Achmat**

ARCHIVE: Cartoon, ''n Poefadder het my gepik'

Fragments from the archives I

Graeme Reid

1985	Cartoon published in *Rapport*
1986	Notes for a speech at the ILGA world conference **Alfred Machela**
1986	Letters from prison **Simon Nkoli**
1986	Letter to Kevan Botha **Caroline Heaton-Nicholls**
1987	Article in *Capital Gay* **Peter Tatchell**
1987	Telex to Peter Tatchell **Thabo Mbeki**
1987	Letters **Ivan Toms, Edwin Cameron**
1988	Pamphlet in *ILGA Bulletin* **End Conscription Campaign**
1988	Call for action in *ILGA Bulletin* **Rand Gay Organisation**
1988	Letters in *Exit* **Glen Shelton, Simon Nkoli**
c.1988	Photographs from Simon Nkoli's release-from-prison party, Barbican Studios, Johannesburg
c.1988	Photographs of GLOW meeting
1989	Photograph of Simon Nkoli and Ivan Toms
1995	Interview: 'Because I'm gay and I believe' **Paul Mokgethi**
1998	Address at Simon Nkoli's memorial service **Mosiuoa 'Terror' Lekota**
1998	Address at Simon Nkoli's memorial service **Kevan Botha**
1999	Simon Nkoli obituary in *Equality* **Zackie Achmat**
1999	Interview: 'My life underground' **Paddy Nhlapo**

The archival material reproduced in Part 1 emerges from and refers back to the turbulent 1980s, a context of intense political struggle when the inevitable meeting between sexual identity politics and anti-apartheid politics took place. It is drawn from the Gay and Lesbian Archives of South Africa and from public and private archives in the United Kingdom and the Netherlands. These 'fragments from the archives' direct us to substantial archival holdings which contain sources of evidence that may support, or contradict, or simply elaborate on many of the issues that are dealt with in the essays.

28

The Delmas Treason Trial was a watershed moment in South Africa's political history. Although 22 activists took the stand on 16 October 1985, it was really the mass democratic movement in the form of the United Democratic Front (UDF) that was on trial. A total of 911 co-conspirators were named in the charge sheet. It was one of the longest running political trials in South African legal history, ending only three years later on 8 December 1988. The central argument in the state's case was that the UDF intended to overthrow the state by violence, independently or in conspiracy with the outlawed African National Congress (ANC). These were serious charges, which potentially carried the death penalty.

One of the 22 charged with treason was Simon Tseko Nkoli, who, aside from being a UDF activist, was also a member of the Gay Association of South Africa (GASA), where he was active in the Saturday Group, a fledgling black interest group within GASA. Simon had a difficult choice to make during the trial – whether or not to come out to fellow activists. When Simon did come out, it caused consternation. Many activists felt that his homosexuality tarnished the good name of the Struggle: some even wanted him to be tried separately. Simon, supported by his lawyers and some fellow trialists, embarked on a long and difficult journey in gaining acceptance and respect from his co-accused.

Simon's letters to friends and, in particular, to his lover Roy Shepherd provide a moving testimony of his experiences in jail. Some of his letters were sent through formal channels, in which case they were approved by prison authorities, as indicated by the prison stamp. Others were smuggled out by visitors and the lawyers representing the accused, thereby evading the prison censor. Either way, Simon made no attempt to disguise his relationship with Roy. Innocuous terms of endearment – 'Dearest Roy', 'Your loving Simon', 'I love you Roy' – in the context of a relationship between an imprisoned black man and a white civil servant were extraordinary at the time.

Simon's coming-out process during the course of the treason trial had a signifi-cant impact on the inclusion of gay and lesbian issues on the political agenda of the mass democratic movement in South Africa. The speech by Mosiuoa

('Terror') Lekota (later Minister of Defence) at Simon's memorial service in 1998 attests to Simon's ability to win the respect and affection of leading political figures embroiled in the trial.

Simon's detention also drew international attention from gay and lesbian organisations and exposed the untenable position of GASA, which strove to be apolitical in the context of apartheid South Africa. This led to ongoing controversy surrounding GASA's continued membership of the International Lesbian and Gay Association (ILGA),[1] a debate which began at its 1986 conference, held in Copenhagen. Kevan Botha represented GASA at this conference. Alfred Machela, founder of the Rand Gay Organisation (RGO), intended to present his perspective on gay engagement in political struggle at the conference, but his sponsorship failed to materialise and he was unable to attend. The essence of the debate on the role of the gay and lesbian movement in the broader anti-apartheid struggle is reflected in a letter written by Simon's lawyer, Caroline Heaton-Nicholls, to Kevan Botha, as well as the incomplete handwritten notes that formed the basis of a speech that was to be delivered to the conference by Alfred Machela.

In September 1987, with Simon out on bail but still on trial, Peter Tatchell published an article based on his interviews with Ruth Mompati and Solly Smith,[2] both representatives of the exiled African National Congress in London. The article caused widespread controversy, notably within the ranks of the anti-apartheid movement. The remarks made by the London representatives were countered in a statement issued by Thabo Mbeki in November 1987, in which he apologised for 'any misunderstanding that might have arisen' and reaffirmed the ANC's commitment to 'removing all forms of discrimination and oppression in a liberated South Africa'.

In 1988, following his acquittal on charges of treason, Simon Nkoli founded the Gay and Lesbian Organisation of the Witwatersrand (GLOW). GLOW emerged as a robust new player in the field of sexual identity politics. GASA was dwindling and teetering towards collapse, out of tune with contemporary South African political developments and mired in internal problems. By con-

1. The International Gay Association (IGA) changed its name to the International Gay and Lesbian Association (ILGA) in 1986.
2. Solly Smith, whose real name was Samuel Khunyeli, confessed in 1991 to spying for the South African security services.

trast, GLOW was at home in the anti-apartheid movement, affiliated to the UDF and participating in political protest. GLOW attracted a new breed of politically savvy activists who combined a strong anti-apartheid agenda with public assertiveness around lesbian and gay identity. A series of photographs thought to be taken at one of GLOW's initial meetings at Lee's Place in Orlando, Soweto, is included here as are snapshots taken at a party thrown in celebration of Simon's release from prison. GLOW rose to public prominence through a series of campaigns, and in 1990 it took the unprecedented step of staging Africa's first Gay and Lesbian Pride March through the streets of Johannesburg.

A glimpse into the experiences of a gay man working within political structures during the 1980s is provided by an extract from an interview with Paddy Nhlapo, which describes a life underground in terms of both illegal political activity and a closeted sexual identity. In another interview Paul Mokgethi, a founder member of both GLOW and the Hope and Unity Metropolitan Community Church (HUMCC), speaks about the tensions between secular politics and Christian conviction.

Homosexuality entered the public domain in South Africa during the 1980s in another form – as part of the apartheid government's attempt to discredit the End Conscription Campaign (ECC). The ECC arose out of a coalition of church, women's, student and human rights organisations in response to a motion passed at the annual meeting of the Black Sash (a group of middle-class women vociferously opposed to apartheid since the early 1950s) in March 1983 calling on the government to end compulsory conscription into the South African Defence Force (SADF). Eighteen organisations rallied together under the ECC banner, united in opposition to the harsh Defence Amendment Act, which prescribed a mandatory six-year jail term for conscientious objectors, and also to the escalating violence in the subcontinent, and the threat of the extension of conscription to coloured and Indian youth.

31

The ECC had developed a carefully managed public profile, a performance of a particular kind of respectability. Neatly cropped hair and suits were more familiar in the ECC than the long hair and jeans characteristic of the anti-

Vietnam War movement in the United States twenty years earlier. Ivan Toms, a medical doctor who worked amongst the poorest of the poor in the Crossroads shack settlement on the outskirts of Cape Town, refused to do any further military camps. He fitted the ECC bill perfectly: he was conventional in all respects except one. While graffiti appeared in Cape Town announcing that Ivan Toms was a 'fairy', the ECC, not wishing to detract from the central focus of their campaign, sought to downplay the fact that he was gay. A propaganda skirmish ensued in which homosexuality was the main contestant. Correspondence between Toms and his advocate Edwin Cameron gives insight into the political complexities of the time – in particular the tensions that existed between personal identity and political strategy. The ECC had been very successful as a 'one-issue campaign' which allowed for the broadest possible consensus in opposition to the Defence Amendment Act. An exchange between Glen Shelton and Simon Nkoli in the pages of *Exit*, a newspaper aimed primarily at a gay male readership, adds another dimension to this intense debate. A decade later, the National Coalition for Gay and Lesbian Equality (NCGLE) was to draw on the success of the ECC model and adopt the 'one-issue' campaign strategy in its efforts to secure equality for lesbian and gay people in South Africa's Constitution, and captured in the slogan 'Equality Means Equality for All'.

The cartoon "'n Poefadder het my gepik' published in *Rapport*, a leading Afrikaans newspaper, in the early years of the HIV/AIDS epidemic illustrates public stigma of homosexuality at the time. It serves as a shocking reminder of how HIV was first perceived and the homophobic environment in which organisations such as GASA and, later, GLOW operated. Such a cartoon stereotypically associating HIV with a stigmatised minority would be unimaginable a decade later when South Africa was faced with a pandemic on an unprecedented scale. The tragedy of Simon Nkoli's untimely death on the eve of International AIDS Day in 1998 is captured in an obituary written by Zackie Achmat. It was at Simon's memorial service that Kevan Botha delivered a tribute in which he reflected on his role in GASA during Simon's detention. This speech self-consciously evoked the Truth and Reconciliation Commission format of disclosure and forgiveness on the road to reconciliation.

Solidarity – with whom?

The international gay & lesbian rights movement and apartheid

Jens Rydström

Jens Rydström draws on unpublished personal and organisational archival material to track the debates at the annual conferences of the International Lesbian and Gay Association (ILGA) from 1983 to 1987 about the Gay Association of South Africa's membership of ILGA.

1983

In 1983 when the Gay Association of South Africa (GASA) applied for membership of the International Lesbian and Gay Association (ILGA),[1] few suspected that this would have such repercussions. But it started a process that would force the international lesbian and gay community not only to deal with apartheid, but also to consider whether it was at all possible for a gay and lesbian movement to disregard other aspects of human rights.

The South African group had submitted a written application for membership, stating that it was a non-profit organisation open to men and women and all races. It was the first African group to apply for membership, but the initial enthusiasm that many in ILGA felt was mitigated by the Scottish Homosexual Rights Group (SHRG), which in 1982 had received a visit from 'a black gay man from Soweto', who alleged that GASA's politics were not inclusive. Ian Christie of SHRG urged the ILGA conference not to accept GASA as a member until the question had been further discussed. His main arguments were that ILGA's international reputation was at stake, and that it was unacceptable to support a white-dominated organisation in South Africa as long as the UN boycott was in effect.[2]

1. The International Gay Association (IGA) changed its name to the International Gay and Lesbian Association (ILGA) in 1986. The current name is used throughout this essay.
2. IGA World Conference Report 1983, p. 101.

However, the SHRG proposal to bar GASA's membership was met by opposition at the 1983 ILGA world conference, which was held in Vienna. It was argued that if ILGA rejected GASA on these grounds, then other groups must be scrutinised for their lack of inclusiveness towards women and racial or ethnic minorities. Two representatives from Israel said that their group worked in an environment much like that of GASA, and they claimed that gay groups by definition are always working against the state. Finally it was decided to refer the question to the following year's conference in Helsinki.[3]

1984 and 1985

In 1984, GASA sent a representative to Helsinki. Pieter Bosman, a tall, soft-spoken, white man, charmed the conference with his mild manner and peculiar South African accent, and won it over on the issue of GASA's membership despite persistent opposition by SHRG and some others. After a long discussion it was decided that GASA would be granted full membership, but that ILGA would issue a statement about its position on racism and apartheid and would express its support of the boycott of South Africa. The statement was referred to in the conference's press release:

> Convinced that the gay liberation movement of South Africa is also a genuine part of the struggle for human rights, the IGA welcomes the membership of the national gay organisation of the Republic of South Africa and declares its opposition to Apartheid [...]. This is the first time that IGA membership extends to the continent of Africa.[4]

By this time, ILGA was growing rapidly, developing from a mainly European network of gay activists to an organisation which could perhaps better live up to its ambitious name. The Helsinki conference also saw the inclusion for the first time of a group from the Soviet Union, and the first representative ever from a Latin American group. At the ILGA conference in Toronto in 1985, a working group against apartheid was formed, but it never seems to have had any influence, and it was the Information Secretariat in Stockholm that coordinated ILGA's anti-apartheid work.

35

3. IGA World Conference Report 1983, pp. 23, 55.
4. IGA World Conference 1984, Press release.

1986

In the beginning of 1986, ILGA began to investigate why GASA had failed to support one of their own activists, Simon Nkoli, who had been imprisoned on political grounds. Nkoli had organised GASA's 'non-racial' Saturday Group in Soweto,[5] but it was for his anti-apartheid activism that he had been imprisoned. In connection with widespread protests against the new South African Constitution in 1984, several town councillors had been killed, and together with 21 other activists, Nkoli faced charges of high treason, terrorism, and murder.[6] When ILGA began to investigate, Nkoli had already been in prison for more than a year, and the trial of his group, known as the Vaal 22, had begun.

Jon Voss, a member of the Swedish national gay organisation RFSL and responsible for contacts with African groups at the ILGA Information Secretariat in Stockholm, wrote letters of support to Nkoli and also wrote to GASA asking them why they had not reported to ILGA about the case.[7] At about the same time, Voss also started the Swedish gay and lesbian monthly journal, *Reporter,* which frequently published articles about the position of gays and lesbians in South Africa. For his journal, Voss could rely on information from his extensive correspondence with many different people in South Africa: first and foremost from Nkoli and his lover Roy Shepherd, but also from Father Don Dowie, who for a short period had been Archbishop Desmond Tutu's chaplain on gay matters and frequently went to see Nkoli in jail. In the beginning the letters came mainly from white men, but gradually more black men and women began corresponding with ILGA. Alfred Machela, Sheila Lapinsky and Glen Shelton are among those who took up correspondence in a later phase. Voss has three or four letters from GASA over the period, from Kevan Botha and Ann Smith.

Some of the ILGA member groups saw the passivity of GASA in the Nkoli case as proof of its lack of sincerity when it had signed ILGA's anti-apartheid statement, and moved to exclude GASA from ILGA. Support groups for Nkoli were organised in Canada, Britain, and Sweden, as well as in other places.[8] But, from his cell, Nkoli wrote that he did not want GASA to be expelled: 'Please don't do that now, not now when I am still in prison,' he told the ILGA

5. 'Sat. Group gets own office', *Link/Skakel*, September 1984. Jon Voss's archive (JV).
6. Amnesty International Urgent Action letters UA 251/84, UA 171/85. JV.
7. RFSL-Stockholm [Jon Voss] to Elizabeth [Nkoli], 20 January 1986; IGA Information Secretariat (IS) [Jon Voss] to the South African Embassy in Stockholm, 20 January 1986; IGA IS [Jon Voss] to GASA, 10 March 1986. JV.
8. Jon Voss to Don Dowie, 1 April 1986. JV.

Information Secretariat.[9] And a month later: 'I really feel bad if IGA is going to expel GASA. Please try to understand, Jon, that there are some individual members of GASA who visit me [...]. And Gasa has been doing so much to bring change in the life of the oppressed gays.'[10]

Founded in 1982, GASA was the only group in the country that could speak for gays and lesbians. When its Saturday Group disappeared after Nkoli's arrest, there was no group that reached out to black people. There was, however, some black participation in the gay Christian community. In 1986 Alfred Siphiwe Machela founded the Rand Gay Organisation (RGO), which the international movement was to regard as a viable alternative to GASA.[11]

Before the 1986 ILGA world conference in Copenhagen, SHRG sent a letter proposing a two-year suspension of GASA's membership, since it had failed to report to ILGA on its handling of the Nkoli case, and because 'the membership of the IGA by a South African organisation which did not condemn apartheid as a part of its constitution would undermine the position of the IGA'.[12] GASA again sent a representative to the conference, Kevan Botha, who succeeded in countering the SHRG initiative. The conference workshop which prepared the issue for the plenary, chaired by Botha, discussed it at length. It was argued that GASA had signed the ILGA anti-apartheid statement in 1984, and that problems of communication could have delayed GASA's answer when ILGA urged them to report on the Nkoli case. Furthermore, Botha 'gave an extensive account of GASA's multiracial work in sport, in its committees, in advice bureaux, in law reform campaigns', and the proposal to suspend GASA's membership was not carried to the plenary. Instead, the conference sent a letter of support to Nkoli, and a letter of protest to the South African president, P. W. Botha, denouncing both apartheid and the lack of gay and lesbian rights. Finally, a petition of support for the Vaal 22 was circulated among ILGA member groups, so that each group could decide whether to endorse it or not.[13]

In the July/August issue of *Exit*, at the time the only gay and lesbian publication in South Africa, Kevan Botha was hailed as a national hero with the editorial claiming that he 'had defended his country and his organisation'.[14] In the next

9. Simon Nkoli to Jon Voss, 25 March 1986. JV.
10. Simon Nkoli to Jon Voss, 10 April 1986. JV.
11. Message from James Willett-Clarke, National president of GASA, 3 July 1986 (a 34-page report on GASA's history and activities); Roy Shepherd to Jon Voss, 18 March 1986; Sipho Ndlangamandla to IGA IS, 9 April 1986; Alfred Machela to Jon Voss, May 1986 (no date). JV.
12. ILGA World Conference Report 1986, p. 24.
13. ILGA World Conference 1986, 'Decisions, actions taken, recommendations', p. 11.
14. 'A bouquet after the vote', *Exit*, July/August 1986, p. 2. JV.

edition, former GASA chairman James Willett-Clarke said that 'the despised "moffies" have succeeded in staying in a world organisation where the respectable straights failed to achieve this so often'.[15] Voss wrote angrily in a private letter: 'If GASA sees itself as a representative of SA – then we shall with joy throw them out of ILGA. SA today is an embarrassment to all humankind – and saying that "gays have succeeded where respectable straights failed" is an insult, both to ILGA and to all blacks in SA. Mr Willett-Clarke must be totally unaware of what is going on in SA – and he should understand that this sort of statement cannot be of help to gays when a new government will take over.'[16] Botha could, of course, not be held responsible for the coverage in *Exit,* but the Copenhagen conference was to have consequences for GASA's international reputation.

Botha had dissociated GASA from the petition of support for the Vaal 22 and pointed out that they were charged with murder, among other overtly political charges. Voss wrote in a letter that he had missed parts of Botha's speech and he tried to check with others what Botha had actually said, but he got conflicting answers. 'Some of the delegates say that he only warned us from "pointing out" Simon and by that making his situation worse. One other delegate said that Botha actually said that it would not be wise to push the Simon–Vaal 22 case so hard since they also were accused of murder.' Botha's speech resulted in a furious letter from Nkoli's attorney, Caroline Heaton-Nicholls. She regarded his statement about the murder charges as an outrageous and ungrateful attack on Nkoli, and made it clear that the state had failed to present any evidence to implicate any of the accused directly with the murder charges.

Botha subsequently explained to the ILGA Information Secretariat that his comments 'were made in the context that there has been no international suggestion that the trial is conducted unfairly' and that his argument simply had been 'that the ILGA should not pre-empt the decision of the court by the petition and that it should await the findings of the court before commencing the action'. Moreover, he assured ILGA that the discussions in Copenhagen had made him understand the necessity to work against apartheid as well as gay rights: 'I must say that I returned home enthused to motivate a direction for

15. *Exit,* August/September 1986, p. 5. JV.   16. Jon Voss to Don Dowie, 1 November 1986. JV.

the association in terms of which we could build on the existing foundations we have laid and thereby achieve a far greater identity with the human rights movement in general and mutually exploit the general air of sensitivity and expectation in return for our support.'[17] GASA also reaffirmed its stand against apartheid and extended an apology to Nkoli.

From his cell, Nkoli wrote letters to ILGA and SHRG, complaining about Botha's actions in Copenhagen. And in an embittered letter to Voss, he wrote: 'I am absolutely difficult now for GASA. I don't want to be used by them to further their own propaganda. They have never supported me, since ever I was arrested. They failed to even organising reading materials for me, so what is there for them to do.'[18] After Nkoli's denunciations, GASA's position was further weakened within the international gay and lesbian community.

Nkoli was also disappointed by the members of his own Saturday Group who had come to visit him. 'There was a white guy there by the name of Robin who was dominating other guys. I was very disappointed when he told me that they will only support me because I am gay, they are not going to support me as a politician.'[19] In fact, the striving to separate gay politics from other kinds of politics would soon become untenable, and as it became increasingly clear that political change would come in South Africa, the question of non-collaboration with the existing political structures became more and more important.

1987

At the next ILGA conference, in 1987, new demands for the expulsion of GASA were made. This time the world conference was held in Cologne. GASA had no representative present, but the Rand Gay Organisation had sent Alfred Machela, who reported that black people felt increasingly excluded from GASA activities. He also emphasised that in South Africa it was impossible for a gay group to be apolitical. The workshop preparing the issue for plenary presented two proposals: the immediate expulsion of GASA was propagated by the Japanese ILGA support group, and by FAGC and EGHAM from Catalonia and the Basque countries respectively; the other proposal was to suspend GASA's

39

17. Kevan Botha to ILGA IS [David Murphy], 21 October 1986. JV.
18. Simon Nkoli to Jon Voss, 2 November 1986. JV.
19. Simon Nkoli to Jon Voss, 2 November 1986. JV.

membership 'while a report is being made by an ILGA-appointed delegate' whose travel expenses would be covered by three Scandinavian national gay and lesbian organisations.[20]

The third plenary session, on 1 July 1987, opened on a highly emotional note when it was announced that Nkoli had been released on bail after three years' imprisonment. Many activists present had worked hard to turn the world's attention to Nkoli's plight, and the news was greeted with extended applause. 'When we heard about Simon's release during the conference we were so happy,' Voss wrote shortly afterwards. 'I and Alfred cried and a lot of us felt like something important had happened. Not just for Simon and Roy, but also for the gay community as a whole.'[21] This triumphant moment, however, was soon tarnished by procedural questions regarding how to count the vote on the GASA issue. In the workshop a simple majority was sufficient to carry a propos-al to the plenary, but in the plenary an 80 per cent majority was needed for all decisions, thus ensuring the widest possible consensus on all matters. It was also pointed out that ILGA lacked formal rules in its constitution for the sus-pension or expulsion of member groups. Since the matter had been discussed thoroughly in the workshop, the chairs of the plenary session cut discussion short and proceeded directly to a vote. The proposal to expel GASA from ILGA was defeated by 37 votes to 19, and the proposal to suspend GASA's mem-bership while investigating its standpoint regarding apartheid was carried with 48 votes to 7 with one abstention.[22]

The question of GASA's expulsion divided the conference. In the discussions, nobody questioned the UN boycott of South Africa, but many delegates felt that one should not confound a gay and lesbian group with the government of the country in which it worked. Why should extra pressure be put on GASA to prove that it worked against its government if such pressure was not put on any other group? Fundamentally, the discussion revolved around the ques-tion of whether it was possible to separate gay and lesbian politics from other kinds of political struggle. At that time, the ILGA member groups for the most part were pursuing their work in the traditions of US-inspired minority-rights activism. But as Hoad (1999) has pointed out, this was not possible in South

20. ILGA World Conference Report 1987, p. 20.
21. Jon Voss to Glen Shelton, 9 July 1987. JV.
22. ILGA World Conference Report 1987, p. 10.

Africa under apartheid, where a minority oppressed the majority, and where consequently the very concept of minority politics was regarded with suspicion by the oppressed majority.[23] Nevertheless, the politically radical groups within ILGA, and particularly those from regions sensitive to ethnic discrimination, such as Scotland, Catalonia, and the Basque countries, forced ILGA to take into consideration a wider spectrum of human rights. As a result of the discussions, the 1987 conference sent a letter of support to Nkoli, congratulating him on his release and asking him to convey a greeting to his fellow prisoners that 'we believe that the struggle for lesbian and gay rights and for human rights are one and indivisible'.[24]

BETWEEN TWO HUMAN RIGHTS MOVEMENTS

If the international gay and lesbian community could not reach consensus on whether to support the struggle against apartheid as well as the struggle for gay and lesbian rights, this reflects a dilemma which was the more acutely felt in South Africa, since the anti-apartheid movement's support for gay and lesbian rights at this time was far from evident. 'Being an isolated gay person among 21 straight people is very difficult – and most of the time I am tense,' Simon wrote in an early letter to Voss. If it had not been for the support of his two friends Gcina Malindi and Johnny Mokoena, life in the cell with the other prisoners would have been even more difficult.[25] And when different gay and lesbian groups around the world declared that they wanted to support the Vaal 22, the other prisoners were reluctant to accept their help. 'Out of 22 of us, only six people would like to get financial help from you,' Nkoli wrote to Voss, 'but five of them would not want that people should know [who] they are getting a financial support from, and that I cannot tolerate.'[26] However, the prisoners were in great need of support, and some of them were the sole breadwinners for their families. Dowie reported that 'Fortunately Caroline, the young lawyer in day to day contact with them, took a tough line. Money is money, an offer is an offer and gays must not be denied credit for it.'[27]

On many levels, there was a concerted effort to reach out to the anti-apartheid movement from the gay and lesbian movement. In February 1986, Voss wrote

41

23. Hoad 1999, pp. 576–7.
24. ILGA World Conference Report 1987, p. 54.
25. Simon Nkoli to Jon Voss, 25 March 1986. JV.
26. Simon Nkoli to Jon Voss, 26 April 1986. JV.
27. Priscilla Jana, Nkoli's attorney, to Jon Voss, 20 May 1986; Don Dowie to Jon Voss, 4 June 1986. JV.

to the ANC office in Stockholm and asked for a meeting to discuss gay and lesbian issues and possible ways for the international gay and lesbian movement to support the struggle against apartheid. But the letter remained unanswered.[28] A year later, the Catalonian group FAGC suggested that the ANC should guarantee GASA's anti-apartheid stance, but Voss had to inform them that '[the] ANC, to our knowledge, is not very concerned about the gay struggle. Please contact your local ANC representatives to pressure them to take a stand on gay issues.'[29] It is not known whether many gay groups made such contacts with the ANC worldwide.

GASA'S COLLAPSE

Botha had told the Copenhagen conference that he had been in contact with Tutu and discussed gay issues. And in January 1987, Nkoli reported that Botha had told him that Botha and Machela had arranged a meeting with the United Democratic Front (UDF), but that Nkoli had not heard any more details about it. This meeting is not mentioned elsewhere in the correspondence.[30]

But even if GASA did take a more active stance against apartheid, and even if contacts were made between the gay and the anti-apartheid movements, the organisation was not able to meet the demands of local politics. In March 1987 Shelton, writing as an independent gay activist from Cape Town, told ILGA that he 'would like to applaud the Scottish gay and lesbian organisation on their stand against Gasa'.[31] And at a meeting in Cape Town at the beginning of April, the Congress of Pink Democrats (CPD) was founded. The new organisation consisted of four groups committed to 'non-racism', 'non-sexism', 'non-heterosexism' and 'non-collaboration with Apartheid's structures and their ramifications in economic, political and social structures'. Botha, representing GASA, attended the meeting, but his association could not align itself with the CPD. Shelton reported to ILGA that the statement of principles had not been acceptable to GASA's members, but noted: 'I must give credit to Kevan for his remarkable handling of the situation and a genuine acknowledgement that GASA was actually racist, sexist and collaborationist.'[32]

42

28. Jon Voss to ANC's Stockholm office, 3 February 1986. JV.
29. ILGA IS [Jon Voss] to GSG in Sydney, FAGC in Barcelona, and SHRG in Edinburgh, 13 February 1987. JV.
30. Simon Nkoli to Jon Voss, 3 January 1987. JV.

31. Glen Shelton to ILGA, March 1987 (no date); cf Jon Voss to Glen Shelton, 31 March 1987. JV.
32. Glen Shelton to Jon Voss, 9 April 1987; Congress of Pink Democrats, Statement of principles. JV.

While GASA did have some conservative members who supported the apartheid system, its main problem at this time was that it was embedded in the political structures of an undemocratic society which was doomed to fall. In an undated pamphlet, GASA boasted of its 'international and national links'. Apart from its ties with ILGA, it mentioned its links with 'government agencies' and 'the South African Defence Force'.[33] This would not be a problem in a democratic society, but in South Africa in the 1980s it was not acceptable.

GASA was thus challenged both within South Africa and internationally, and after its suspension from ILGA and the founding of the CPD, it did not take long before GASA collapsed. At a meeting in Johannesburg on 25 and 26 July it was announced that GASA no longer existed. According to the newsletter *LAGO News*, Botha had 'been claimed by burn-out', and the only functioning branch of GASA was the Cape Town chapter, which was about to change its name. The Gay Alliance was formed, but progressive gays refused to participate. GASA's last acting national chairman, Eddie de Beer, confirmed that GASA's relationship with ILGA was now a dead issue, since GASA no longer existed. 'It is understood that should any former GASA branch wish to apply for membership of ILGA it would then do so as an independent separate organisation,' the newsletter concluded.[34]

1988

GASA's membership of ILGA had been suspended by the conference in 1987, but the report clarifying GASA's position on apartheid was never written, and no delegate was sent to South Africa to investigate matters. At the 1988 conference, in Oslo, when Machela again represented the RGO, the plenary decided as follows:

This conference, noting that GASA
no longer sees itself as a member of ILGA;
has ceased to exist;
has not paid any membership fee for two years;
states that GASA is not a member of the ILGA and would be required to

43

33. Undated pamphlet. It mentions IGA, which dates it to after GASA's admission to IGA in June 1984, but before 12 July 1986, when IGA changed its name to ILGA. JV.
34. *LAGO News*, 28 August 1987. JV.

reapply for membership should it wish to participate in the ILGA in the future.[35]

Commenting on the new situation, that the collapse of GASA saved ILGA from having to expel the South African group formally, the Scottish delegate said drily that it was a pity that ILGA 'had been let off the hook from taking a political decision that should have been made years ago'.[36] One is forced to draw the conclusion that GASA was thus never officially expelled from ILGA, despite the continuous efforts of many activists. Instead the issue dragged on for years, and there was a marked reluctance from the majority of ILGA representatives to hold a member group responsible for its stance on apartheid. GASA silently vanished from the ILGA scene, and ILGA missed its opportunity to take a firm stand against apartheid.

Conclusion

The question of GASA's membership of ILGA had haunted the organisation for five years. During that time it provoked heated debates and internal conflicts more than once. In 1983 an Israeli group left ILGA in protest because GASA was *not* admitted as a member. In 1984 GASA's admission made it necessary for ILGA explicitly to condemn apartheid for the first time. And GASA's presence in ILGA was constantly challenged by member groups in different countries. But, as Voss pointed out to some of GASA's most persistent foes, 'I have not yet received any requests from anyone in South Africa asking us to expel or suspend GASA – no organisation and no individual. Expelling GASA would then mean that the international body should take a serious decision concerning the gay community in South Africa without getting the support of either black, coloured or white gays or lesbians in South Africa.'[37] And this was certainly true. Not only did no one from South Africa demand the expulsion of GASA, but Nkoli, Shepherd, Dowie and Machela all wrote explicitly that GASA should remain in ILGA.[38] And even in an open letter to ILGA from the CPD, in which they scathingly criticised GASA for its collaborationist politics and declared that they could not seek membership in ILGA if GASA remained a member, they stated that 'We are not actively campaigning for GASA's expulsion'.[39] In a

44

35. ILGA World Conference Report 1988, pp. 11, 14.
36. ILGA World Conference Report 1988, p. 14.
37. Jon Voss to GSG in Sydney, FAGC in Barcelona, and SHRG in Edinburgh, 13 February 1987. JV.
38. Simon Nkoli to Jon Voss, 25 March and 20 April 1986; Roy Shepherd to Jon Voss, 18 March 1986; Don Dowie to Jon Voss, 19 March 1986; Alfred Machela to Jon Voss, 9 June 1986. JV.
39. Open letter from the Congress of Pink Democrats and supporters to the ILGA, September 1987 (?) (no date), signed by Tseko Simon Nkoli, Glen Shelton, Keith du Toit, L. R. Sihiya, and an illegible signature. JV.

letter to Voss, Shelton explained to him: 'Ironically, while reading your letter, I realised that we have been waiting on each other to make a move on GASA. None of the groups here has felt they wanted to actually ask for GASA's removal from the ILGA although most of us have agreed that they are what we have called "sell-outs" or collaborationists. We were hoping you would make the decision.'[40]

The GASA issue certainly had an impact on the gay and lesbian movement, worldwide. Voss explained to Dowie, that 'For us, working with Simon and against the apartheid system, is not only a gesture of solidarity. It is also a great help to our community, in making it aware of the complexity of oppression: that you can not isolate one oppression from another. It also makes it possible for us to try to work with gay issues not only from a white middle-class European perspective.'[41] The discussions about GASA's membership made the international lesbian and gay community question whether it was possible to form a broad alliance around one specific issue, and also forced the anti-apartheid movement to acknowledge the presence of gays and lesbians in the struggle for equal rights. Slowly a new kind of trust grew up between the two movements.

In the long run, GASA risked compromising the gay and lesbian movement in the eyes of the future leaders of South Africa, and those who did not stay clear of GASA would also be regarded with suspicion. Ever since Machela founded the RGO, he had criticised GASA for its non-inclusive politics, but he also tried to keep a dialogue with them and influence their attitudes, and this made him vulnerable to attacks from two sides. In the summer of 1986 he was scheduled to go to the Copenhagen conference, but one of his South African sponsors withdrew its support because of a rumour that his intention was to 'edge GASA from the world body', according to a report in *Exit*. Machela confirmed to Voss that an air company had promised a return ticket but declined its offer because of this rumour. 'Despite attempts to explain that there was no truth in the story, they were no longer interested,' Machela explained. In October 1986, Botha wrote to ILGA that 'Alfred Machela has won my personal respect and confidence as a pragmatic leader who I believe identifies the need for

45

40. Glen Shelton to Jon Voss, 9 April 1987. JV.
41. Jon Voss to Don Dowie, 1 April 1986. JV.

unity at all costs'.[42] And before going to the Cologne conference in 1987, Machela was quoted in *Exit* that he would fight to keep GASA in ILGA. He claimed he was misquoted, and at the conference he did quite the opposite, but Shelton criticised him for 'his peculiar insistence on helping GASA' and said that this was the direct reason that Machela did not get a visa to Sweden, since the ANC did not endorse his visa application.[43] (Because of the UN boycott, Swedish policy was to deny South African citizens entry unless they were vouched for by the ANC.)

At the ILGA conference in July 1987, Machela reported that the ANC had responded to the RGO's questions in a negative way and said that it would treat every social problem as it arose, and that the RGO had demanded the ANC's unconditional support.[44] He had planned to go to Stockholm directly after the conference, but could not get a visa. Whether it was for his conciliatory attitude toward GASA, as Shelton suggested, or simply because the ANC did not care much for gay and lesbian politics at the time, he had to cancel the trip. At about this time, Shelton had an argument with Machela and criticised him for not understanding the importance of non-collaboration. 'As I mention above, the reason for the cancellation of the visas was that gay politics are considered to be reactionary. Especially in the light of GASA's project. [—] Alfred understands the importance of not collaborating *outside* of gay politics very well, but, like many left gays in SA, he doesn't emphasise enough the need to ensure the non-collaborationist status of gay politics as well.'[45] Later that year, however, Swedish gay group (RFSL) managed to get support from the Swedish International Development Agency (SIDA) for a joint AIDS prevention project, coordinated by RGO and RFSL and financed by SIDA. Machela was invited by SIDA, and could finally visit Sweden in October 1987. During this visit, two meetings were arranged with representatives of the ANC. On the first occasion, Machela met with Jerry Matsile in the office of the *Reporter*, a meeting which was surrounded by great secrecy, and everyone else had to leave the premises during the meeting.[46] Machela, however, was not satisfied with this meeting, and after some pressure from SIDA he was allowed to meet with Lindiwe Mabuza, then chief representative of the ANC in Sweden.[47]

42. Kevan Botha to ILGA IS [David Murphy], 21 October 1986. JV.
43. 'Machela will fight to keep Gasa in Ilga', *Exit*, June/July 1987; Glen Shelton to Jon Voss, 16 June 1987. JV.
44. ILGA World Conference Report 1987, p. 19.
45. Glen Shelton to Jon Voss, 17 July 1987. Emphasis in original. JV.
46. Personal communication with Jon Voss, 27 December 2004.
47. Personal communication with Alfred Siphiwe Machela, 10 January 2005.

It seems that it was around this time that the ANC began to show an interest in gay and lesbian issues. According to a document from the Organisation of Lesbian and Gay Activists (OLGA), distributed in 1990, a number of supportive ANC statements from 1987 onwards made it possible to work for the inclusion of lesbian and gay rights in the Constitution. In November 1987, Thabo Mbeki said that 'The ANC is indeed very firmly committed to removing all forms of discrimination and oppression in a liberated South Africa [—] That commitment must surely extend to the protection of gay rights.' In another statement the same year, Frene Ginwala commented: 'The ANC is a broad church [—] Our membership reflects South African society and overwhelmingly the oppressed majority within which there are gays and lesbians, but also within which there are people who do not have, as yet, a developed understanding of the need to eradicate all forms of discrimination against gays and lesbians in society.' And she went on to say that the ANC must fight discrimination 'and deprivation of gays and lesbians cannot be excluded from that process'. At a press conference in Stockholm in March 1990, Nelson Mandela was asked to comment on the attitude of the ANC to progressive lesbian and gay organisations in South Africa. He replied: 'We have already indicated that we are presently addressing the issues of uniting all anti-apartheid forces, drawing no distinctions whatsoever concerning anti-apartheid organisations. Whether we are going to succeed in bringing about that united front depends on the response of the organisations involved. But all I can assure you is that we will leave no stone unturned in our effort to unite the oppressed people of our country.'[48]

With hindsight, it is striking how unprofessionally the whole GASA issue was dealt with by ILGA. The position of the association shifted according to whether GASA sent a representative or not; procedural questions obstructed a firm dealing with the issue; and the discussions in the workshops were often poorly structured. At one point, the workshop was not aware whether it had passed a recommendation or not, since it did not know how many votes were necessary to carry it.[49] On the other hand, the association was not made up of professional lobbyists. The difficulties in handling the GASA issue were due largely to the fact that ILGA was a highly democratic association. Its structure was open and flat, inclusive towards women, and sensitive to questions of racism, sex-

47

48. OLGA's proposed amendments to the constitutional guidelines/draft constitution of the African National Congress, p. 5. JV.
49. ILGA World Conference Report 1987, p.19.

ism, able-ism, ageism and so on. But ILGA was also vulnerable and easily disrupted by conflicts. Although ILGA activists were mostly highly experienced and competent, the difficulties inherent in bringing together activists and groups from different continents, with distinct political and organisational traditions, were often overwhelming. The GASA issue exposed all these weaknesses, but also forced it to deal with issues that influenced the future of the movement. And the most important result of the entire affair was perhaps that it contributed to South Africa becoming the first country in the world to include the protection of its gay and lesbian citizens in its Constitution.

Note on the sources

The main sources for this article are my own memories of the ILGA conferences, conference reports, and the private archive that Jon Voss kindly has given me access to. There is of course a risk that the Swedish perspective gets too much emphasis, given these sources.[50] Simon Nkoli corresponded with gay and lesbian groups in more than a dozen countries, and at one point he reports that his mother had received over 300 letters of support from all over the world. It is important to remember that support for Nkoli and opposition to apartheid was an international movement. The international political movements of the 1980s, which laid the ground for worldwide political changes around 1990, allowed such a broad movement to develop. All those who wrote to the ILGA Information Secretariat had different interests to defend, and wanted to explain the situation in South Africa from their particular viewpoint. Accordingly, the information in the letters is not necessarily objective. I have tried to balance the sources against each other, in order to establish the most likely interpretation of the chain of events. All quotes are rendered with the exact wording, but I have standardised the spelling. All letters referred to are in the private archive of Jon Voss, Stockholm, and the conference reports are to be found in the private archive of the author. Copies of *Link/Skakel*, *Exit*, *LAGO News* and various pamphlets are all in Jon Voss's archive.

50. For an exhaustive account of Swedish involvement in the South African anti-apartheid movement, see Sellström (2002).

ESSAY

Works cited

Hoad, Neville (1999). 'Between the white man's burden and the white man's disease: Tracking lesbian and gay human rights in Southern Africa.' *GLQ: A Journal of Lesbian and Gay Studies,* 5:4, 559-84.

Sellström, Tor (2002). *Sweden and National Liberation in Southern Africa: Solidarity and Assistance, 1970–1994.* Uppsala: Nordiska Afrikainstitutet.

49

Personal testimony: A lesson well worth learning

Kevan Botha

Kevan Botha provides a personal context for his approach, as the GASA representative, to the proposed expulsion of GASA from ILGA at the 1986 ILGA conference, and reflects on the consequences for his development as a gay rights
activist.

I have been privileged over the past twenty years to have been part of movements that have played meaningful roles in securing the rights of the lesbian
and gay community in South Africa. My formative introduction to the politics
of the gay rights movement as national secretary of GASA and the events of
the 1986 ILGA conference were salutary lessons which served as a solid foundation for the lobbying work that followed through the Equality Foundation and
the seminal work of the National Coalition for Gay and Lesbian Equality. Over
the past two decades I have worked with individuals whose insight, dedication
and commitment to justice have played important roles in my own development as a gay man, as an African and, more importantly, as a human being.

The documents and narratives contained in this book seek to provide greater
clarity about events that gave rise to the constitutional covenant by South
Africans to accord equality to all irrespective of their sexual orientation.
As is often the case with recording relatively recent history, there is no single
perspective; achievement of constitutional protections in a bill of rights is the
result of many struggles involving the commitment and dedication of many
organised groups and individuals in South Africa and across the globe. Each
of those organisations and individuals holds their own determinative perspec-
tives of events forming salient historical markers in that struggle.

I was asked by the authors to provide a personal perspective on one of those
markers in the struggle for gay rights: the international isolation of GASA
through the campaign for its expulsion from the ILGA and its eventual demise,
which ultimately served a key strategic role in forcing its members and the
wider gay and lesbian community in South Africa to accept unequivocally that
gay rights were inseparable from larger questions of liberation, in particular
the eradication of apartheid. I was asked in particular if I would record my feel-

ings on receiving the letter from Caroline Heaton-Nicholls which is published in this compendium. The letter and the events which gave rise to it stand as a marker on my personal journey of political awareness and understanding of the pervasive effects of apartheid. It also stands to my eternal embarrassment as a marker of my naivety in formulating a fallacious argument that should never have been made. The observations which follow are therefore intensely personal.

In recording these thoughts, I do not seek to justify or contextualise the historical record in the wider debates of that time. That is the role of commentators and researchers, and my proximity to many of these events deprives me of the objectivity necessary for that enterprise. However, the depiction of one of the arguments I made at the 1986 ILGA conference stands in sharp counterpoint to my wider commitment to the struggle for human rights. It is appropriate therefore that I should provide my own perspective.

For me, the passage of years has not dimmed Caroline's forthright and eloquent advocacy on behalf of Simon and his co-accused in the Delmas Trial or the force of its impact on me. Her quintessential point, that the trial was predicated on a fiction of common purpose unsupported in any evidence at the trial and that I had not made appropriate and sufficient inquiry about those facts, singularly undercut the otherwise carefully nuanced position that I had adopted at the 1986 ILGA conference. Her point was well taken; for had I prior to the conference stepped back and asked those questions, as I pointedly and correctly should have done, a very different history would be recorded about those events. That failure was not only a personal and professional failure but a disservice to my own sense of fairness.

However, underneath the personal embarrassment there was a more important personal realisation that played a central part in my understanding of the broader struggle in South Africa. Central to my upbringing was a belief that courts were honest arbiters of the issues before them; that they could implicitly be trusted to dispense justice based on the evidence before them. However, following the ILGA conference and Caroline's intervention I was forced to starkly confront the fact that my then belief had been shaped and filtered through the prism of my experiences as a white, male South African. In so many cases the daily reality for the majority of South Africans was that justice could not be assured by simple recourse to South African courts. My utopian confidence was not only misguided but intrinsically flawed.

51

At the ILGA conference I had supported without any reservation a letter of support from conference to Simon, had no difficulty in supporting the resolution condemning apartheid and personally sponsored the suggestion of a letter of protest to PW Botha, who through a quirk of fate shared my surname and therefore probably an ancestor. In relation to the resolution of solidarity and support for the 'Vaal 22', as the Delmas Trial defendants were known, my argument was not that such support should never be forthcoming but that it should follow clarification and not 'pre-empt the decision of the court'. It was an argument that recommended a stance of 'not now' rather than 'not never'. Yet it was an argument too far. At first hurdle it offended the principle that everyone was entitled to be regarded as innocent until proven guilty by a competent court. Underpinning my misguided argument was a reliance on the legitimacy of the legal process and the courts that was naïve and at odds with the manifestly political nature of the charges, the paucity of evidence and the daily experiences of Simon and so many other South Africans. I did not know those facts about the evidence at trial at the time; yet I could so easily have acquainted myself with those facts if I had simply asked about them expressly.

Apartheid was pernicious and pervading in its impact on the lives of the majority of South Africans. By repeated indignities and perpetual classifications of human beings into categories of difference it defined generations of South Africans and caused immense harm. It dehumanised people and desensitised others, including me, to its magnitude and effect on fellow citizens and institutions that are taken for granted in democratic societies. That it did not occur to me at the time to thoroughly cross-check each of those facts was not a conscious strategy. Yet in its simple omission it was a failure to accord to Simon and his fellow co-accused the most basic of human rights: the right to the same treatment as I would have wished and expected for myself. That omission on my part had a hugely hurtful impact on Simon, his then partner Roy, Simon's fellow accused in the trial, their family and friends at a period when my actions unnecessarily added to the stress of defending themselves against unjust charges in an unjust trial. Over the intervening years I have been afforded affection and friendship by many of them disproportionate to the indignity that my spurious and thoughtless argument in 1986 caused to each of them.

Too few white South Africans have taken the opportunity to acknowledge their failings and thoughtlessness about the daily indignities and suffering perpetrated by them or in their name under apartheid. I was fortunate, through the unfolding events of the ILGA conference in 1986, to have had to confront publicly and in an international forum my own insensitivity in the way in which I presented that argument. That insensitivity had its genesis in a wider failing to identify earlier in my life the dehumanising and pervasive effect that apartheid had had on me. It constituted a personal marker in understanding myself and the world around me. However, my personal lesson came at a cost borne in the effect that my actions had on Simon and his comrades. For the quiet dignity and patient understanding that Simon showed to me over the next fifteen years, I will always be grateful.

I hope that in some small way my enduring commitment and contribution to the cause of human rights, including the equal rights of every human being irrespective of their sexual orientation, have gone some way to redeem the misguided position I adopted in relation to the Delmas accused at the 1986 ILGA conference. It was a lesson that on a personal level was well worth learning.

These incomplete handwritten notes were made for a speech to be delivered at the 1986 International Lesbian and Gay Association's annual conference by Alfred Machela, representing the newly formed Rand Gay Organisation. Machela was not able to attend the conference when sponsorship of his airfare did not materialise. The notes are in the Alfred Machela collection at the Gay and Lesbian Archives of South Africa.

Since our inception, at the beginging a lot of people could not understand us or our stand for gay rights as well as broader human rights. We were taken as trouble makers and people who were trying to move two mountains to come together. Our being was interesting, but also frustrating in part.

To those who critised us, we made it clear, that we were committed to making the gay community aware of the realities of life for everyone, in this country. Far too many of South Africans still live in a dream-world, in which, they see, or are made to see, what they want to see. So long as they are left undisturbed and enjoy the sort of contact they want. They float along merrily, forgetful of the cold reality, that many of our members continue to suffer as victims of injustice. They also seem to ignore that the present state of affairs could become infinitely worse.

But we are glad to inform you that since a R Go was started some few months ago, we have been able to point out to other groups that

Since South Africa is in Crises
it does not make Sense to claim
that "our group is apolitical."
Nothing in this Country can be apolitical
We have also pointed out that, the
gay community can not afford to be
relegated to the margins of the Struggle.

With these point gay groups ~~to~~ are
now starting to realise the nessasity
of being part of the Struggle. ~~To~~ GASA
has also joined the band wagon of this
struggle ~~for human~~ for the political
necessity for human Survival. Though
their ~~pace~~ is pretty slow, but we
as NGO believe that with More Mortivin-
tion they will ~~it~~ Come right. With
NGO insight we trust that they will
over Come their fears.

We are aware of frustrations and
embarrassement of ILGA Member group
because of GASA's presence in this
international body and Maybe that
is the reason Some groups have
expressed their wish to resign if
GASA is not kicked out. We Understand your reasons very well and
we Can not blame you for taking

Such a punitive action.

    Should I L G A take such action
there is nothing we can do but other
than pointing out that you shall have
punished the gay community here (mainly
white gays.)
We believe that GASA can be made
to change with the International demand
and cooperation. Throwing them out will
not solve anything.

    RGO and LAGAO (Lesbians and gays
against oppression have proposed an alliance
which will be non as Progressive gay and
lesbian alliance which will aim at
politicising the gay community. GASA
have requested to be a member of this
alliance which is a thing they would have
never wanted to be part of before.

    However this is a plea from RGO
me and RGO to the I L G A and all
its member groups not to expell GASA
from I L G A. We also would like to
place on record that we are at
your disposal should you want to
know more about the happenings in
South Africa.

We are also

At the moment we are compiling a
document on South Africa which we
hope to table at the next ILGA
Conference should we be able to attend.
The document is composed of
vidio tapes and interviews with people
from different organisations and politician

Yours gayly

Alfred Machele

Where was I in the eighties?

Ann Smith

In this personal testimony Ann Smith responds to the intentionally provocative
question 'Where were you in the eighties?' by examining her shifting identity in
relation to unfolding political events.

Where was I in the eighties? For me this question has less to do with an
enquiry about my literal geographical location twenty years ago than with where
I would place myself along the continuum of the identity I now claim for myself
in order to answer it. In other words, 'Who was I?'

In this personal testimony I will try to present and represent myself, as honestly
as possible, as I was then, in relation to being a founder member of GASA, the
Gay Association of South Africa, the first national association of its sort.

In an effort to convey to my students the complexity of what is included in the
notion of 'identity' I get them to list a few of the positions, in no particular
order, they occupy in the world that they think best capture what it is that
makes them uniquely themselves at that moment. They come up with lists
which include woman/man, daughter/son, mother/father, student, musician,
lover, friend, etc. In similar spirit I would list for myself, as writer of the personal testimony, and in no particular order, the positions of lesbian, mother, academic and activist. While these positions are no different in name from those
that I may well have thought of myself as occupying two decades ago, even if
I did not ever articulate this explicitly, what has changed is my understanding
of what is implied by my appropriation of these terms and, perhaps more
importantly, of the relationships between and amongst them.

It was in June 1974, on my 30th birthday, that I met the first woman I ever fell
in love with. I was married and had three children – surely and obviously(?) a
heterosexual mother. But suddenly, according to my understanding of the term
then, I was a lesbian! Most of the women-loving women I got to know at that
time called themselves 'gay women'; the term 'lesbian' was still thought to be
somewhat extreme and unnecessarily 'in-your-face' then, but I loved the idea
of being something so outrageously explicit as a lesbian! This decision to be a

'lesbian' rather than a 'gay woman' had no political basis at all since I had no knowledge of the politics behind the lesbian refusal to be grouped with homosexual men under the common adjective 'gay'. Furthermore, of the implications of seeing myself as both 'lesbian' and 'mother' I remained blissfully unaware (at the cost, I later discovered, of a certain amount of well-being in my two younger children). In February 1976 I went to university for the first time; my youngest child started school that same year. Long before I had any sense at all of the various implications of considering myself a student, I was a lesbian student mother. Immediately after I completed my BA Honours degree, I accepted the invitation to take up a junior position at the university; so now I was a lesbian academic who was also a mother. In 1982 I went to a meeting, which resulted, quite soon afterwards, in my being a founder member of GASA; so now I could add the final description of myself to the list – I was an activist.

It was with the sincerest of good intentions that I threw myself into what I saw to be worthwhile gay activism. After all, I was a 'mother' – therefore I knew about being a member, however erstwhile, of the heterosexual enemy. And I was in love with a woman so I knew about being a lesbian, didn't I? This, I then believed, qualified me to be an 'understanding and competent gay activist'! That I was also an academic simply added to the existing qualifications, and I was not alone in the belief that this was an admirable combination of 'identities' for a 'gay activist' in South Africa in those dark days. The University of the Witwatersrand had long been considered one of the hotbeds of revolutionary activity, and this did, in some ways, add to my credentials as an activist, in spite of the fact that we saw no necessary connection between this sort of revolutionary activity and the establishment of a gay association. This was genuinely ingenuous naïvety, based on honourable ignorance of what it actually meant – or in hindsight now, of course, what it should have meant – to be any kind of activist, gay or other, in the early 1980s in South Africa.

In those heady early days of what we thought of as 'gay liberation' in South Africa, we, the founder members of GASA, saw ourselves as courageous – and we were. The National Party government of the day – with what I now recognise to have been its entrenched religiously, politically and socially upheld heterosexism – was strongly oppressive, and we were in danger. But we were determined to make a difference. Sexual acts between members of the same sex, along with masturbation and bestiality, constituted, under the law, punishable behaviour in its turning of permissible procreative sex into impermissible recreational sex. Gay-bashing was an institutionalised right, as the fairly common homophobic bumper stickers such as 'Kill a queer for Christ' and later 'AIDS is God's way of punishing queers' made clear. The right of gay men and lesbians to self-expression, privacy and freedom of association fuelled our efforts. What is so very obvious to me now never occurred to any of us then – we did not see oppression as a continuum. We did not see the now glaringly obvious connections between homophobia and racism. It was not that we were blind to this relationship: we simply did not see it. I was a brand-new 'academic', very recently graduated from the old canonical school of English literature and with no training at all in the social or political sciences. We all 'knew' about racism, but the term 'heterosexism' had no place in our lexicon. Much less did we have any understanding of the ramifications of a social order so overwhelmingly based on its unquestioned inevitability. Nor, moreover, did we see the link between this inevitability and that on which racism is based.

I think, looking back, that we saw homophobia as existing in a kind of vacuum, but also, unlike racism, as something that we could tackle. We had no intellectual awareness at all of the dynamics of political power structures of any sort. If we saw any connections at all between 'gay liberation' (at least we did not speak of 'gay lib', which was something, however small, in our favour – we were much too serious for that) and any other liberation movement, it was between what we (thought we) were doing and (a crudely understood) kind of basic feminism. As we saw it, women were fighting for equality and so were we. The relationship between feminism and civil rights movements was not apparent to us then at all. That any kind of activism needs academic analysis was not one of our insights. We plunged into the deep end, bravely, it is true, but without any intellectual or academic understanding of what we were doing, or of the possible implications or consequences.

We sincerely believed that what we needed to do, as activists, to effect this 'gay liberation' was to create a safe space in which gay men and women could

meet and interact without fear of being condemned, brutalised, shamed, humiliated or arrested. This is how we interpreted those rights to self-expression, privacy and freedom of association. For us this constituted what we described as a liberation movement. While I continue to be astounded, now, that this kind of naïve ignorance – or would it perhaps be more correct to call it innocence? – could actually have existed, I know that it did. It is most important to remember that there is always a relationship between supply and demand, and the dynamics between a given segment of society and the clubs, organisations, associations, etc. that it gives rise to, reflect this relationship.

Those early 1980s meetings revolved around creating this safe space – quite literally a physical meeting place as well as an association which would uphold these principles of liberation. That the principles were flawed did not occur to us: this is what we thought we all wanted, and this gay association was geared up to try to provide it.

Of course we knew that GASA had far, far more white members than black, but we did not see a way out of this except to make the GASA premises a racially integrated space. Although there was one GASA event (which I later heard of) that did take place in a venue which turned out to be racially segregated, contrary to what was thought to be the case when the event was planned, we were scrupulous in refusing to frequent places that did not allow racially mixed visitors or audiences. But it is true that we were afraid, in our white liberal safety, to rock the boat too much: it was dangerous enough in those days to defy the tenets of apartheid by having an association open to people regardless of their colour. A founding principle of GASA was that we would – and here I must, yet again, refuse to suffer the seemingly expected embarrassment of having been so politically naïve in that I will also, yet again, defend the very circularity of this naïvety – 'keep out of politics'. What we understood by the word 'politics' was overt opposition to the apartheid laws of the government. What we understood by 'keeping out of politics' was the same as that which we understood our function as 'liberals' to mean – a way of opposing the system from within it, so we would have a racially integrated association – but we would not link 'gay liberation' to any civil rights liberation initiative. We thought that such a stance would guarantee us at least some measure of protection from the draconian laws which frequently led to the banning of organisations and individuals. Although some of us were involved in the more radical civil rights movement, as GASA leaders we believed that creating this space of safety for lesbians and gay men was not just the best we could do, it was all we could do. We didn't have the 20/20 vision of hindsight then, and we failed to realise that enacting our acceptance of the mandate of our members to keep GASA 'apolitical' meant that we perpetuated the myth, with all its consequences, that it is possible to compartmentalise forms and expressions of oppression.

As a founder member of and energetic worker in GASA, I was, I now know, most certainly not an activist in my present understanding of the term, and I most certainly was not at all an academic activist either. Neither was I a 'lesbian' as I now understand the term, in at least some of its political

nuances. I think, too, that my being a mother somehow gave me, and by implication the GASA leadership, a kind of 'heterosexual respectability' which may
well have furthered our cause. This is not something that I could definitively
demonstrate, but I do have a sense that it may well have been true. However,
in spite of all this, I was then what I thought I was, in that I fulfilled in good
faith the terms, as I understood them, in which I then identified myself. I may
now be a far more effective lesbian mother who is an academic activist,
because I have a different and more comprehensive understanding of the
implications of describing myself thus, but is this not part of what the emergence of sexual identity politics is all about? South Africa has come a long way
in relation to the politics of sexual identity in general since those early 1980s,
and I like to think that through my lasting involvement with gay and lesbian
issues, if not with GASA specifically, I have had some influence on a few of
those, perhaps more courageous than I, who went on to help effect these
changes.

Because I'm gay and I believe

Paul Mokgethi

In this verbatim extract from an interview conducted by Graeme Reid as part of his MA research, Paul Mokgethi reflects on the 1980s, a period during which he negotiated the tensions between his political and his Christian convictions. The audiotape and transcript are in the Hope and Unity Metropolitan Community Church collection at the Gay and Lesbian Archives of South Africa.

I started being involved recently after I knew that I was gay and at that time it was 1986. Thereafter it was a time whereby we had friends and as friends we just knew that we were gay but there was nothing that was happening around, as young guys from Soweto. Up until the time that I met Tsidi, that's one of my friends, and Tsidi sort of like spoke to me that he knows of a gay organisation here in town. But the gay organisation, he didn't know where to contact the people or how to contact them. So somebody gave him the address that he could contact Simon [Nkoli]. But at the time it was the collapse of that organisation, I don't know what it was called, where Simon belonged earlier on. Yes, it was called GASA at the time. But it was at the time Simon decided to pull away from GASA because of some of the things that he was not satisfied with.

Then in 1988 Simon had been arrested but he was out of jail at that time. Simon and other people started having meetings in Soweto and the place is called Lee in Orlando. That was a shebeen that was called Lee. It's not there now. So Tsidi then invited me to one of the – it was on a Saturday evening when they had a meeting. I went there with Tsidi and I sat there and I was listening to – there was Simon and Zaza and other gay people from Soweto, and they were talking about starting to organise themselves and they wanted to have a black gay and lesbian organisation whereby they could meet together and share their problems as gay and lesbian people, and whereby maybe they can also, if they've got problems, they can help each other, maybe in the way of counselling one another. So the meeting went on for a while and I was a bit bored, so I went home.

Then the next meeting was arranged and I went there to the meeting. Two issues were brought up: as gays and lesbians in Soweto we don't need to separate ourselves from other gay and lesbian people, white people in town, and we don't have to make an organisation of our own. We need to be in contact with other people so that we could also help each other.

In one of the meetings Simon decided that we should sort of like publish this in *Exit* and ask people who are willing to come and attend the meeting, to come and attend the meeting which was going be at Wits. At that time, it was the time whereby things were not – we didn't know where we were going. I can remember it was in October/November 1988 when we met at Wits University. A few white people were around and there was a lot of discussion about how to form this organisation. It wasn't easy. There were problems here and there and there were a lot of disagreements here and there. After a while we decided let's just conclude the meeting and we will meet again next time.

The next meeting was when we decided that we should form an organisation and give it a name. The elections started after a while and things started going. That was when I then started being active in GLOW and I attended meetings. I supported GLOW everywhere. Even when the first gay march was started, I was there, trying to organise with Bev [Ditsie] and Simon and other people, and it went on like that, and I was one of the gay people who were active in GLOW.

But the problem was GLOW was like a political organisation, dealing with political issues. It was good for it to be there, but on the other hand, the problem was GLOW is not a Christian organisation. That was the problem because most of the time it would come to a point whereby Roy [Shepherd], when he was at the meeting, would raise something of a Christian issue and he would just be cut off. They would say, No, no, Roy, now you're out. Here we're not dealing with Christian issues. GLOW is not a Christian organisation. We are dealing with political issues. There was that difference now.

So I felt, as a Christian, as gay and lesbian people we also need to have a place whereby we meet as gay and lesbian Christians, because gay people, most of the time when you speak to them and tell them about Christianity, they don't want to hear a thing about that. And unfortunately that's the problem that the church has brought. The church has rejected them so much and it has said so many things, and they feel that they don't want to belong to a church because they've got no room in the church. The church has just left them out as human beings, so they don't want to have anything to do with the church.

So that was the time – that has hurt me so much, because I always ask myself the question, because I'm gay and I believe and I'm a Christian, and seeing other people don't want to hear about Christianity. And while other people were so much involved in the church, but due to the oppression that they got from the church, now they decided to pull away from the church. I felt that, no, we really need to do something, even those who have just cut themselves away from the church, they need to come again now. We need to come together and talk this thing out and maybe from there we can see where we are actually going to.

That's when a church thing started, and that was the time when Cecil [Nyathi] was still around. We had so many discussions with Cecil and other gay and lesbian people in general. Every time when we met we used to discuss about that until we felt that it is about time, even if we are two or three, because if we are going to wait for a group of people we cannot really do it. But if we start, even if we are two or three, the other people will come, they will follow us. That's when we started meeting in this flat.

We were about two or three, we would meet for maybe 30 minutes, just to take our own Bibles and open them and maybe read from a certain verse. Then each and every one would relate and interpret how he understands that verse that we have opened on that evening, and then maybe we sit down and ask ourselves what is it that we did during the week. Or maybe if there is something that has hurt you during the week, or maybe in your relationship there were some problems, then we would sit and talk about that. And afterwards we would praise and it would be finished.

It went on like that for some time and then other people started coming and joining us because they said what we were doing was something interesting. And even though we no longer belong to any churches, even though maybe we were out of the church for some time, but if we come back and talk and we relate, maybe from there we can start again, our spiritual beings feeding each other so that we should grow spiritually again. That was then the time whereby things started progressing, up until where we are now.

The problem now is the thing that we formed, we want to see it succeeding. I no longer have enough time because as a GLOW member and as a GLOW founder, as somebody who was dedicated that much, now that there is this Christian church, which I also want to see being a grown up church and see it being successful, that is why I have given myself a break for a while from GLOW, to make this thing be a success until I can say the church is strong and they've got a destination where they are going. That's when I can feel very happy to see it progressing.

Maybe next year some time we'll have a very big and grown up church. I still attend some GLOW meetings but it's no longer the same as before because now the church is demanding on the other hand. So that is why I've got that bit of separation with GLOW.

22 June 1995, Hillbrow, Johannesburg

My life underground

Paddy Nhlapo

In these extracts from a 1999 interview conducted by Zackie Achmat, Paddy Nhlapo talks about life 'underground' – which for Nhlapo meant not only his experience within the political structures of banned organisations, but also the clandestine ways that he found to express his sexuality. The interview was conducted for the Idol Pictures documentary film *Apostles of Civilised Vice*. The videotape is in the Idol Pictures archive.

The day we were supposed to start our examinations I got arrested at four o'clock in the morning. I was studying at home, and suddenly it was these police vehicles and lights and everything. Then I got arrested. At that time what they accused me of, they wanted to know as to where there was a guy called Mabiscuit, he was an MK soldier and it was known that they had information that he is training people and establishing cells in our township. So they thought I might be one of the people in that, and unfortunately I couldn't talk, I couldn't say anything on that, you know.

So, people finished examinations and it was 1989 all of a sudden, and I was still doing that Standard 8. So I went back to school in '89 to continue my Standard 8 and there was lots of things happening at that time. Politically I had developed, I was involved in many other activities. I was in the Southern Transvaal region of the student congress and I couldn't concentrate on my books. It was a case of me being busy politically and the work that we were doing and knowing that there was much repression at that time as well. So the police were looking for me. I had to move from one safe, I mean, place of safety to the next, you know safe houses and all that, and when examinations came I couldn't go back to school and write because I was afraid I was going to be arrested.

So then finally 1989 I did my Standard 9 and passed. And then in '91 I passed my Standard 10, but I got an 'F', so I said, no, I want to go to university. So I went back again, now in a private school, assisted by someone who was a boyfriend of mine who was working for the French Embassy. So he paid for me to go to the private school, then I passed my Standard 10 in '92.

Well, the first time I saw gay people it was in my school. They were, I could call them now because I have an understanding, they were transgendered youths who were at my school, who I hated so much. I hated them, they know me very well, Bennie and Themba, why I hated them. Because I thought they are behaving like girls. They think they are women, they're putting make-up on and the way they behave. They only hang out with girls and all that. So I had that very strong hatred against them.

And mind you, at that time, I was also underground, having something going on with a friend of mine, and we also had girlfriends, you see. With a friend of mine, we would have sex together, and sometimes we would have sex with our girlfriends. We would go out together to do, what we called in the township, to 'check your girlfriend'. But we would have sex, and every time we had sex we never talked about it, we never discussed it. We never even mentioned it, we just do it and that's it.

And then later on, I think, about a year later, that was about '86, then I started knowing, you know, having information on gay people, that there are people who are gay. We were doing biology, and so this biology teacher of mine who is up until today gay, he like mentioned, because we were talking of bisexuals, then he explained to us nicely as to what do we talk of when we talk of gay people, bisexual people and what's happening. The type and form of sex that takes place. Then it dawned on me as to, oh, oh seemingly I might be part of, you know, this kind of thing.

So because of, I think, my own curiosity, I heard of this shebeen which was 31 Majolo Street, that lots of 'moffies' hang out there. So because of the interest we would go there, because it was a mixed shebeen, but sit outside, just to watch them coming in and going out. I was doing that with this person that I have been going out with for like two or three years, and we would say maybe we are just like them. We just have to start befriending them. So then there was a nicer way, I mean, there was I think a gateway which was open.

Our comrades within the organisation, in fact they were from KWAYCO, which was KwaThema Youth Organisation, they raised up an issue saying there are people doing devilish things and blah, blah, blah, and they need to be beaten up. So they said we need to beat them up. That's when I suddenly said 'No!' So I remember very well, it was in 1987, late '87, it was shortly before I got rearrested, then they wanted to like beat these people up who were hanging

69

out at 31 Majolo Street. And things that they were doing were devilish, and there were something that they said that 'They were selling sperms', because there was always an ambulance waiting outside there. And unfortunately the guy who was driving the ambulance, he worked for the Fire Department and he was gay, so he used to come there for a beer or something if he was not busy. So seeing that this ambulance comes every time to buy sperm, because they were saying, 'These gay people are selling sperm,' and all that type of thing.

So I started objecting, and fortunately our chairperson at that time, Siyabonga, just said no, he doesn't think it is okay. And he knew, he had information that there is an organisation called GLOW whatever, he had information, second level information, that we need to support such people, we need to get closer to them to know exactly what they are doing, because he doesn't think there is anyone who can sell sperm. So then it gave us a chance, because we were deployed at 31 to go and hang out there and see exactly what these people were doing. So we went to 31, we were drinking as well, I remember that time I was drinking stout beer. So we were buying beer and that's how I got closer to gay people. And then I had someone that I met there. Then we, like behind everybody's back, had a relationship going on. Then I came to terms with myself as to, 'Gosh, this is what I am exactly.'

But it was very difficult for me then because I did not have information as to declare myself as gay, but I knew exactly what my feelings were, but I continued having girlfriends. I think it is a well-known factor, mostly with activists, you have lots of girlfriends, lots of female comrades, which we called 'structures'. Well, you had your structures around. So I had my structures and also had my gay relationships underground. So that's how I came to know about gay people and gay life.

If we can't dance to it, it's not our revolution

Julia Nicol

In answer to some questions put to her by Anthony Manion, Julia Nicol explores the relationship between gay and lesbian politics and anti-apartheid politics in the 1980s from the point of view of a grouping of gay and lesbian activists in Cape Town. The interview was conducted via email and has been edited.

What were the main objectives of LAGO and its successor, OLGA?

In both organisations our aim was to be an openly gay presence within the struggle for a non-racial, democratic South Africa.

LAGO was formed in mid-1986 by six lesbian and gay friends who saw crying needs in two areas.

Firstly, we felt it was essential for a specifically gay/lesbian voice to be speaking out against apartheid. The Gay Association of South Africa (GASA) had emphatically failed to do this, and nor was it being done by any of the other smaller gay organisations at the time. We felt that to do so was vital both for the sake of our self-esteem as lesbian/gay individuals, and for the sake of the image of the gay community in the eyes of the anti-apartheid movement.

Secondly, we were strongly aware that within the anti-apartheid activist circles in which we moved, lesbians and gay men were closeted to an almost total extent. The climate within the democratic movement was such that lesbians and gays did not feel comfortable about being open about their sexual orientation. We were not prepared to sit back and accept this: we felt that it was anomalous that a movement based on principles of liberty and justice should have a homophobic ethos. As the slogan has it, 'Gay rights are human rights'.

In South Africa in the eighties that was an extremely novel idea. And we had to live with accusations from within the Left that we were hijacking the anti-apartheid struggle for our own partisan ends. The fact that both LAGO and OLGA had approximately 90 per cent white membership made us especially vulnerable to such perceptions. But it helped that three of our members had something of a profile as anti-apartheid activists – Ivan Toms, Sheila Lapinsky and Derrick Fine.

Why did it come about that LAGO terminated itself and was replaced by OLGA?

This happened in October 1987. LAGO at that time comprised ten members, and the group was divided along ideological lines to the extent that the organisation was paralysed: proposals from the one school of thought would be blocked by the other one. The ideological differences were simple: while a majority of the members positioned ourselves firmly within the broad democratic struggle, others adopted a purist gay liberation approach which held that the anti-apartheid movement was as much the enemy as was the Establishment, because both were equally homophobic. These members disagreed with our majority view that left-wing homophobia was an aberration which didn't logically belong in the Left: that inasmuch as the Left was homophobic, it could be called to account for betraying its own principles, while the same could certainly not be said for the ruling sector.

LAGO's constitution laid down that all decision-making must be on the basis of complete consensus. So it was a deadlock situation, and LAGO decided to dissolve itself. That was on 16 October 1987. A sad day, not only for sentimental reasons but because LAGO had built up something of a profile and that went west.

OLGA had entirely the same objectives as LAGO. When the eight like-minded former LAGO members formed OLGA, we adopted LAGO's constitution more or less as it stood. We just altered the rules about decision-making so that majority vote replaced consensus.

73

How did LAGO, and then OLGA, make their presence felt in the Western Cape?

We issued pamphlets which situated the lesbian/gay struggle within the context of the broad liberation struggle. We produced T-shirts and badges bearing slogans such as 'Dykes for Democracy' and 'No Liberation Without Gay–Lesbian Liberation'.

Opportunities for distributing these were limited because the period from mid-1985 to early 1990 was a time of extreme repression. Hundreds of activists were in detention at any given time. A State of Emergency was in force and virtually all anti-apartheid political activity was banned. Anti-apartheid organisations replaced their political rallies with cultural events and fêtes, and at these events in the Western Cape, we would set up a stall.

It is difficult to know what effect we had; certainly we didn't have people coming forward expressing an interest in joining our organisation. But in my view the vital thing is that we were there: an explicitly lesbian and gay presence at a 'Struggle' event.

There was quite a bit of curiosity about us; I think that many people didn't quite know what to make of us. And because homosexuality has to do with sex, I think some people felt embarrassed by us and ignored us for that reason. For nearly everyone, it was a new experience to be faced with the words 'gay' and 'lesbian' in huge letters on our banners, T-shirts and so on; one must remember that South Africa's first-ever Gay Pride march was as late as October 1990. This, of course, post-dated President De Klerk's landmark liberalising measures of February 1990.

One of the most fascinating reactions we got at our stalls was from personal friends of ours who were gay or lesbian 'lefties': almost without exception, these individuals studiously ignored us! People whom we knew well as friends, would walk past our stall looking steadfastly ahead. I must confess that this sometimes had us in stitches because their closeted unease was so obvious, especially in contrast with our straight friends who used to stop and chat. Laughter aside, though, this was pretty disillusioning.

Did LAGO and OLGA have allies in the form of supportive organisations or individuals?

Yes – both here and, very importantly, overseas. Here in Cape Town, our first organisational ally was a group of the same small size as ourselves, called the Organisation of People Against Sexism (OPAS). They were committed to combating sexism in society in general, but also inside the democratic struggle. Their blood used to boil at the frequently heard rhetoric-laden references to women as the wives and mothers of the Struggle – as if there were no women who were activists in their own right. We used to collaborate with OPAS in writ-

ing letters of protest to newspapers, and at cultural events our two organisations always attempted to have our stalls next to each other. Their support was
a great boost to our morale.

Most of us were former members of the Cape Town branch of GASA. We
had friends within the organisation, but had no formal links with it. I had
great respect, though, for the counselling service which they ran.

In the early period our main source of moral support came from overseas
gay organisations and individuals. The most important was the Scottish
Homosexual Rights Group (SHRG), which was the most vocal group within
the International Lesbian and Gay Association (ILGA) with regard to support
for South Africa's anti-apartheid struggle. The SHRG's international secretary,
Ian Christie, was a devoted friend and correspondent. Ian also, incidentally,
gave much moral support to Simon Nkoli during his imprisonment.

Peter Tatchell in London was our other vitally important ally. He provided much
encouragement, as well as publicising our stand in the British gay press. Peter,
too, was an important support for Simon Nkoli, as it happens.

From the late eighties we benefited also from supportive ties with the Swedish
organisation Riksförbundet för Sexuellt Likaberättigande (RFSL), the Norwegian
organisation Arbeidsgrupper for Homofil og Lesbisk Frigjfring (AHF) and the
Danish organisation Det Norske Forbundet av 1948 (DNF-48).

These individuals and organisations were of great importance in reminding us
that in the big world out there, there were people who shared our vision and
who believed our work was important. I can't overstate the importance of this
to us, particularly in the early days, at a time of such repression.

**Did you have ties with other progressive lesbian and gay organisations
inside South Africa?**

In early 1987 LAGO became aware of and set up links with the African Gay
Association (AGA), based in the black townships of Cape Town. The Group
Areas Act was of course then still in force, confining black people and white
people to their own racially-demarcated residential areas. AGA's agenda was
chiefly social, though its members were aligned with the democratic struggle.
There were about 30 members, mainly male.

Then, also in early 1987, we established links with the Johannesburg-based Rand Gay Organisation. The RGO was a small organisation like ourselves. They had a mix of black and white members and their agenda was both social and political. The chairperson of the RGO, Alfred Siphiwe Machela, further opened up the window to the overseas world for us, because he had attended ILGA conferences in Europe and had established important ties there. The relationship between the RGO and ourselves was fruitful and a morale-booster for us, certainly, and I hope for the RGO too. Another comrade in Johannesburg was Roy Shepherd, the then partner of Simon Nkoli. Simon was in prison at that time: the treason trial was still in progress. At this stage we had never met Simon, but we wrote letters to him in prison.

What was the Congress of Pink Democrats?

The CPD was established at a conference in Cape Town in April 1987 held under the joint aegis of LAGO and the RGO. It was an alliance of progressive lesbian and gay organisations. The other members were AGA and the University of Cape Town's Gay and Lesbian Association (GALA); and some months later, the University of the Witwatersrand's gay organisation (Wits Gay Movement) joined. The CPD was an ill-fated venture which didn't last long. A second conference was held in October 1987, but some months after that the alliance fizzled out.

Why do you think the CPD failed?

Our mistake was to try to formalise the alliance too much. A loose, informal network could have worked, but the CPD had its own constitution and rules of operating, and attempted to formulate collective policy and action. This just was not practical given the large geographical distances between the member organisations, and also their lack of administrative and financial resources. None of the member organisations, barring the student groups, had our own offices, and each of us operated on a shoestring budget.

The failure of the CPD was a shame, as lots of energy went into it. And there was a lot of publicity about its launch in the overseas gay press. Two organisations – the SHRG and DNF-48 – came forward with offers of sponsoring CPD membership fees for the ILGA. But the CPD simply never got off the ground. In fact, the second and final CPD conference, held in Johannesburg, was something of a fracas because of internecine tensions between on the one hand, LAGO delegates, and on the other, disaffected LAGO members who attended under the banner of GALA. It was awful. These events in fact prefigured the dissolution of LAGO, which took place within a week of the CPD conference.

The other dreadful thing about that conference, and indeed the first CPD conference, was that speaking time was overwhelmingly dominated by the organisations whose membership was predominantly English-speaking and university-educated. This was, I believe, avoidable; but it happened.

**In LAGO's dealings with the Left,
did you encounter any explicit homophobia?**

Explicit, no, except for an episode involving the End Conscription Campaign. One of our core members, Ivan Toms, was also a committed activist in the ECC. This was a nationwide organisation devoted to the abolition of the system whereby all white males within a certain age group had to serve in the apartheid regime's army. The army call-up was in fact a leading cause of emigration among young white men in those days.

In mid-1987, Ivan received notification that he must serve in the army for a three-month period early the following year, and he made a decision that he was going to refuse. This was, of course, illegal and made him liable for a prison term. In the event, Ivan served nine months in prison in 1988.

But I'm jumping ahead. In the several months preceding Ivan's call-up date, the ECC launched a nationwide campaign focusing on Ivan's stance as a conscientious objector. He went on a speaking tour sponsored and organised by the ECC. LAGO formally backed Ivan's campaign, with some of our members becoming ECC activists to assist with the campaign work.

But a problem arose a few weeks into the campaign. The Western Cape ECC made a ruling that Ivan must exclude all reference to his homosexuality in his speeches and pamphlets. The ECC believed that it would be non-strategic for his sexual orientation to be publicly known: that homophobic South Africans would dismiss Ivan and all he stood for if they knew he was gay.

LAGO held formal talks with the ECC leadership in an attempt to shift their position, but we met with failure. Needless to say, this was a painful time for

77

Ivan. In his campaign material up until then, he had described how his experience of homophobic oppression had helped him to identify with the racist oppression experienced by black people. But when LAGO's representations to the ECC failed, Ivan had to go along with their ruling. He was accountable to the ECC, and so he didn't have much option.

So at that point, LAGO formally withdrew our support from the campaign. Most of us continued to work in the campaign in our individual capacities; and LAGO publicised Ivan's stand as a conscientious objector amongst lesbian and gay organisations both in South Africa and overseas. But it was unfortunate that LAGO had to withdraw from supporting the ECC campaign. Interestingly and sadly, the individuals within the ECC leadership who were most vociferous in urging silence on the gay issue were two gay men.

Despite that unfortunate episode, Ivan Toms' stand as a conscientious objector was excellent for the progressive gay and lesbian movement in South Africa. We in LAGO knew that there were many, many lesbian/gay individuals active in the broad struggle, but with precious few exceptions they were closeted. So Ivan's stand was wonderful for our cause.

OLGA became an affiliate of the United Democratic Front, the ANC-aligned alliance of Struggle organisations. Tell me about that.

We took the decision to apply for UDF membership in December 1989. Most unfortunately, our organisational wheels turned so inefficiently on this matter that we lodged our application only in late February 1990 – some weeks after President De Klerk's landmark announcement of 2 February 1990, in terms of which Mandela was released and the ANC unbanned, along with all other anti-apartheid organisations, including the UDF. The timing of OLGA's membership application can have done little to bolster our credibility as committed participants in the Struggle!

Why did OLGA decide to join the UDF only some three years into OLGA's history?

Two reasons. Firstly, we felt that OLGA was possibly too small to qualify as an affiliate organisation. Our comrades in OPAS had applied to join the UDF in 1987, but had simply been ignored.

Second, we were reluctant to join the UDF for fear of chasing away potential OLGA members who, although opposed to the apartheid regime, were not as far to the left as the UDF. In fact, we lost one of our founding members because of the increasingly apparent pro-UDF tendency within the group. He, incidentally, was a universal pacifist.

The UDF was not acceptable to all in the anti-apartheid camp, one of the main stumbling blocks being its support of the armed struggle and the fact that violence had been associated with the UDF in some parts of the country.

This is why the decision to seek membership was not taken hastily.

It was a relief when our application was accepted. At the UDF Western Cape General Council where OLGA's application came up for consideration, a delegate posed the question: 'But is OLGA a mass-based organisation?' Fortunately for us, this was responded to by one of the UDF office-bearers – Cheryl Carolus – who suggested that one of the UDF's existing affiliates, the Call of Islam, arguably was not a mass-based organisation either. So, we were duly notified that we were in. In fact, one of the delegates had stated that it would be advantageous to have OLGA in, as gays are talented in media design!

OLGA's membership of the UDF was of more importance to ourselves and our image on the landscape than it was to the UDF. On a practical level, the main result was that we sent OLGA delegates to UDF meetings, which were famously lengthy affairs.

Our membership of the UDF was important also in that it enabled us to spread knowledge about the gay rights issue. On one occasion, two OLGA members went on a long trip to a national conference in Johannesburg amongst a busload of UDF people, and they found that for large parts of the journey they were answering curious enquirers, some of whom did not even properly understand what the terms 'lesbian' and 'gay' meant.

Particularly amongst black people, there is a lack of knowledge about this. While I don't of course subscribe to the 'homosexuality is unAfrican' view, the fact is that lesbian/gay *culture,* as we know it today, is an import from the West. Historians have described how, in Europe, the term 'homosexual' gradually came to denote not just a type of psychosexual behaviour but a type of lifestyle, a type of person. And a stereotypically homosexual *lifestyle* is something which we have not seen emerging indigenously in Africa, to the best of my knowledge.

It's instructive that a high-profile gay man such as Simon Nkoli was often told by fellow blacks that he was 'letting whites control my mind'.[1]

Despite the collapse of the CPD, did OLGA maintain its ties with your fellow Capetonians in AGA?

Yes, we held joint gatherings. Many of the AGA members were unemployed and many still lived in their parents' homes despite being adults. So they had a very hard time trying to conduct any sort of gay social life and I think that their chief needs centred around material deprivation rather than abstract principles of gay rights. On this theme, I'd like to quote from an interview with an AGA member, Siphiwo Tukulu:

> Because of all the other forms of oppression which affect black people, the problem of gay rights is a very small issue to them. Even black people who are gay do not see it as a big problem, because they are so heavily oppressed in other ways that it won't make that much difference in their lives if they have gay rights … It will make hardly any difference.[2]

That quote is noteworthy in its own right, but the point I'd like to make here is that AGA did not have precisely the same underlying motivation as OLGA.

And so working together as two organisations did not come easily. We also had huge transport problems when we wanted to meet together. And there were language difficulties in that the home language of the AGA members was Xhosa, and OLGA members were not fluent in Xhosa.

So, although there was much enthusiasm initially in the links between the two organisations, this waned after a while. In fact, AGA members simply did not feel at home at OLGA gatherings. Siphiwo Tukulu, in the interview I've mentioned already, said the following:

1. In 'The Slow Race to Freedom', *Glowletter*, March 1990, Johannesburg
2. In *OLGA News*, February 1991, Cape Town

And have you ever asked yourself why so few of us come to OLGA forums? When the CPD first started there were a lot of us – we filled about three car-loads. Then somehow after a while, people were not interested any more. Some of them I had to interrogate: 'Why aren't you going there any more, what's happened?' Some would say to me, 'We don't find enough comradeship; there isn't *any* warmth there. Although we're supposed to see ourselves as their equals, there is that vast difference: they are intellectuals and we are "just black people". What we say is not valued. They are using us so that the ANC or whatever political organisation can see that there are black gay activists, so it's not a myth that there are black gay activists.' This was how they felt. Why should they want to go to yet another place where they are made to feel inferior?[3]

This, of course, is quite an indictment of OLGA. Different home languages and different levels of education were part of the cause, I'd say, along with the enforced geographical separation of black and white residential areas for decades. In other words, the apartheid system worked very successfully. But nevertheless it is an indictment of OLGA.

OLGA played a role in the process leading up to the protection of lesbian and gay rights in South Africa's new Constitution.

Yes. It's difficult for me personally to know to what extent OLGA's contribution featured in bringing about the happy end result. OLGA's role fitted chronologically somewhere in the middle of a lobbying process that lasted from 1987 through 1994. The lobbying involved various parties and took place both in Europe and here in South Africa.

Most important in Europe were the initiatives of London-based writer and gay activist, Peter Tatchell. He engaged the ANC-in-exile about their policy on gay rights in various initiatives from late 1987 through 1990, in a focused and directed way which was extremely fruitful. Peter's early initiatives were especially important in that they resulted in the ANC publicly confronting the issue of gay rights for the first time.

81

3. In *OLGA News*, February 1991, Cape Town

Garry Wotherspoon from Sydney, Australia, also approached the ANC in London. And it is important that Alfred Machela met with the ANC when he travelled outside the country to ILGA conferences. He met them in Stockholm and also in an African country, I'm not sure where. This was brave, given that the apartheid regime had security police outside the country. Even I was not allowed to hear of these meetings until long after they took place.

OLGA's contribution was a written submission to the Constitutional Committee of the ANC, then newly unbanned, in September 1990. In this document we motivated for the inclusion in the ANC's draft Constitution of provisions protecting lesbian and gay rights. It was important that we were able to make this submission as an affiliate organisation of the UDF: it came from within the broad ANC camp, as it were.

Our submission met with success: the ANC's draft Constitution issued in November 1990 included a gender rights clause which prohibited discrimination on the grounds of, amongst other things, sexual orientation.

We were, of course, overjoyed about this. We had by no means been certain of success. As late as May of that year, Albie Sachs of the ANC's Constitutional Committee had said to OLGA in a meeting with us: 'There is no guarantee that you'll be heard, but if you don't speak you certainly won't be heard.'[4]

The supportive attitude of a senior ANC person such as Albie Sachs – the fact that he was prepared to meet with OLGA – was wonderfully encouraging. A very interesting statement by Albie at that meeting was that the ANC policymakers were much influenced by the knowledge that people such as Simon Nkoli and Ivan Toms were gay: the fact that comrades were being affected by gay oppression did much to get the gay issue considered on its merits, Albie said.

After the victory of the ANC's draft Constitution, we were strongly aware that work needed to be done to ensure that the sexual orientation provision survived through the multi-party negotiations into the final version of the Constitution. OLGA sent written representations to all the other political parties.

4. In 'Report of meeting with Albie Sachs, 14 May,' OLGA, 1990, Cape Town

We also continued to lobby for acceptance of our cause amongst the ANC grassroots, at branch level. But the really important work from this stage on was done by two Johannesburg-based activists, lawyers Edwin Cameron and Kevan Botha, acting under the aegis of a newly-formed gay funding body called the Equality Foundation. Edwin and Kevan attended the multi-party negotiations held at Kempton Park near Johannesburg, and lobbied intensively amongst the various groupings there. Thankfully, the sexual orientation provision survived and made it into the final version of the Constitution.

The Constitution came into operation after the watershed 1994 elections, but was formally adopted by the Constituent Assembly only in 1996. On that occasion, OLGA was one of the groupings formally invited to attend the adoption proceedings and the celebratory banquet afterwards.

GLOW was established after Simon Nkoli's acquittal in 1988. What were OLGA's relations with GLOW?

OLGA and GLOW were both engaged in the same struggle, and OLGA members knew Simon well as a friend and comrade from the times he visited Cape Town after his acquittal. But strangely enough, OLGA's dealings with GLOW turned out to be pretty formal, and few in number.

Tell me about the last years of OLGA.

In 1992 to 1993, OLGA formulated a Charter of Lesbian and Gay Rights, a document which set out in concrete detail the various areas of civil life where we wanted protection. We circulated this amongst all the South African lesbian and gay organisations which we knew of, and at a national conference held in Cape Town in late 1993, the Charter was formally adopted by fourteen organisations.

83

After that OLGA never had another meeting, although it carried out protests against two instances of homophobia – both successful – in 1994. Thereafter, in Cape Town, the organisation to join was ABIGALE, the Association of

Bisexuals, Gays and Lesbians. ABIGALE was established in 1991. Some OLGA members left to join ABIGALE. I was a member of both organisations, though was unable to attend meetings at that stage owing to a health problem. There was a degree of rivalry between the two organisations, including some tension at times. I was relieved to read in Eric Marcus's book *Making History*[5] that in the US too, there was some less-than-friendly rivalry between organisations in the early days of the Gay Liberation Movement.

Do you see a need for lesbians and gays to continue organising in South Africa today?

Yes, certainly. There is still a lot of homophobia in our society. It's a sobering fact that we don't have a single Member of Parliament who is openly gay or lesbian. Thank heavens for high-profile South Africans such as entertainer Pieter-Dirk Uys and Judge Edwin Cameron, who are uncloseted.

There is suffering in particular for homosexual youth living in small towns or rural areas. Their isolation is extreme. How to reach them, though, is of course not a simple matter.

I assume you'd disagree with those who say that in today's South Africa there is no need for people to assert a gay or lesbian identity?

Definitely, I'd disagree. For as long as one single teenager anxiously asks, 'But what do I tell my parents?' there is a need for people to stand up and be counted as lesbian and gay.

5. Eric Marcus. 1992. *Making History: The Struggle for Gay and Lesbian Equal Rights 1945–1990*, New York: HarperCollins

The International Lesbian and Gay Association (ILGA) published this End Conscription Campaign pamphlet about Ivan Toms along with the Rand Gay Organisation's 'Call for action', in its *ILGA Bulletin* (number 2, 1988). These reproductions are courtesy of Homodok-Lesbisch Archief, Amsterdam. Copies of the *ILGA Bulletin* are also housed in the Ivan Toms and LAGO/OLGA collection in the Gay and Lesbian Archives of South Africa.

CALL FOR ACTION

group calling for action	*send letters of protest to*
Rand Gay Organization of South Africa	The Minister of Defence, Box 47, Cape Town 8000, Republic of South Africa;
	& your local South African Embassy or Consulate-General

ACTION NUMBER 88:8 ILGA

On page 13 of the Bulletin you can read more about the campaign to save IVAN TOMS.

The Call for Action from the Rand Gay Organization only arrived after the Bulletins have been printed. In the next Bulletin we shall publish information from the letter from Alfred Machela of the R.G.O..

We hesitated to include this as a Call for Action when we received the material from South Africa, as we did not then have sufficient information regarding the veracity of the pamphlet. R.G.O. has now confirmed the strong anti-apartheid stance of Ivan Toms, and we therefore accept this Call for Action.

HOW TO CALL FOR AN ACTION:

1. Send a letter to the Information Secretariat;

   a) Describe the incident or the situation.

   b) Give the exact date and circumstances.

   c) Give the addresses to which to direct letters of protest.

HOW TO RESPOND TO A CALL FOR ACTION:

1. Send letters of protest to the addresses given in the Call For Action.

2. Send copies of your letters to:

   a) Action Secretariat c/o GLF-Cologne P.O. Box 270501 D-5000 Köln 1

   b) The group calling for action.

   c) Other relevant Secretariats or Information Pools (Women's Sec, LGPP, EEIP, IMIP etc). Addresses see back cover.

The pamphlet below has been sent to the Informatio
of Lesbian and Gay Activists) in South Africa, of
up for military service...Ivan declared his refusa
accomplice in the violence of apartheid." OLGA al
ty) on several platforms, explaining how the onpre
strengthened his commitment to the work for the li
sexuality has been used by the state security appa
harassment."

In many respects Ivan Toms is like any other ordinary white South African. Born in Germiston, raised in Durban – where he captained his rugby team and was deputy headboy in an illustrious school career – Ivan eventually graduated as a medical doctor from the University of Cape Town in 1976.

From there it was into the army where he was commissioned to the rank of lieutenant. And like many of our young men in uniform, Ivan entered the SADF reluctantly.

It was not the sweat and drudgery of military life that concerned him. It was rather a deep rooted sense that it was wrong to serve in the SADF. His religious, moral and political convictions told him that the SADF was being used to defend apartheid. But the alternatives of leaving the country, living as a fugitive, or even facing the prospect of going to jail were too harsh to consider.

Now, after nine years of experiencing the harsh South African reality, Ivan calmly faces the possibility of up to thirty months in prison. This is the punishment which confronts him if convicted for refusing to serve a one month camp in November.

"I, like many other young white men who love their country, find that I cannot ignore my conscience. I am prepared to go to jail for this stand," says Ivan.

"The reality of the injustices in our country have convinced me of the impossibility of continuing with any form of service in the SADF."

Ten years have passed since Ivan did his basics in the Medical Corps. Here he tells of some of the experiences he has had which have led him to the point of refusing to serve and possibly to go jail:

"I have served in the SADF as an officer, and these experiences have greatly influenced my decision to object.

"I was sent twice to the operational area and served on the Angolan border for six months. My contact with the Namibian people convinced me that they do not want the SADF in their country; international law says that South Africa has no right to be there. The local people feel that they are oppressed by an invading army. For them, curfews and security force harassment are the way of life in the SADF-imposed war zone.

"I have worked as a doctor for six years in Crossroads, and know that I am able to do real national service working with the poor and disenfranchised.

"In September 1983, Administration Board officials and police would come in, day in and day out, for three weeks, to demolish 'illegal structures'. What this actually meant was that innocent people who had come from the homelands of Transkei and Ciskei

because there was no food or work there, were being attacke by these officials. Old women and babies were being left in and cold of a Cape winter because, to the South African gove they should not have been in Cape Town. When the women onto the flimsy branches that formed the base of their plastic shelters, this constituted a 'riot'. Rubber bullets, teargas, sne powder and police dogs battered the people into submission had to treat the casualties in the clinic."

In June 1986 Crossroads was destroyed by "witdoek" conse vigilantes with backup from the security forces. On 16 June SADF took over the clinic where Ivan worked: "Now what ha community clinic run by a Christian staff team was used by to try and win the "hearts and minds" of the people. I don't b National Servicemen who were forced to be part of this occu the clinic. Some of the doctors had actually worked in the cli their final year at UCT and were very unhappy about what the do. The blame must be directed at the SADF.

"Since October 1984 troops have been used to control the black townships of South Africa and to suppress resistance to apartheid. The border is no longer thousands of miles away in Namibia, but right on our doorstep in Langa, Guguletu, KTC. Friends who might have gone to the same church school are now facing each other across the barrel of a gun in the townships. For most conscripts this is the first time they have entered a black township, and they drive in high up in a buffel with teargas, grenades, rifles – and with fear welling up within them.

"After working in the townships and developing real friendships with the people, I cannot believe that the children and youth being chased by patrolling buffels are the enemy.

"I really do believe that I have been doing true national service in my work in the poorest squatter areas of greater Cape Town. This is the kind of service that I believe will help to build a South Africa that we can all be proud of."

88

ISSUED BY THE END CONSCRIPTION CAMPAIGN

riat from ALUTA CONTINUA of OLGA (Organization
n Toms is a member. OLGA writes "when called
e...beacuse of his unwillingness to act as an
s that "Ivan has spoken about (his homosexuali-
ch he has experienced as a gay person has
of all oppressed peoples. And Ivan's homo-
a futile campaign of attempted smears and

voice echoes the concern of many other
ripts. Some have publicly been prepared to
their opposition to serving in the SADF. For others
s sincere in their beliefs – it is families and friends
ir their frustrations. Conscripts are not the only
of the law. An entire community has been caught
web of war and conscription in South Africa.

ne of many unhappy and unwilling
pts who have to make very difficult
s," says Ivan.

some refuse to serve, many simply find it
ble to do anything but go into the SADF
tly, angry that they are not given any realistic
ves.

d with all conscripts who support the End
iption Campaign's call for constructive alternative
l service.

v provides for community service only to conscripts who
religious and pacifist. They are forced to do six years of
in a government structure.

uctive alternative service should be the same length as
service and be available to us in church, welfare and
nity organisations.

se conscripts who see no option but to go unwillingly into
F, the choice should be given not to serve in the townships
mibia.

"I hope that my stand will contribute to the pressure
on the government to introduce constructive
alternative national service for all conscripts.
"I believe I must make a stand.
"I am committed to South Africa and believe
that the truly patriotic action for me is to go to
prison rather than deny my faith and my
beliefs.
"South Africa is in a state of civil war and we
have to take sides. I believe that the side of
justice and truth is the side of the poor and
disenfranchised in our country. I stand on that
side."

You can support Ivan and other conscripts by
sending the following message to:

The Minister of Defence
Box 47
Cape Town
8000

"I call on your government to change the law
so that conscripts are given the option of
doing constructive alternative National
Service. This service should be the same
length as military service and be available in
church, welfare and community
organisations. I also call for soldiers to be
given the choice of not having to serve in the
townships or Namibia."

89

The public correspondence between Glen Shelton and Simon Nkoli, both members of the Gay and Lesbian Organisation of the Witwatersrand, was published in

the August 1988 edition of *Exit*. All the issues of *Exit* are in the *Exit* collection in the Gay and Lesbian Archives of South Africa.

Shaft 88: that stripper tainted proceedings

Were you proud?

TOGETHER with gay people in the rest of the world we celebrated Gay Pride Week. Here it culminated in Shaft 88, an open – and very proud – event in a prestigious venue.

Yet the support was surprisingly disappointing. After all, even at a conservative estimate there are more than a quarter of a million people of our proclivity just on the Witwatersrand.

There should have been thousands upon thousands of people thronging that arena.

Where were you?

We cannot help but wonder what value gay pride has in this country. We also wonder how many of you know what it means.

Next year we shall make sure that it is at least spelled out in this paper in detail – well before the time.

In the meantime we would like to ask you to let us know why you were not there. Were you ashamed? Or were you scared?

Do not hesitate to write and tell us. We, and everyone who is fighting your battle, and establishing your dignity, would like to know.

Group vs club

SIMULTANEOUSLY in Pretoria and Johannesburg we see a new phenomenon: open and strong friction between groups and clubs.

The circumstances are somewhat different, as are the reasons, it appears.

But in the battle a strong emotion is being expressed. The expression is in the voices of

TAT WOLFEN, Hyde Park, Johannesburg, writes:

Shaft 88 was, on the whole, an enjoyable and successful means of celebrating the gay lifestyle.

The organisers of the Pageant might, however, consider the following criticism, in the interests of improving the show in future:

• Those pregnant pauses between turns, which ruined the momentum of the show, could have been eliminated with finer planning and rehearsal.

• I found the excessive song-and-drag a trifle tedious. There must be some gay magicians, ventriloquists, etc. knocking about

Gay pride? My ass

Charles Lampbrecht of Hillbrow writes:

The Shaft 88 effort gave me a whole new perspective on gay pride. I mean, as if two heterosexually based fashion parades were not enough, we had to sit for hours watching drag queens miming to recorded music.

And to add insult to injury, their offering included a badly done, unending selection of James Bond movie themes – that ultimate in heterosexual stereotypes.

The Shaft 88 Dancers were quite good, but once again oh so heterosexual. If there is no pas de deux for two male dancers to be found somewhere, for heaven's

I was ashamed

BRIAN MULDER, Yeoville, Johannesburg, writes:

I attended Shaft 88 partly because I wanted to show

out there somewhere (or straight entertainers with 'progressive sympathies', for that matter).

• Finally, there was an event that tainted not only the Pageant, but the whole day's proceedings – was 'exotic dancer' Nico really an appropriate choice for a gay pride gathering?

sake, be proud to be gay and create one!

The day was an absolute bore, with nothing happening hour after hour. No wonder so many people had already left by the time their ticket numbers were called for prizes. They came, they saw, they went. And no wonder the bar was the only stall that really had a successful day.

I, however, stayed on in the hope that somewhere something could happen to stimulate my gay pride. The closest we got was a recorded version of 'I am what I am' to end the day and a hangover the next day.

Gay pride? Glad to be gay? My ass.

Was Oasis racist?

ANTON ENUS, 123 Eighth Avenue, Bezuidenhout Valley, 2094, writes:

As one of the Togs' runners participating in the 1988 Two Oceans Marathon, I was fortunate enough to be in Cape Town at Easter. That city's famed hospitality was, however, marred by a rather unsavoury incident at a local club.

Wanting to celebrate Togs' excellent showing in the race, I arranged to meet some friends at The Oasis. On arrival, however, my companion and I were bluntly refused admission on the grounds that we were not card-carrying members of this 'private' club (No one else appeared to be carrying these membership cards).

No amount of reasoning by us or our fellow runners, who at that stage had already been allowed in, would

Send your letters to Input, ☒ 57386, Springfield 2137. Please keep your letters short and to the point.

His first lapse in taste was to remove his clothing undaunted by the lack of rapturous applause for this grisly exposure, he hauled a member of the audience onto the stage whence began a spectacle of degradation. I chose not to watch any further once this sleazy performer began thrusting his barely-clad nether regions

into his unsuspecting victim's face.

Apparently, this alleged entertainer proceeded to suck his prey's toes, fiddle with his fly, and, believe it or not, sit on the guy's face! Such an act ought to have been booed off the stage; sickening public displays like this can only cause grave damage to the gay image.

Taylor replies on Shaft 88

• DAVID TAYLOR, convenor of Shaft 88, replies:

With a show of this nature, like with most entertainment, it will always be impossible to please everybody. One must operate within the parameters of the majority's likes as well as the realities. Where possible one must try to cater for those discerning patrons. The pas de deux was a classic example with a touch of class and a possible wide appeal. As for variety, we appealed widely to artists personally and through Exit to participate. Most artists were either under contract or could not confirm until the last minute. Those that did appear, were the people who responded. We apologise if any section of the programme offended anybody, but not all the

Perhaps as a result a spate of new venues are trying their fortune. We predict that they cannot all last that well – the specific-market is too limited there. But we wish them luck.

The sheer speed of developments in Johannesburg made one thing clear: that the gay collective is no longer content to be silent and be at the mercy of what is more and more often being termed exploitation.

While this need not in all instances be true, it signifies a new chapter in attitudes towards commercial concerns.

They have been riding high on a well-heeled society. They would do well to heed the signs.

Editorial and Display Advertising
✉ 57386, Springfield 2137 ☎ (011) 683-5477

Smalls Ads and Subscriptions
Henk Botha
✉ 18938, Hillbrow 2038; ☎ (011) 643-8088

Smalls rates   See Smalls page

Subscription cost
Southern Africa: R10 per year
Airmail overseas; rate per year: R32, US$16
Aus$25, £10, FF95, Yen2 400, DM2?

Advertising rates
Black and white –   R3,50 per column cm
Spot colours –   add 50c each (min R50 extra)
Full colour –   R5 per col cm (min R150 extra)
Special positions   Front page +300%
Back page +100%; guaranteed position +25%

Managing editor – David Moolman
Assistant editor – Alex Robberze

Exit is published by Exit Publications at the above address.

Contributions in the form of news items, articles, suggestions, letters, photographs, etc. are welcome. The editor, however, reserves the right to edit contributions if necessary.

Opinions expressed by contributors to *Exit* do not necessarily represent the opinion of the publishers.

Publication of the name or photograph of any person or any organisation or establishment in articles or advertisements in *Exit* must not be regarded as any indication of the sexual orientation of such persons or members of such organisations or patrons of such establishments.

Printed by Seculo Printers, 8 Kay Street, Marshalltown, Johannesburg.
Copyright reserved.

Glen Shelton: use energy more creatively

GLEN SHELTON, 68 De Korte Street, SAIRR, Braamfontein, Johannesburg, writes:

When a journalist writes an article on the individual that individual is usually allowed to give his or her perspective on the circumstances.

When Exit wrote about my resignation from Glow they did not allow me this privilege. Instead I was judged entirely according to the dictates of a few marginal participants. Just to set the record straight I would like to offer the alternative of the story that Exit ignored.

First of all there was no decision to suspend me from Glow. Such a decision would have to have been taken by the rest of the executive and the membership and that would have entailed a meeting.

This meeting never occurred. If any person claimed that a decision was taken they are acting beyond their mandate to the group. Exit could have checked this, and all the other issues, with me before deciding on their version of the truth.

Secondly, I never 'acted without the knowledge of the group's executive'. The particular document that was sent out to various groups and magazines was merely the minutes of a meeting at which we agreed to question whether Ivan Toms is or is not a gay activist.

No-one suggested that he should not be supported, but merely that the issue needed debate.

As secretary of the meeting I was told to write up the minutes and to despatch them to the different venues. This was all done with the full knowledge of the executive. The motion against Ivan also came, not from me, but from AGA in Cape Town.

Finally, my resignation was not caused by the document. It was caused by a blood-thirsty and relentless attack from Olga (which is Ivan Toms' support group).

It would seem that this group objects to freedom of speech and decided to silence any debate on the topic.

They also attempted to isolate Glow, unless Glow toes their party line. Under these circumstances it became impossible to function in solidarity unless we became obedient to Olga's demands.

Not being a performing circus animal, I dislike being told what top say and how to behave, so I resigned to alleviate the difficulties for Glow and to attempt to unite a fractious gay left.

We can only hope that unity is now possible. Although, personally, I have become cynical.

Olga's vendetta has has successfully put back the project of the gay left by at least three years.

The CPD (Congress of Pink Democrats) which was the national representative body for the gayleft, is in disarray and is unlikely to continue. Instead ethics become expedient as people as people whose actions have been questioned formally and constitutionally are given moral ascendancy in the new Big Top.

Meanwhile Olga gloats on its little 'success'. What a pity they couldn't put their obviously endless energy into a more creative area instead of working so hard to generate the intellectual wasteland in which they no longer feel threatened.

To end a quote from a little recognised gay poet, (why is it that ex-centric gay activists and writers – the most immediate example being Jeremy Zipp who Exit suddenly eulogises after yearsofabuse – seem onbyto gain recognition after death); Thomas Gray:

Alas, regardless of their doom,
The little victims play.

Gray was not referring to the heterosexual community. Unfortunately, I am not.

But perhaps I had better shut up before that ominous Ringmaster cracks her whip again to ensure obedient silence.

• The letter below should cover most of this writer's points – both journalistically and otherwise more than adequately – Editor.

Simon Nkoli replies to Shelton

SIMON NKOLI, chairman, Glow (Gay and Lesbian Organisation of the Witwatersrand), replies to the accompanying letter from Glen Shelton:

Although the meeting (which is referred to in the letter) did not take place to suspend Glen Shelton from the executive committee of Glow,

I personally told him on the day that he handed in his resignation to me that we were considering to ask him to suspend his membership from the executive committee.

I remember well that he was very angry about that and he suggested that I did so because I was afraid that Olga (the Organisation of Lesbian and Gay Activists in Cape Town) will be very disappointed in me and that the rest of the International Lesbian and Gay Organisation won't support Glow.

Anyhow, there was absolutely no decision taken to suspend him from Glow.

That was only a suggestion coming from me, and since he resigned I did not feel I should bring that suggestion to the meeting.

Zsa Zsa, Tshidi and Reggie (members of the executive) know about this suggestion.

Glen says that he had never acted without the the knowledge of the group.

Well, I don't want to argue about that. But I want to say that when he was asked to write letters overseas to inform them about the launching of the new gay organisation which was to be launched, he went on in the report back talking about Ivan Toms who was not even part of the agenda. As far as I remember, the Ivan Toms issue was not part of the agenda at that meeting.

I thought the issue under general since I was concerned about Ivan Toms and Olga had written a letter asking for a support for Ivan to me as individual.

Anyway, the issue was discussed at the meeting of Glow after it was launched and only one person who was a member of Glow was against the motion of his support – and someone else supported him.

I don't want to talk about this, but people who attended there are my witnesses.

They know exactly what took place then.

It is quite interesting to hear that the motion against Ivan did not come from Glen Shelton alone, but also from AGA.

By AGA Glen means one individual person, Monde Mazibuko, whom I did fear saying, 'We can't go on like this. We need to be known that we're gay and that we're also fighting for human rights'.

Of course he talked about other progressive gay organisations being and not accepting.

But all the same, my argument is: Monde Mazibuko was not supposed to be part of that meeting and he was not speaking for the AGA since he did not have the mandate of the AGA to be at that meeting. That meeting was an action committee meeting for the launching of Glow, that's all.

I once again refuse to admit that Olga had tried to influence us and silence any debate on that topic.

But delaying tactics were being used and I could not figure why should we keep on postponing the matter.

I am also not aware that they were trying to isolate us unless we follow their footsteps; but I think they would do so if they feel we were trying to victimise a victim who at the present moment has got no power to say anything.

A victim of apartheid (Toms) can't be a victim of other victims (gay people, especially when they think they are being more progressive and concerned).

I however respect Glen Shelton for speaking up his mind, and I do not suggest to him not to think that there is any one or organisation against him.

If he thinks his resignation will bring unity in the gay community (organisation) it is okay.

That unity he is talking of also demands his understanding of what is happening in gay politics – and he needs to be patient and challenge whatever is taking place.

Well, most unfortunately I can't respond on the CPD's (Congress of Pink Democrats) and Olga's behalf.

And since I am not intelligent enough or a lawyer for that matter, I can't quote from any book of gay law.

All I can say is gay unity must be brought along.

END CONSCRIPTION CAMPAIGN

PO Box 208
Woodstock
7915

1st July, 1987.

Edwin Cameron
Johannesburg

Dear Edwin Cameron,

This is just a short note of thanks for your assistance in
the ECC campaign that was to be run around my refusal to
serve in the SADF, and an update on the latest situation.

On Friday, 26th June, a Major Vorster from my unit [3
Medical Battalion] telephoned to say that my call-up had
been withdrawn. When asked for more details by my lawyer,
Allan Dodson, she said they had called up too many doctors.
Yet she was only instructed to phone me and she did not know
the names of any other doctors who were phoned!! Later I
was sent a telegramme saying that my call-up had been re-
secheduled to November 1987.

Another interesting detail is that the threatening and
sexually abusive telephone calls stopped from Friday
morning, even before I was informed of the re-scheduling of
my call-up! This is after they had reached a peak of 25
calls in one day on 23rd June!! Obviously the callers are
either the military intelligence or the security branch or
informed directly by them.

So it would seem that the military have backed off - but are
leaving their options open for later in the year. The
campaign group in the Cape Town ECC has issued press
statements and have now disbanded.

I want to thank all the organisations and individuals who I
was able to meet personally for their support, interest and
willingness to involve themselves and their organisation in
the campaign. Also thanks for the suggestions you made
which would be used in the campaign.

There were a number of organisations and individuals,
especially in Cape Town, that I was still to meet
personally. May I thank you all for your interest and I
will definitely get to see you before the November call-up -
if it ever arrives!

ECC

I find the present situation a mixed blessing. On one hand
I had "psyched" myself up for this and feel a bit deflated
and depressed. On the other hand it is a definite victory
for those opposed to the SADF, and I was able to build and
strengthen relationships between ECC and you.

I hope that the good working relationship that ECC has with
you will remain strong, and I hope that if they call me up
in November 1987, I will be able to depend on your support
again. Once again thanks so much for all your help.

Aluta continua!

Yours in the struggle for a just peace,

Ivan.

DR IVAN TOMS
FOR: ECC CAMPAIGN GROUP IN CAPE TOWN

PS: Thank you so much for your support &
help. Everywhere I have gone, people have commented
on your ability as an advocate — so I felt in
very safe hands.

The "gay issue" continues here in Cape Town. Today
"the enemy" put up large posters on lamp posts
in the city & suburbs saying: "TOMS AIDS TEST POSITIVE"
(a lie) and "ECC PROBES GAY MEMBERS.".

Congratulations on Simon's release on bail.

Once again thanks for everything. I hope it
might be possible to next time meet in less
formal circumstances.

Regards,

Ivan.

93

UNIVERSITY OF THE WITWATERSRAND, JOHANNESBURG

1 Jan Smuts Avenue, Johannesburg

CENTRE FOR APPLIED LEGAL STUDIES

Dr Ivan Toms
P.O.Box 208
WOODSTOCK
7915

P O WITS
2050, SOUTH AFRICA

Uniwits
4 27125 SA
(011) 716-1111

Reference: EC:CMT

Enquiries: Mr Cameron

(011) 716 5671/2

Date: 25 August 1987

Dear Ivan,

Thank you for your note dated 1 July 1987 which I received at
least ten years ago. Ironically, had I regarded your letter
as purely 'business', I would have answered much more
promptly.

I was most distressed to hear that these people seem to be
trying more of their malign tricks on you. I have suggested
to Alan at Mallinicks that we should institute legal
proceedings should they try the same trick again in November.
We may well lose - the application I have in mind is one for
an interdict restraining the army authorities from further
harassing you by fake call-ups which are then only withdrawn -
but the principle of the thing will be important and that will
be established, I think, even if we lose.

The other harassment you have suffered around the gay issue is
deeply disturbing. I have been sticking out my neck recently
and criticising some prominent judges. This has aroused some
overt security police interest. (A plain clothes constable
called at our Centre on the Monday after I had given the speech,
asking for a copy of it and on the Thursday I received a call
from a security police major from headquarters in Pretoria.)
The uneasy thought that crosses my mind is that they may well
try to do to me what they did to you.

Tomorrow (Saturday) we are holding a meeting to try to see
whether 'progressive' gays in Johannesburg should form some
sort of alliance or organisation and, if so, what. I feel
quite ambivalent on the issue. I find the inherent reactionary
nature of most gay organisations, here and in the United States,
repellent; and I find the deep-going chauvinism of many of
the liberation organisations and local democratic organisations
disquieting. But is there really a role for progressive gays
outside and apart from the other progressive organisations?
Does our role not lie in 'conscientisation' inside them? I
don't know.

94

It would be good to see you. I have to come down to Cape Town
at the end of November for a meeting, and plan to stay a little
longer. That, of course, is just the time when your own army
crisis will be at its peak. (My meeting is over the last
weekend of November.) We will obviously be in touch before
then through Mallinicks, and I hope that circumstances will
be such that we can see each other in 'just peace'.

Warm regards,

Yours sincerely,

EDWIN CAMERON

The photograph of Simon Nkoli and Ivan Toms was taken by photographer Mike Hutchings in Cape Town in January 1989 on the occasion of a visit to South Africa by repre- sentatives of Norway's Arbeidsgrupper for Homofil og Lesbisk Frigjøring. It is in the Simon Nkoli collection in the Gay and Lesbian Archives of South Africa.

96

COMRADE ASHLEY KRIEL
OCT 1966 — JULY 1987
NO
LIBERATION
WITHOUT
LIBERATION

ARCHIVE

Cape Town activists remember sexuality struggles

Mikki van Zyl

Based on author Mikki van Zyl's recent interviews with gender activists in Cape Town in the 1980s and early 1990s, this essay explores how various strands of human rights activism came together or pulled apart at that time, and still influence the life and work of the activists today.

Overview of political organisation in Cape Town in the 1980s

In the early 1980s, gender analysis played almost no part in broad political mobilisation in the Cape Town area. Of the groups affiliated to the two prominent mass organisations, the United Democratic Front (UDF) and the Federation of South African Women (FedSAW), very few publicly adopted a feminist stance. This was primarily because anti-racism was the central political discourse.

Even within women's organisations there was a wide range of attitudes to gender and sexuality, some of them openly expressed, some not. The Black Sash, for example, made up of predominantly liberal women, simply discounted women's oppression altogether.

> From my involvement in the Black Sash there was a strong denial that there existed any discrimination against women or that there needed to be any focus on gender rights. (Anne)[1]

Older women in the UDF expressed hostility to feminism and even more so to homosexuality:

> Working with older black women in the UDF was often difficult because they were strongly anti-feminist and very anti-gay. One had to hide that part of oneself and work with them anyhow. (Victoria)

1. Quotes are from the author's survey material. On request, some names have been changed.

The one large organisation dealing with issues immediate to women was the United Women's Congress (UWCO), which concentrated on grassroots work among women in oppressed communities, encouraging women to solve the problems facing them. As a non-racial organisation with branches from Gardens to Khayelitsha, its aim was to unite all women to oppose apartheid, to fight for the full recognition of all women, and to bring to an end all laws, customs and regulations that discriminated against women (Van Zyl 1991: 10). But even UWCO espoused the 'two-stage' theory of revolution, in which women's emancipation would follow national liberation.

> From my involvement in UWCO and FedSAW, there was a recognition and celebration of the role women could play and the power of women. But there was also a strong perception that the anti-apartheid struggle came first and that we would worry about women's equality later. (Anne)

If there was little dialogue about gender-based oppression in the political and social movements, there was even less about sexuality and sexual abuse:

> Gender and the oppression of women by society and by men were discussed freely, but sexuality issues were taboo. It was seen as an issue that would cause confusion and deter from the urgent struggles we were involved with ... apartheid, the pass-laws, violence and non-participation in homebuilding and child-care ... these were articulated by grassroots organisations and women and contained in the political discourse of the time. (Jenny)

An exception was at the University of Cape Town (UCT), where women student activists began to reset the agenda for themselves. Initially they started a women's movement because 'they believed there was a reluctance by the men to address women's issues in politics' (Van Zyl 1989: 2). In 1978 many of these women joined Rape Crisis, inspired by the need to 'do something real for women'. Rape Crisis was run by young, English-speaking, educated middle-class women, and provided a lay counselling service for rape survivors.

> ... setting up Rape Crisis I felt that this would be a good way of working really closely with black and coloured women and finding ways to help each other create a more feminist and less violent South Africa. (Victoria)

99

The feminist analysis of rape adopted by Rape Crisis was not appreciated by those with a political activist background:

> The Struggle was dominated by black men who blamed rape on colonialism. Others said that it was their culture to beat their wives. Rape Crisis was too small and white for anybody to pay us attention. I knew feminist issues would be ignored. (Diane: author's notes from telephone conversation)

> ... some of them saw us founder members who had been battling so bravely for two years, as 'silly women' who did not have political sophistication and who were really not up to the work of building an organisation. (Victoria)

In 1987 UWCO and other women's organisations took the initiative to revive FedSAW. Many community women's organisations were members of FedSAW. Rape Crisis was also a member. The Black Sash had observer status.

After some years of debate, Rape Crisis had redefined itself as *first* a 'feminist organisation', but one which recognised that 'democracy is a process located in a social context ... a struggle for democracy is integrally linked with the struggle to end sexism, racism and economic exploitation ... responsibility to become part of the process of change ... keep in touch with the issues that concern the majority of people in this country' (Van Zyl and Anderson 1989: 19). This broader commitment was Rape Crisis's rationale for joining the UDF and FedSAW. However, many members left the organisation at that time, feeling it had lost its feminist focus.

Several gay and lesbian organisations were formed in the Cape Town area during the 1980s. Some were student organisations, some focused on counselling, and others concentrated on creating safe social spaces for lesbians and gays:

> A lesbian campaigning group formed called Lilacs ... an outreach and social group that held social evenings once a week ... and [later] set up a lesbian telephone help line. (Victoria)

> In 1981/2 we – several gay men – tried to start a gay and lesbian counselling organisation at UCT. The university opposed its establishment for

years, and in the meantime we started 6010. ... I left 6010 a year
after its establishment because it was subsumed by GASA (started in
Johannesburg), which I thought was a mistake that would make it (as a
national organisation) vulnerable to government oppression. I was wrong.
... My involvement with trying to set up a counselling service at UCT continued, and eventually we catalysed the establishment of the Gay and
Lesbian Association [GALA]. (Duncan)

Although GASA and GALA were non-racial national organisations, black members felt uncomfortable or unwelcome in their predominantly white context
(Kleinbooi 1994; Jara and Lapinsky 1998: 48–9).

In 1986, Lesbians and Gays Against Oppression (LAGO) was started in Cape
Town, mainly by white intellectuals who identified gay oppression as part of a
broader struggle. It later changed its name to Organisation for Lesbian and Gay
Activists (OLGA), and became a UDF affiliate. LAGO was later to link up with
the Gay and Lesbian Organisation of the Witwatersrand (GLOW) to draw up the
brief on sexual orientation which was eventually incorporated in the Equality
Clause in the Constitution.

The Association of Bisexuals, Gays and Lesbians (ABIGALE) was started at
about the same time in Cape Town as a support group, mostly for black
and coloured men. It also became concerned with political issues (Jara and
Lapinsky 1998: 51). OLGA was admitted, albeit reluctantly, to FedSAW's
annual festivals.

My experience was in FedSAW and with working on the committee of two
or three FedSAW festivals. There was initially an objection, mainly from
UWCO, to OLGA being an affiliate of the federation and to OLGA having
a stall at the festival. But the objections were overridden and there was,
I think, an uncomfortable acceptance of OLGA. (Anne)

Some lesbians were hesitant to join gay organisations, because they believed
many homosexual men still bought into the domination and subordination
embedded in heterosexual relations through the centralisation of 'male' desire
in patriarchal discourses (Jeffreys 1990: 146).

There were definite differences between the women and men in the group
[OLGA]. Most of the men were very politically correct in front of us, but

when you overheard some of them on their own they were deeply misogynist … apart from the orientation clause, we really didn't seem to have the same agendas. (Marié)

Lesbianism posed a challenge for the women's organisations that did not question the nexus of oppressions in sexism, Western familial ideology and Christianity.

When the organisation found out that we [two women members] were having a relationship, some members wanted to *skors* [expel] us. There were meetings and even a disciplinary hearing, but we were allowed to stay. (Linda: author's notes from telephone conversation)

The heterosexual women decided that the lesbian feminists were giving the movement a bad name. (Victoria)

Also caught up in sexual politics was the End Conscription Campaign (ECC), which organised against the military conscription of white men, although it had many active women members. The ECC was banned in 1988, indicating the threat that resistance to militarisation posed to the government. Smear campaigns against the ECC explicitly linked it to homosexuality, characterised as femininity, thus demonstrating the deeply gendered nature of the military (Van Zyl et al. 1999: 61).

How they came into the struggle

Family and social backgrounds of respondents to the survey varied widely, from conservative racists to communist sympathisers.

Values within the family were quite classically *Boer*. Dad was a farmer and ruled with the required iron hand – and sometimes fist – otherwise, according to him, 'they' get *hans* [a designation for tamed animal, but with connotations of being cheeky]. (Amiene)

I grew up at the end of the colonial era and, as a child, I was not aware of the simmering anger against my people (British) and myself as a representative of these people. (Victoria)

My family was politically inactive, uninterested … My politicisation only really started once I got to high school. Until then I was ignorant of why the student uprisings were taking place. (Debbie)

My family was typical of white middle-class liberals – voted Prog [Progressive Party] but had a 'girl' in the kitchen and a 'boy' in the garden. My own politicisation only really started once I went to UCT as a student in 1972. (Carol)

My father came from central Europe and his experience of the rise of Nazism profoundly shaped his thinking. He was opposed to political oppression and anything that smacked of a police state. (Jenny)

I grew up in a family with parents who had been SA Communist Party sympathisers as students at Wits, a politically disaffected Afrikaans father and a mother active in Progressive Party canvassing. (Duncan)

Politically conscious and active family, parents and siblings – self politically aware at early age (early primary school ... with anti-apartheid, anti-racist political school essays) and active from end of standard five (adolescent detentions, etc.) (Berne)

Gender awareness of their 'otherness' came at an early age to all the respondents.

I wanted to be a boy. (Marié)

I had a strong awareness of the unfairness of gender stereotyping from about eight or nine when I couldn't/shouldn't do things my brothers did because I was a girl. I resisted by becoming a 'tomboy'. (Anne)

I learned about men first hand, in experiences of sexual abuse by my cousin, uncle and schoolteacher – all in primary school. (Amiene)

... during onset of puberty I realised I was a girl ... mortified by the implications, but determined not to marry and buy into female oppressions and always to be independent. (Berne)

I experienced a very traumatic attempted rape. ... I was seven years old ... it affected me badly. I had nightmares for years after. Counselling children who had survived sexual abuse was not done in those days and my parents believed that if they said nothing about it I would forget about it. I never did of course. (Victoria)

Sexuality was a primary factor in identifying their 'otherness'.

Lesbianism was a word whispered in the corridors – as something awful and disgraceful. (Jenny)

I realised I was a lesbian when I was about fourteen, but did not do anything about it until I was in my early twenties. (Carol)

In my final year of junior school, I realised I was homosexual (well, a moffie actually) and spent the next seven years in active denial. (Duncan)

… born a dyke. (Diane: author's notes from telephone conversation)

I was quite separate from my peers … Became somewhat of an 'outsider' at 'varsity (Stellenbosch) – not sitting around the same fire like most – maybe due to increased awareness and acceptance of my own 'deviant' sexuality. (Amiene)

From about the age of six I was aware that I was 'different'. I tended to fall in love with my girlfriends. I wanted to be a boy so that I could do the things boys were allowed to do … I was about eleven years old when I discovered a label for my sexuality – lesbian. It was a big headline in a local newspaper, 'Navratilova Lesbian'. I looked at this and said 'Nope, that's wrong, she's Czechoslovakian'. (Debbie)

Early experiences of 'otherness' formed a basis for later sympathies and alliances with oppressed people, especially among the white respondents.

At high school I ran into anti-Afrikaner 'racism' … called me names like 'rock spider', 'hairyback'. (Marié)

School was difficult because I was an oddball, a foreigner, I had not had the same grounding as the other children, I was way behind them in the syllabus, and it was a Catholic convent and I was not Catholic! (Victoria)

Two Afrikaner women from typical households where men 'wore the pants' both mentioned that an early source of their political conscientising was working out their personal contradictions about the Dutch Reformed Church. An English-speaking woman from the Catholic Church was influenced by hearing apartheid being questioned by the church:

> Tried to make sense out of the NG Kerk [Dutch Reformed Church]/Christian contradictions at an early age – who are the 'chosen ones'? ... why do the 'coloureds' and 'blacks' attend a separate church? (Amiene)

> The *dominee* [minister] came to warn my parents that I would be expelled from the *katkisasieklas* [confirmation class] – for questioning his interpretations of the Bible. They prayed together for my salvation. I had to 'recant' to keep the peace. (Marié)

> The church's social teaching questioning the apartheid social order was discussed in the household ... In high school, politics was discussed, and we were encouraged to get involved in social 'upliftment' projects ... Sexuality issues were never discussed at home or at school. (Jenny)

For others, the defining politically conscientising experience was student politics, and its direct confrontations with police brutality.

> In Standard 6, 1985, I was sort of thrown into the deep end of the student side of the anti-apartheid struggle ... injustices that were being perpetrated by the regime ... racism, segregation and the host of inequalities and oppressions associated with apartheid. Suddenly, many things started to make sense to me, like why we had to sit upstairs in the bus, and why there were separate toilets for whites and blacks at the train station, and why we could only go to certain beaches. Until then my parents had told me that this was just the way it was and I had to accept it. (Debbie)

> My politicisation took place in first year at UCT, 1972, the year of the police attack on students at St George's Cathedral ... a large protest crowd was broken up with teargas, dogs, truncheons, and a concrete mixer driven deliberately through the crowd. After that I attended various anti-government demonstrations, but ... it was only in 1981 that I found a channel for my accumulated frustrations and anger by getting involved in gay activism. (Duncan)

I became involved in student politics in a peripheral way … police brutality made my mind up. A stint overseas shaped my political views into a strong feminist and anti-apartheid stance. My return to SA in 1976 just before the Soweto uprisings had a radical impact on my political commitment to the Struggle. (Marié)

When I first went to university in 1976 in Johannesburg, I was exposed to the events of June 1976. The reality and 'wrongness' of political oppression, and social disadvantage struck me deeply. (Jenny)

All the respondents were motivated by notions of social injustice, and joining political organisations was a way to work for change.

When I was 22 years old, I became involved with another woman, with a similar political commitment … involved in the same 'Struggle organisations' – for which we spent the whole of the 1980s committed to building and fighting for a transformed South Africa. We were also political detainees together. (Jenny)

… my opportunity to bring about change. I attended area meetings, mass meetings, marches, distributed pamphlets, stoned Casspirs and police vans, was chased by the police and their dogs, scaled walls and fences, inhaled copious amounts of teargas, ran away as my friends had the shit *sjambokked* [whipped] out of them and then had to deal with the feelings of guilt because I didn't stay to help. (Debbie)

Secrets and disjunctures

Political work – meeting times, names of comrades – meant secrets had to be kept because of security. Sexuality, especially homosexuality, was a secret too – a taboo subject in organisations, as much as in families. Some had to admit their sexuality to peers and comrades for security reasons, so that the police could not blackmail them if they were detained.

The 1980s was an era full of intense activity and political intrigue. Secrets and lack of full disclosure about activities, involvements and people in organisations and social circles were part of the social and organisational climate of the day. I did keep secrets, around the nature of my primary relationship with a woman, and my political involvements. I did not disclose the former to my work, the organisations I was part of, or my family. Likewise the full extent of the latter was not disclosed to anyone. (Jenny)

I was 'discreet' about being a lesbian in the Women's Alliance and Coalition but not in the Black Sash. There was an unspoken pressure not to 'dilute' the struggle agenda (race being the primary battleground!) with secondary struggles/identities, such as sexual persuasion. (Amiene)

Homosexuality was often a disruptive political positioning, for individuals and organisations alike.

He threatened to expose me publicly as a lesbian, and discredit Rape Crisis because he said that it would become public knowledge that the organisation was being run by 'a pervert'. (Victoria)

At one level I didn't think that [my sexuality] was something I had to share with others ... also a fear of people's reactions or rejection of me because of my sexuality, so I 'normalised', spoke of guys that I liked, even went on dates with guys and tried to do all the 'girlie-things'. (Debbie)

It became clear that my choice of a primary partner would not be tolerated by my church colleagues and that I therefore had no future in the church. ... Many '80s activists were more concerned about political secrets than their sexuality. Many realised that being in the closet with one's political peers risked exposure and blackmail by security forces. (Jenny)

I was fortunate to work in, and be part of, progressive organisations, and have friends who were all activists, so being a lesbian wasn't a problem. The only secrets I kept were about my friends' and my partner's under-ground activities. I also didn't discuss my political views or activities with my family, though they knew about them. (Anne)

Because of my involvement in activism, by the early 1980s I was publicly out. Secrets? After my energy-sapping closethood of the 1970s I didn't have time for secrets. Parents, friends and colleagues either accepted me as I was, or not. I try to live an open but non-confrontational life. (Duncan)

Kept my sexuality secret from most ... Kept my political persuasions 'at a distance' from my parents, i.e. no in-depth accounts of my activities. I did share some of my experiences in the States with them (arrest for protesting) … necessitated by the fact that they were receiving menacing phone calls from the security police and that a previous house of theirs was targeted with graffiti. (Amiene)

[They] were aligned with the democratic struggle and supported the anti-apartheid movement [but] they were homophobic and it was very uncomfortable working with them. (Victoria)

There were standards of political correctness and honourable behaviour in political organisations, but beyond these boundaries lay another terrain of self-censorship, secrets and silences.

I felt that I had to put my personal feelings aside for the good of the struggle. (Debbie)

During the late 1970s while I was active in women's organisations I also worked as a sex worker … no one knew. When I later became involved with women, I often hid my previous history with men … I became alienated from my family during the anti-apartheid struggle (because of my politics) – only my one sister knew about my relationships with women. (Marié)

Caucusing … was not approved of within OLGA … that might have been seen as secretive activity. (Duncan)

That gender rights remained marginalised was evident in the many covert 'anti-rape' campaigns that some of us got involved in, such as slogan painting on public buildings and attempting to 'out' known rapists and batterers. (Debbie)

During the 1980s, feminists found themselves having to differentiate between the feminist cause and the political cause.

After starting a campaign for the resignation of a male teacher who was sexually abusing female students at a neighbouring primary school, I realised that issues relating to women were of lesser importance. (Debbie)

During my involvement with Rape Crisis I worked hard to help politicise people in the organisation to becoming part of the anti-apartheid struggle. (Marié)

We had a very interesting experience in the Black Sash when some of us formed a 'women's group' and were criticised for being 'aggressively feminist'. There were also mutterings that the women's group was 'dominated by lesbians', which led to the women's group holding a meeting/workshop to discuss the 'lesbian issue' in the Black Sash ... we had a very fruitful workshop, which brought up not only the issue of marginalisation of lesbians, but also of others, such as Afrikaans-speaking members. (Anne)

After my arrest in 1989 I withdrew from student politics. I never ever went back to the mainstream political arena but got involved with issues relating to gender and gender-based violence. There were several reasons for my withdrawal, one reason was the distrust of my comrades when some of them turned out to be police informants ... I was not prepared to put myself at risk of arrest and harassment in a climate where I could not trust my comrades. The second reason was the sexism and sidelining of gender issues in the political arena ... there were constant promises of addressing issues of women's roles and raising women's profiles in the movement but no real effort was put into it. (Debbie)

For activists of homosexual orientation, the labelling of deviance positioned them as 'other', whether they were black or white. Often having to fight women's gender stereotyping in their personal lives, they found a home in organisations fighting for women's rights.

Some female comrades who were far more assertive than I [was] managed to get their voices heard and respected. I only developed that level of assertiveness and confidence once I got to Rape Crisis, in the early '90s, an environment that was for women by women, where my voice and contribution were valued and affirmed. (Debbie)

Liberation for one would be liberation for all. I still think however that the pink agenda was strategically kept secondary so as not to dilute or detract from the primary struggle ... Today the link is irrevocable and constitutionally guaranteed. The social perceptions and attitudes of the majority of South Africans might not, however, agree with the sentiment of the law. (Amiene)

The Constitution and the normalisation of homosexuality

OLGA members, though middle class, had allies in the anti-apartheid movement, and strategised to get the sexual orientation clause included in the draft Constitution. Even so, there was an awareness that this needed to be done somewhat surreptitiously.

> There was a consensus amongst my friends that we wanted an Equality Clause in the Constitution. In OLGA we set about drafting such a clause. There were enormous battles for power and control in the process. It ended up as a men vs. women battle. Our strategy was to get a top ANC official (or several) to support the clause, which happened with Albie Sachs and Frene Ginwala. My feeling was that the nitty-gritty work was done in Cape Town, and then GLOW in Johannesburg took it up and did the 'marketing'. By then I was so pissed off with the petty fighting and bickering that I withdrew from the organisation. Like some of my friends, I felt that OLGA was not facing grassroots problems in the lesbian and gay community in the way that ABIGALE was doing. (Marié)

> [The sexual orientation clause] involved an enormous amount of lobbying and even people in the ANC were opposed to it at times. It is great that it is there, that is a great victory. It is a tool that can be used to gain more rights for gay and lesbian people. Through a legal process, rights for lesbian and gay people can now be gained – like the right to adopt children, pension benefits, recognition of relationships, etc. It is true that popular opinion does not support the clause – but that is true of many things, like the death penalty. It can be used to mobilise support for gay rights. (Jenny)

> We were aware that if we made too much noise, the clause would be rejected. We also knew that, given the opportunity, the majority of people would not support it. (Marié)

> It definitely has made a huge difference, especially for black people and black women, to normalising our queernesses and institutionalising our rights. Opinions will shift over time. The clause guarantees that it will, and pushes opinion in that direction. (Berne)

All the respondents applauded the Equality Clause, even if the reality of equality still lags behind.

I thought and still think that lesbian and gay rights were peripheral to the anti-apartheid struggle. My sense is we sneaked in through the (largely white liberal) back door, which was strategically clever. It leaves us vulnerable to grassroots prejudice and popular political change. My impression is that we squeaked into the Constitution largely through the efforts of a few powerfully connected individuals. They did a good job. (Duncan)

I think there is quite a gap between the ideal the Constitution stands for and the actual beliefs and attitudes. There seems to be a correlation between the degree of homophobia and whether one lives in a rural or an urban setting. Attitudes in city centres like Cape Town seem to be more positive and affirming whereas rural areas seem to be more conservative. The same correlation exists in terms of religion i.e. the Christian and Muslim faiths' condemnation of homosexual 'acts'. (Amiene)

All the respondents felt a deep respect for the few 'out' public figures, and believed these people played an important role in normalising homosexuality.

We need more textured knowledge about gay and lesbian public figures so that young people can see that being gay is part of a range of being human, and OK, and successful. (Jenny)

Awesome the ones who are out ... and the CGE's [Commission on Gender Equality] explicit adoption of sexual orientation in their list of things greatly helps these women too. Those not out, they should combat their internalised homophobia and live normally, acknowledge their relationships, families and lifestyles in a relaxed way (e.g. not play the pronoun game and be paranoid) – this will help other younger people to follow suit. (Berne)

I think that everyone should be out, whatever it is they are hiding, but acknowledge that for many, this would be an act of courage greater than they can countenance, due to the inherent and dangerous inequalities which pervade our society. (Carol)

People like Zackie Achmat are fabulous examples of brilliant and ethical gays; Judge Kathy Satchwell is a very important role model for both women and lesbians ... Edwin Cameron, who is HIV-positive, is an inspiration, and we need more public figures like them. (Victoria)

With victory achieved in the adoption of the Constitution, some of the impulse was lost. Some organisations dissolved. Some of the respondents broke away.

> ... The rich capitalist lesbians did not feel comfortable amongst what they called the 'dowdy', more socially conscious, feminist lesbians; the racist, white lesbians did not feel happy when the coloured lesbians joined the socials at the pub. The feminist lesbians were delighted when the coloured lesbians arrived, but they often found that some of the coloured lesbians had no social consciousness and were not feminists in any way. The coloured lesbians complained that they did not feel comfortable because they experienced racism. Lilacs died! (Victoria)

> I think I became too frustrated with the intra- and inter-organisational politics, especially where personal agendas supersede the objectives of the organisation. (Debbie)

> By that time I was also pissed off with gay and lesbian politics, especially the internecine warfare that threatened to sink every positive development, and I decided to leave gay activism to others. (Duncan)

> Once the Equality Clause had been drawn up, I decided to focus on gender and development – important because we were entering the period of reconstruction. (Marié)

The Struggle continues

For everyone in this study, gender and politics has been a way of life. Though their political mobilisation was initially motivated by self-interest, it widened their views on other oppressions. For them, the liberation struggle was part and parcel of their personal development. All of them are still involved in civil society activism.

> I believe that the struggle for gender rights, the lesbian and gay rights struggle, and the anti-apartheid struggle are one and the same – a human rights struggle. I do believe that those who brought gender rights to the political platforms did a marvellous job in getting women's contribution recognised in the new South Africa. (Victoria)

[Politics influenced my life] very considerably during the 1980s. It purged my anger and gave me focus. In fact, it also formed the backbone of my socialising. I made some very good friends through gay activism. (Duncan)

For us lesbians it was heaven to work in an organisation where we could be totally ourselves and not have to hide in any way. But I felt in some ways it became self indulgent, we should have been more professional about the organisation, and been more concerned about spreading the knowledge to all kinds of women and making all kinds of women feel welcome. (Victoria)

Politics coloured my early life. It was the major determinant of the course of my life as an adult. My political commitments determined how I spent my time, my friendships and my work. I still feel that a commitment to equity and solidarity with exploited people and societies will continue to drive my work for the rest of my life. (Jenny)

Once one comes to understand that everything in life – oppression, poverty, crime, one's sexual orientation, etc. – [is] political, it is all consuming. My lifestyle and political persuasion inform each other. I am grateful for my exposure and opportunities to inform myself and for having taken action to help contribute to change. (Amiene)

Involvement and identification with feminist and anti-apartheid politics has made me who I am, it has affected every level of my life. (Anne)

At a personal level I have benefited immensely … I have grown as a person … and without the assertiveness and self-confidence/belief gained through my process of conscientisation and politicisation I probably would not have gone to university nor travelled. But I also find that it brings with it a great deal of stress and expectation … once you've become politically active there is almost an expectation for you to continue … I know that this is more a self-imposed expectation than anything else … where I feel I should be campaigning, should be active on the issues I believe in … and it really freaks me … especially when all I want to do is bury my head in the sand and focus on me and my life, live a normal 'blinkered' life. But I suppose that once the blinkers are removed, they are removed forever.

113

When I tried to do this a few years ago, I found myself riddled with guilt, especially when I saw or read the news, because I was not doing something to change the injustices I saw. Sometimes I think I feel indebted to the notion of 'struggle' or obligated to be an activist because of the opportunities afforded to me through my activism. Perhaps I am simply an activist at heart and I am trying to resist my 'nature'. Whatever it is, it frustrates me no end. (Debbie)

The Struggle gave me a reason to live through some really deprived years without food and with bad education, etc. My idealism kept me alive through the darkest days. It still does. I am because I dream. I am because I challenge both my ever-evolving self and other edifices. I live for peaceful change. I live for the realisation of dreams – *egalité*, liberty and siblinghood. While there is still much to be done, we have already achieved so much, especially in South Africa. *La luta continua – victoria es certa!* (Berne)

The rights-based cohering rhetoric of the 1980s dissolved after the democratisation of the 1990s, but something like the discourse of that struggle is emerging in the mobilisation process against the HIV/AIDS pandemic. This process closely follows identity-based politics but also incorporates rights struggles based on the Constitution. (Parker, Barbosa and Aggleton 2000: 10). This new struggle may evolve to forge the alliances needed to address ongoing oppressions such as gender, sexuality, poverty, discrimination against people living with HIV/AIDS, and community health.

The HIV/AIDS pandemic has forced a focus on sexuality that could not be imagined twenty years ago, deeply disrupting many African cultural assumptions about the secrecy and privacy of sexual discourse. It has also forced us to refigure norms of family arrangements. The campaigns around people living with AIDS have a strong resemblance to progressive identity politics (Kraak 1998: viii–ix). One of the strongest challenges will be how men's control over women will be transformed.

... for all the excellent changes that have taken place and the progress that is all around us, I am disappointed in the inertia that has set in, and the fact that the new government is becoming like the old government in many ways. I am afraid of the way Mbeki and his clique are entrenching themselves. If they were white, they would never get away with what they are doing to the people of South Africa. (Victoria)

Oppressions are indivisible. Resistance becomes part of a search for personal authenticity. For these respondents, this authenticity has a strong ethical component, which binds them into the broader South African community.

My political origins in faith-based movements, with their universal commitment to liberation – political, social, economic and personal – was the framework for understanding oppression. So personal liberation – freeing the bonds imposed on ourselves by society, our families, and discovering one's own authentic sexuality and identity – was part of living an authentic faith. Similarly, involvement in anti-apartheid struggles was part of that commitment and faith. For me on a personal level, they were part of the same process. (Jenny)

115

Works cited

Jara, Mazibuko and Lapinsky, Sheila (1998). 'Forging a representative gay liberation movement in South Africa'. *Development Update*, 2:2.

Jeffreys, Sheila (1990). *Anticlimax: A Feminist Perspective on the Sexual Revolution.* London: The Women's Press

Kleinbooi, Hein (1994). 'Identity crossfire' in Gevisser, Mark and Cameron, Edwin (eds), *Defiant Desire*. New York, London: Routledge

Kraak, Gerald (1998). 'Editorial: Class, race, nationalism and the politics of identity: A perspective from the South'. *Development Update*, 2:2.

Parker, Richard, Barbosa, Regina Maria, and Aggleton, Peter (2000). 'Introduction: Framing the sexual subject' in Parker, Richard, Barbosa, Regina Maria, and Aggleton, Peter (eds), *Framing the Sexual Subject: The Politics of Gender, Sexuality and Power.* Berkeley and Los Angeles: University of California Press

Van Zyl, Mikki (1989). 'Herstory' (Rape Crisis training dossier). Cape Town: Rape Crisis

Van Zyl, Mikki (1991). 'Feminism' (Rape Crisis training dossier). Cape Town: Rape Crisis

Van Zyl, Mikki and Anderson, Pat (1989). 'Democracy' (Rape Crisis training dossier). Cape Town: Rape Crisis

Van Zyl, Mikki, De Gruchy, Jeanelle, Lapinsky, Sheila, Lewin, Simon and Reid, Graeme (1999). 'The aVersion Project: Human rights abuses of gays and lesbians in the South African Defence Force by health worker during the apartheid era'. Cape Town: Simply Said and Done

Homosexuality and the South African left: The ambiguities of exile

Gerald Kraak

The subject of Gerald Kraak's essay is the disjuncture between the conservatism of the South African liberation movement in exile and the ANC's later support for gay and lesbian rights. Kraak's own experience as a gay man and anti-apartheid activist in South Africa and in exile, and his interviews with other gay men who were in exile and in prison, provide a personal perspective.

For friendship, such an unrequited longing
Text engraved into the marble of the Gay Monument in Amsterdam, from a poem by Jacob Israel de Haan

This essay is a contribution to a slim but emerging body of work in gay South African historiography – the hidden, largely unacknowledged role played by gay men and lesbians in opposition politics and in the anti-apartheid and liberation movements.

Mark Gevisser, in particular, has sought to chronicle the lives of such people, initially as co-editor of the seminal *Defiant Desire* (1994), in which there are partial biographies of political activists such as Zackie Achmat, Ivan Toms and Derrick Fine, and later in his film documentary, *The Man Who Drove with Mandela* (1998). The documentary is a biography of Cecil Williams, a member of the proscribed Communist Party and a contemporary of Mandela and others, later indicted in the Rivonia Trial of 1963. Gevisser's posthumous outing of Williams and his account of the way he straddled the spheres of anti-apartheid politics and the homosexual underworld of 1950s Johannesburg, is a history rich in contradiction. Like Williams, many gay men and lesbians hid their homosexuality – not only from the authorities, but also from their comrades – for fear of marginalisation or oppression, even while committed to the liberation of others.

The experience of progressive gay men and lesbians in South Africa is not unique in this respect. The link between the agendas of the progressive political movements in the US and Europe and gay liberation over the last decade and a half belies a longer, more enduring tradition in the left. Notwithstanding some brief epochs where groups and governments such as the early Bolsheviks tolerated a degree of emancipation, historically the left has proved as homophobic as the right. So, for example, in the socialist countries of the Soviet bloc, homosexuals were persecuted, even as centre-right governments in the West decriminalised same-sex behaviour.

Awe

History is an interpretive discipline and inevitably subjective when it involves autobiography, as this interpolation into the work of Gevisser and others does. Like Gevisser, I am still struck with awe at the quantum leap from the ante-diluvian criminalisation of homosexuality under apartheid, to the full citizenship of gays and lesbians under the government of the African National Congress (ANC). The awe derives from an apparent lack of connection, the absence of a historically explicable discourse linking the past to the present, so that the change has the quality of miracle. Returning to South Africa in 1993 after thirteen years in exile, I was struck not only by the contrast between the repression of homosexuality of the country I had left in 1979 on the one hand, and the pre-election debate on the indivisibility of human rights on the other, but also by the contradiction between my sometimes negative experiences as a gay man in the ranks of the exiled liberation movement and the ANC's latter-day support for an emancipatory agenda.

There's a gap that seeks explanation. Gevisser has tried to provide one:

> The primary reason why the notion of gay equality passed so smoothly into the Constitution is most likely that the ANC elite has a utopian social progressive ideology, influenced largely by the social-democratic movements in the countries that supported it during its struggle: Sweden, Holland, Britain, Canada, Australia. In exile in these countries key South African leaders came to understand and accept – and in the case of women, benefit from – the sexual liberation movement. Foremost among these were Frene Ginwala, now Speaker of Parliament; Albie Sachs, now a judge on the Constitutional Court; Kader Asmal, now Minister of Education; and Thabo Mbeki himself, South Africa's second democratically-elected President. (2000:118)

This exposition of the ANC's encounter with homosexuality needs further interrogation. While Gevisser's tribute to some of the more libertarian and open-minded members of the movement may be valid, he discounts two other strong ideological traditions which competed with social democracy in the ANC

119

– those of Africanism and Stalinism, both hostile to the variants of gender politics framed by Western feminism and the proponents of gay liberation.

For me as a closeted political activist inside South Africa and, later, as a member of the ANC in exile, there was more of a resonance and a continuum of experience in these latter traditions, than in the ANC's late embrace of social democracy and full citizenship for gays and lesbians.

After my own, late, coming out, it was something of a revelation to discover how many of my fellow activists in the late 1970s and early 1980s were gay and had led lives of partial subterfuge, keeping their sexual identities secret in their political lives. This has even led me to speculate that assuming the resolutely *political* identities required by the style of anti-apartheid politics amounted to a sublimation of sexual identity and a deferral of coming out that was a subtle form of internalised homophobia. Or even that the subterfuge of the political underground allowed for a parallel secret sexual life, otherwise difficult to express.

'Mystic crystal revelation': The student movement and the counter-culture

I was active in the left-wing National Union of South African Students (NUSAS) from 1975, taking up the post of National Media Officer in 1978. Many of my predecessors in the Union's executive were gay. Yet this was never disclosed. Ironically, the NUSAS of the mid-1970s aped the counter-cultural revisionism of its European contemporaries – the era of 'free love', expressed in a flowering of (heterosexual) promiscuity, long hair, flowing batik clothing, rock festivals, cannabis use, nascent feminism and other challenges to social mores on the campuses. The cultural wing of NUSAS was even dubbed Aquarius – after the signature tune of the musical *Hair* (Rado and Radni, 1969).

120

> *Harmony and understanding*
> *Sympathy and trust abounding*
> *No more falsehoods or derisions*
> *Golden living dreams of visions*

Mystic crystal revelation
And the mind's true liberation
Aquarius! Aquarius!

Thankfully these cheesy sentiments were mitigated by a more realistic and hard-nosed leftism in the ranks of NUSAS, but neither allowed for the homosexuality celebrated in another track from *Hair* (Rado and Radni, 1969):

Sodomy, fellatio, cunnilingus, pederasty.
Father, why do these words sound so nasty?
Masturbation can be fun
Join the holy orgy
Kama Sutra Everyone!!

Homosexuality was so deeply buried in the movement that the notorious Schlebusch Commission – established in 1973 to investigate the threat posed by NUSAS to the state (the Prime Minster at the time had called it a 'cancer in society' to be rooted out) – failed to discover or note that the NUSAS president and three of its executive members were gay men or lesbians.

The Commission highlighted – and condemned – the promiscuity of NUSAS's heterosexual office bearers and the fact that they lived in communes! These and other such moral digressions were sensationalised by the media at the time and were used as partial justification for the Calvinist government's subsequent restrictions on NUSAS.[1]

Neville Curtis, the NUSAS president, was banned, later went into exile and played a prominent role in the Australian Anti-Apartheid Movement. Sheila Lapinsky, a member of the executive, also served with a banning order after the Schlebusch Commission issued its report, re-emerged as a United Democratic Front (UDF) activist in the 1980s. Another executive committee member went into exile and helped found the Committee on South African War Resistance (COSAWR). Yet others, whose political involvement began with NUSAS, helped establish the nascent trade union movement or became involved in the ANC underground.

121

1. NUSAS was declared an Affected Organisation, preventing it from raising funds abroad. Eight members of the organisation were served with five-year banning orders. Several members of the organisation were later tried for treason.

Home

In the 1980s NUSAS abandoned the excesses of the counter-culture and embraced the more sober conventions of anti-apartheid politics of the day, seeking alliances with the emergent trade union movement and black students and scholars. Yet the implicit homophobia persisted.

James Barrett, a student at the University of the Witwatersrand, was a founding member of the Wits Alternative Service Group, which challenged compulsory military conscription and questioned the role of the South African Defence Force (SADF) in the repression of anti-apartheid opposition.

> There were about eight of us. I was the only gay man. It was quite a schizophrenic experience. I had this sense of needing to split my gay identity from my work against racism. Politically, at a gut passionate level it felt right to be involved, but the meetings, dominated by straight, socially conservative couples, were uncomfortable. (Interview with author, July 2001)

Barrett's experience mirrored those of a contemporary, Rupert Smith (a pseudonym) studying at Natal University, later a founder member of COSAWR.

> I think my sexuality has always held me back in some ways, because of a general fear that being 'out there' politically, making things happen, all opens you up to scrutiny of who you are and what you do in your spare time. (Interview with author, May 2001)

I have given this absence of a discourse about sexuality in the student movement a great deal of thought, confounded as I am by its progressivism on every other front while failing to mirror its Western contemporaries, which allowed space for the emergence of gay liberation. This lacuna bears further exploration. It could not have been the Africanist denial of homosexuality expressed more strongly in the late 1980s by spokespeople of the liberation movements – the student movement's links with these were tenuous and clandestine until well into the second half of the decade.

Perhaps the homophobia had two sources. Maybe it lay in the student movement's developing embrace of Western Marxism, which in its more derivative aspects derided homosexuality as 'bourgeois deviance', inimical to a robust working-class culture of hardy men supported by dutiful women.

Or perhaps it lay in that most debilitating aspect of 'being gay' – the internalised homophobia of gay and lesbian student activists themselves. Their terror of discovery delayed the student movement's coming to terms with homosexuality, in contrast, say, to the way that separatist feminists challenged the sexism of the male leadership in 1978 and forced the movement to adopt more progressive policies on gender.

And there was crucially, too, the absence of a meeting point between the open expression of gay identity – in the early 1980s confined almost entirely to the white, gay male club scene – and anti-apartheid politics. James Barrett incisively captures the schizophrenia of gay anti-apartheid activists in this period.

> I really struggled. I endured homophobic jokes and remarks in my political work and then went to gay clubs in Hillbrow where there was the most grotesque racism. I had a one-night stand with someone, in fact my one sexual encounter in two-odd years. We finished having sex and this guy talked about what a terrible time he was having at work. He said that he was treated worse than the 'kaffir girls'. It was just dismal. You had a sense that the few black men that were allowed in the clubs were only there because they were with much older white men. (Interview with author, July 2001)

Barrett's experience reflects that of many gay and lesbian activists of the time – the sense of a life half-lived, of sublimated identity, the truncation of a discourse on the relationship between class, race and sexual oppression, that was implicit, but never realised, in the notion of struggle.

> The white gay community was racist. There was very little sense of a black gay community. So for white gay political activists the spheres of political and gay identities just did not come together, as they might have in a Western country. (Interview with author, July 2001).

Exile

I left South Africa in 1979 to avoid conscription and lived in Europe for thirteen years. So did Rupert Smith and James Barrett – the latter after his flat was raided by police and other members of the Alternative Service Group were detained. Some were later charged with membership of the banned ANC, and treason.

123

Exile proved no different. Exile politics in the United Kingdom of the 1980s was shaped by the London structures of the ANC and by the solidarity campaigns of the Anti-Apartheid Movement (AAM). In both there was, again, a curious silence on the issue of homosexuality, the more marked because in British society there had been an upsurge in progressive mobilisation against the policies of the Conservative Party government of Margaret Thatcher. These included further restrictions on gay men and lesbians.

Path-breaking alliances were being struck between the conventional, socially conservative formations of the left, such as the trade unions, and gay and lesbian organisations. According to James Barrett:

> Lesbians and gays were supportive of the miners' strike – there was extraordinary coalition politics; gay and lesbian groups raised funds for the miners. The 1983 Gay Pride march was led by a colliery band belting out Tom Robinson's anthem 'Glad to be Gay'. (Interview with author, July 2001)

Although the ANC and AAM structures were closely allied to the Labour Party and other left-wing groups, which were at least nominally libertarian, the exile community seemed hermetically sealed against outside influences. Why was this? Was it a typical exile response, a fear of integration, the loosening of the bonds with home, a cultural regrouping around essential identities? Or did the homophobia have roots elsewhere?

We found little evidence of the exposure of 'the ANC elite to a utopian social progressive ideology, influenced largely by the social-democratic movements in the countries that supported it during its struggle', cited by Gevisser.

Rather we encountered a certain defensiveness: that in adopting or opening up to issues other than the racism of apartheid, the movement would be deflected, led astray. The notion of oppressed groups other than blacks expressing themselves, or organising separately, somehow constituted a betrayal of the imperative of national liberation.

The stronger influences here were the ANC's – always latent – Africanism and the extreme social conservatism of Stalinism that its alliance with the South African Communist Party brought to the movement. As I have written before,

[The ANC] rejected feminism as a western unAfrican concept ... feminist
debate may not have been openly suppressed, but it was sublimated to
the intrinsic logic of the strategy for liberation: the first struggle was for liberation of the nation; the second for the liberation of the working class;
and at best third down the line might come the struggle for the liberation
of women. (Kraak, 1998:7)

The more conservative women's sections of the liberation movement
[even] held that it was the primary task of women to provide support to
the front ranks of the Struggle – the men – and to care for their children
... (Kraak and Simpson, 1998:viii)

In the pubs of London

In the many discussions with 'comrades' in the ANC's leadership and membership structures – in the pubs of London, inhibitions loosened by pints of beer –
the responses were always the same when the issue of homosexuality was
raised.

Most often the subject elicited revulsion, ridicule or discomfort. More intellectu-
ally or ideologically-considered responses held that homosexuality was deca-
dent, a bourgeois deviation of Western capitalism that would disappear under
socialism. Or that while homosexuality might well occur in the white community, it was alien to African culture. Where homosexual practices existed in
African communities it was by contamination, or as a consequence of apartheid institutions such as the migrant hostels, which broke up families and confined men in urban barracks. An explicit project of the anti-apartheid struggle
was to restore the sanctity of family life.

For others still, homosexuals posed a risk to the movement – they could be
blackmailed or compromised by the regime and for this reason could not be
trusted as comrades.

In the absence of more rigorous research, what I am recounting can only be
anecdotal and risks stereotyping. But there is other more compelling substanti-
ation that these views were prevalent among the membership. The assertion of
the unAfricanness of homosexuality, or of homosexuality as contamination,
struck other chords. Activists from inside South Africa, passing through London
at the time, recounted that at least some of the victims of the notorious neck-

lacing phenomenon of the 1980s were homosexuals, rejected by their communities.

Gevisser, in his compelling account of the inclusion of the Equality Clause in the Constitution, cites a debate – on whether the ANC government ought to recognise gay partnerships – that took place in the Cabinet in 1998, and confirms the homophobia abroad in the ANC even in the late 1990s. He cites Sbu Ndebele, currently the leader of the ANC in KwaZulu-Natal and

> a former political prisoner with Nelson Mandela on Robben Island, [who] declared that it was outrageous for the ANC to support homosexual activity. He reminded his comrades that anybody caught doing this on 'The Island' was automatically expelled from the party. (2000:120)

This squares with the experiences of Indres Pillay (a pseudonym), sentenced to imprisonment on Robben Island for activities in Umkhonto weSizwe (MK), the ANC's armed wing, in the late 1980s. One of the prisoners' hard-won concessions was that the authorities allowed them to watch videos on weekends. After screenings of 9 1/2 weeks (in which there is a brief lesbian scene) and Kiss of the Spiderwoman (an account of the relationship between a straight political prisoner sharing a cell with a transvestite in an unnamed Latin American dictatorship), the leadership group on the island issued an edict that videos with gay scenes not be shown. Prisoners also had to agree to a code of conduct that disallowed antisocial behaviour. Pillay learnt to his cost that this included homosexuality. He was later ostracised by his fellow prisoners (Luirink, 2000:38–9).

Jack's story

Gevisser also cites Dumisane Makhaye, an ex-MK combatant present at the same cabinet meeting, who is reputed to have said that MK cadres discovered to be homosexuals were shot (2000:120).

There is nothing to suggest that such executions took place, but this resonates with a chilling encounter I had with a comrade in the late 1980s – let's call him 'Jack'.

Jack joined MK and was part of a group that smuggled arms into the country and had begun to plan acts of sabotage against military targets when they were betrayed and arrested. Jack recounted later that in the course of an operation, the group needed a car that they intended to use for reconnoitring purposes, and then abandon. Jack had a certain rugged, blonde attractiveness and the group hit upon the idea that he could pick someone up in a gay bar, go home with him, kill him and take his car. For reasons I can't recall, the operation was aborted, but the homophobia and the hostility to homosexuals – seen as dispensable solely on account of their sexual orientation – that the group's strategy displayed was deeply alienating and accelerated my own coming-out to my political peers.

The Anti-Apartheid Movement, an organisation of predominantly British people and rooted in the politics of the British left, seemed no more open. A prominent member of the movement recounts:

> A march had been organised by the AAM to mark the Soweto uprising.
> I had taken part and was acutely disappointed with the turnout, bearing in
> mind the nature of the occasion being commemorated. On the same day
> Gay Pride had organised a huge demonstration. It was obvious that the
> two events had competed for support. I was subsequently in the AAM
> office and stressed the importance of establishing links with the gay com-
> munity. Though one person in that office agreed with me, others agreed
> with the ANC VIP who was there, who insisted that being gay was not a
> natural thing. That in any case it didn't occur in South Africa. Somebody
> else suggested it was a result of the public school system in the UK. It was
> also pointed out that women would be the sufferers if this gayness were
> accepted. (Interview with author, June 2001)

A poverty of debate, a dissection of identities

Such was the poverty of the debate on the issue of homosexuality in the discourse of national liberation. This placed those of us who were white, gay and anti-apartheid activists in the uncomfortable position of living a sometimes conflicting dissection of identities: racial (in relation to our black comrades), sexual (in relation to our straight contemporaries) and political (in relation to the overwhelmingly politically conservative communities from which we had come).

This was perhaps most vividly expressed in the internal politics of COSAWR – an organisation of exiled conscientious objectors, draft dodgers and military

127

deserters, established to undermine the SADF by encouraging internal resistance to the draft and international isolation of the apartheid regime.

The ANC and COSAWR developed a close political relationship, and the ANC included the work of COSAWR in its broader strategy to undermine the South African military. Some of the COSAWR leadership participated in the ANC's clandestine structures, exploring ways of infiltrating the military and police, broadening the campaign against conscription and undermining the morale of the white community.

An army of lovers?

At least a third of the executive membership of COSAWR were gay, as was a much larger proportion of the broader war resister community – perhaps because in addition to our moral and political objections to military service, many of us feared participating in as avowedly homophobic an institution as the military.

For many of us who had come into exile in this way, our primary social, political and sexual relationships were with fellow war resisters. And yet even within the confines of the organisation our common homosexuality was never an explicit part of the discourse, even where our brief might have dictated otherwise – in particular, when it came to the treatment of gay men in the military.

Rupert Smith, a founder member of COSAWR, said of being gay in the organisation:

> It was possible but it wasn't welcomed. I've always been pretty discreet/
> straight-acting/fucking boring and closeted, so I wasn't a threat 'cos I toed
> the party line. But a friend of mine who was much more out was definitely
> seen as being a bit ... what's the right word? Just not quite the right
> image, really. COSAWR was never overtly homophobic, but the liberation
> struggle was never really about sexual politics, not even feminist politics!
> Basically, pretty heteronormative. (Interview with author, May 2001)

James Barrett struggled with exile:

> I felt screwed up, messed up, not finding a niche to think about my gay
> identity. I found the general spirit in the war resister community destructive

– many of the South African refugees were very depressed, living in bad conditions, really struggling with their loss of comfort. I gradually drifted away. I got involved in the London Gay Workshop, a group of gay men who got together to discuss political issues. It had a broad left-wing agenda and was trying to reach out and establish coalitions with other groups and draw gay men into political activity. This was formative for me and drew me away from anti-apartheid work and into the field of HIV/AIDS.

Ultimately I was put off the closetedness of some of the leading members of COSAWR, who saw being gay as a shameful thing that might be used against COSAWR – you know, fags who were too wussy to do military service. (Interview with author, July 2001)

Terry Shott, also a founder member of COSAWR, echoes Barrett's response, but chose a different course of action. As a student in London in the mid-1970s, Shott was drawn into Okhela, a clandestine group loosely associated with the ANC, that sought to infiltrate South Africa, recruit additional members and carry out sabotage, but was quickly rounded up, making it impossible for Shott to return to South Africa.

An 'out' gay man, Shott found the homophobia of the ANC and the AAM alienating and chose instead to become involved in groups which welcomed gay members – initially, the Southern African Liberation Support Committee and, later, the Namibia Support Committee. He also helped establish the End Loans to South Africa Campaign:

I chose to work in these groups. I sought out groups that I thought would be sympathetic to my sexual orientation and a broader politics that embraced gay rights, women's rights and so on. In the ANC and the Anti-Apartheid Movement, these issues were seen as a distraction. (Interview with author, May 2002)

Shott confirms that, as in NUSAS, an insidious form of internalised homophobia prevailed – a fear not only that our homosexuality would alienate us from our comrades in the movement, leading to our marginalisation,

but that it would somehow confirm the propaganda of the regime, that in fleeing military service we were cowards, not real men. (Interview)

Always the link with home

In the mid- to late 1980s there was something of a cultural and political shift. This shift was dictated from inside South Africa, where the rise of the United Democratic Front (UDF) – which, although closely allied to the ANC, was not characterised by the same ideological rigidity as its exiled counterpart – allowed a broader debate.

But it was the courage and actions of Simon Nkoli that broke open the silence around homosexuality in the liberation movement. Simon Nkoli, an African gay man, was a UDF activist from Sebokeng in the Vaal Triangle. He was arrested and put on trial for treason as part of a dragnet that included some of the UDF's most prominent leaders. With extraordinary personal courage, Nkoli came out to his colleagues in prison, at first inspiring opprobrium and later, through sheer persistence, respect.

One of the trialists, Patrick Mosiuoa ('Terror') Lekota – later South Africa's Defence Minister – speaking at Nkoli's funeral in 1998, said:

> all of us acknowledged that [Simon's coming out] was an important learn-ing experience … His presence made it possible for more information to be discussed, and it broadened our vision, helping us to see that society was composed of so many people whose orientations were not the same, and that one must be able to live with it. And so when it came to writing the constitutions how could we say that men and women like Simon who had put their shoulders to the wheel to end apartheid, how could we say that they should now be discriminated against? (Gevisser, 2000:119)

Nkoli's actions not only challenged the notion that homosexuality was unAfrican, but demonstrated the presence of gay men and lesbians in the anti-apartheid movement. Nkoli's arrest and trial came at a point where the scale of the uprising against apartheid and its brutal repression by the security forces had captured worldwide attention and sparked a revival of anti-apartheid soli-darity in the West. Gay groups in the US and Europe took up Nkoli's cause, demanding his release, and brought the issue of gay and lesbian identity into the foreground of anti-apartheid politics.

Nkoli emboldened gays and lesbians in other formations of the anti-apartheid and liberation movements, including a group of gay men in COSAWR, who launched a campaign in solidarity with imprisoned conscientious objector Ivan Toms. Toms was a prominent member of the End Conscription Campaign and of the Western Cape branch of the UDF. A medical doctor who tended to the victims of police brutality and shootings in the squatter camps and townships of Cape Town, he spoke with particular authority about the consequences of the State of Emergency. Clandestine elements of the security forces tried to discredit him by pointing to his homosexuality in pamphlets and posters circulated in Cape Town.

Toms, who had until then remained silent on his homosexuality in his public life, became increasingly open, pointing to the similarity of experience of oppression shared by homosexuals and black people. Toms's coming out was a signal for the gay membership of COSAWR. When Toms was jailed for refusing to obey his military call-up, COSAWR organised a campaign of solidarity with him, specifically profiling Toms as a gay activist, targeted at and winning support from gay groups in the UK.

The Dutch connection

There were other shifts.

Bart Luirink and other openly gay executive members of the Dutch anti-apartheid movement were disconcerted by the absence of a discourse on homosexuality in the liberation movement, and with some of their colleagues began to raise the issue with the senior leadership of the ANC. Some executive members of the Dutch movement were uneasy about this stance. The Dutch movement had very close ties with the ANC, was one its mainstays of support in Western Europe, and could not be easily discounted.

This invisible debate, this samizdat discourse, that went on behind closed doors between senior leaders of the ANC and gays in implicitly trusted anti-apartheid movements, was brought to a head in 1987 when the gay London weekly *Capital Gay* interviewed senior representatives of the ANC in London on the movement's position on gays and lesbians.

The publication was responding – in part – to the assurances which had been given to a delegation of students who had sought contact with the ANC's headquarters in Lusaka, Zambia. This was part of the dialogue that was opening up between internal groups and the exiled movement, which presaged full-blown negotiations three years later. The ANC stated that while the ANC had no policy on gays and lesbians, it was 'open-minded on the issue'.

> ANC policy grows as it confronts social questions that need to be addressed. A democratic state should restructure and accommodate issues related to oppression ... (*Capital Gay*, 18 September 1987)

But Solly Smith, the ANC's representative in London, responded to *Capital Gay's* question thus:

> We cannot be diverted from our struggle by these issues. We believe in the majority being equal. These people [lesbians and gays] are in the minority. The majority must rule. (*Capital Gay*, 18 September 1987)

An executive member of the ANC, Ruth Mompati, went on to say:

> I cannot even begin to understand why people want gay and lesbian rights. The gays have no problems. They have nice houses and plenty to eat. I don't see them suffering. No one is persecuting them. We haven't heard about this problem in South Africa until recently. It seems to be fashionable in the West ... They are not doing the liberation struggle a favour by organising separately and campaigning for their rights. The [gay] issue is being brought up to take attention away from the main struggle against apartheid ... They are red herrings. We don't have a policy on gays and lesbians. We don't have a policy on flower sellers either. (*Capital Gay*, 18 September 1987)

Mompati's views betray the much wider thinking in the ANC at the time – that all gays were white. This says a great deal about the visibility of black gays in the liberation movement, a subject to which I will return.

What if 1990 hadn't happened?

How far this process of discussion and opening up on the issue of sexuality in the ANC would have gone had the events of the late 1980s and early 1990s not transpired, is open to question. But the focus of debate on the future of gays and lesbians shifted to the halls of the constitutional negotiations at the World Trade Centre in Kempton Park, where Kevan Botha, appointed by the Equality Foundation, a gay and lesbian group established to promote law reform, pressed for the inclusion of the clause on sexual orientation in the Constitution. The rest is part of a remarkable and unprecedented story which others have covered in detail.

What, then, to make of the role of gay men and lesbians in the liberation movement and the contradictory experience of commitment to an apparently emancipatory project that took no note of their oppression? In this, their most critical endeavour, the one that is likely to have shaped them, they led half-lives.

Of course, most cadres in the movement also did so, sacrificing their youth, sacrificing the possibility of sustained relationships and many, also, their lives. Women in particular endured the suffocating patriarchy of the ANC's exiled structures, and have been vindicated by the explosion of an indigenous femin-ism in post-apartheid South Africa. We have all gone on to claim full citizenship of a democratic country.

But for gays and lesbians specifically, it might so easily have been different. Were it not for the 'miracle', for the actions of a few brave individuals who had the foresight to seize the historical moment of the negotiations, South African gay men and lesbians might endure the oppression of those in Zimbabwe, Namibia and Uganda, where Africanism has held sway.

At the same time this has of necessity been a white history, a story about some white gay political activists. Emerging historiography has now established that the notion that homosexuality is unAfrican is a fallacy, called into question not only by the flowering of black gay and lesbian organisations, but by the rich emergent histories of gay life in black communities. Yet we can count on the fingers of one hand the 'out' black gay political activists in the history of the Struggle. This very lack of the visibility of gay and lesbian cadres in the move-ment points surely to the persistence of homophobia in the political commun-ity, which colours the memory of the Struggle. What was the experience of black gays and lesbians in the formations of the liberation movement and its armed formations, in the trade unions and the affiliates of the UDF? We need to know in order to be able to reclaim our pasts.

This brief history of some gay men and lesbians who worked in anti-apartheid structures and in the liberation movements tries to do that. It seeks to add to the complexity of our experience. It tries to pose critical questions about how

133

we arrived in this safe haven, so that our history is not appropriated into some bland notion of Rainbow Nation in which the needs of all have been accommodated and the real difficulties, pain and alienation of reaching this point are airbrushed into the rosy-hued background.

Inasmuch as truth and reconciliation are motifs of the post-apartheid society, we need to look back and proselytise for the union of the political and personal, so that the politics of the future embraces all those who seek a role. The indivisibility of human rights for all is a standard that should never again be questioned, compromised or contoured to fit ideology.

Works cited

Cameron, Edwin and Gevisser, Mark (eds) (1994). *Defiant Desire: Gay and Lesbian Lives in South Africa*. New York: Routledge.

Gevisser, Mark (2000). 'Mandela's stepchildren: homosexual identity in post-apartheid South Africa' in Drucker, Peter (ed.). *Different Rainbows*. London: Gay Men's Press.

Luirink, Bart (2000). *Moffies: Gay Life in Southern Africa*. Cape Town: David Philip.

Kraak, Gerald (1998). 'Class, race, nationalism and the politics of identity: a perspective from the South.' *Development Update*, 2: 2.

Kraak, G. and Simpson, G. (1998). 'The illusions of sanctuary and the weight of the past: notes on violence and gender in South Africa.' *Development Update*, 2: 2.

Schiller, Greta (1998). *The Man Who Drove with Mandela*. New York: Cinema Guild.

Mystifying history:
The thing that goes bump in the night

Tim Trengove Jones

Tim Trengove Jones asserts the historical and political inevitability of the Equality Clause in this response to Gerald Kraak's essay.

Gerald Kraak's essay, *Homosexuality and the South African Left*, is revealingly axiomatic of post-1994 gay history writing in a number of ways. In its reliance on personal testimonies and witnessing, it fits in neatly with the kind of projects fostered by the Gay and Lesbian Archives (GALA). In fact, much of Kraak's paper involves that commitment to a special kind of gay and lesbian micro-history: making audible previously inaudible voices, making visible previously invisible lives. As such, it is one more strand in a process of democratisation.

But it is, of course, a very specific sort of strand. It is intensely autobiographical, with Kraak acknowledging the advances we've made, yet struck by the 'contradiction between my sometimes negative experiences as a gay man in the ranks of the exiled liberation movement and the ANC's latter-day support for an emancipatory agenda'. The seemingly definitive quality found in Kraak's *ex post facto* analysis lies in this perceived 'contradiction': well-rehearsed evidence of hostility or indifference to a gay and lesbian agenda, and the 'awe' at the inclusion of the Equality Clause in the new Constitution.

In a way, Kraak's 'final' position is not one that is gay-specific. And his final dissatisfaction is symptomatic of a key 'gay' dilemma: 'we' want a history that is 'exclusively' ours, just as 'we' want also to be incorporated into the mainstream. Such 'inbetweenness,' registering a not always unawkward blend of sameness and difference, is responsible for some of the disconcertment informing Kraak's positions. His perception of an inexplicable gap is, inevitably, symptomatic of his own subject position: while committed to political change, his identity as a gay white male was either hidden, ignored or derided during much of his struggle experience. It is this dissonance that largely constitutes his perception of 'a gap that seeks explanation'.

He writes of the absence of 'a historically-explicable discourse linking the past to the present, so that the change has the quality of a miracle.' Here he invokes the standard discourse used to characterise South Africa's transition, the idiom of 'miracle'. But, in concluding, Kraak does not find this idiom of miracle entirely adequate. (Who would?) There is a note of nostalgia and some bitterness, there is more than a hint that Kraak's own perception of 'the gay condition' remains one driven by intimations of exile. He wants, he writes, to 'pose critical questions about how we arrived in this safe haven' so that the 'real difficulties, pain and alienation of reaching this point are [not] airbrushed into the rosy-hued background.' (In downplaying a standard rhetoric of rainbow-ism, he runs the risk of diminishing our great achievement.)

Rightly unsatisfied by the 'miracle' non-explanation, Kraak casts around for something more solid. Oddly for what seems to be a materialist critique, he dabbles with the influence of a few significant individuals. The usual suspects are presented: Cecil Williams, Ivan Toms, Simon Nkoli. But, surely, as an his-torically plausible explanation for the advent of the Equality Clause, we can't rely on the fact that Cecil Williams was a generous and useful gay white male, that Toms was a philanthropic one, and Nkoli was a courageous activist who just happened to be black and gay.

Searching for the key, Kraak confirms his own prison. The thing that goes bump in the night is not the influence of a single, pivotal individual. Nor is it attributable to some radical change of heart by powerful figures as yet undis-closed. Kraak is in 'awe' of the Equality Clause's arrival, remains in pursuit of some Holy Grailish explanation, because he frames the question wrongly. His own feelings of exclusion understandably issue in his attributing an almost magical aura to the inclusion of the clause.

Speaking at a GALA dinner in the Johannesburg City Hall on 20 September 1999, Justice Albie Sachs of the Constitutional Court pointed us in the right direction. He recalled attending the first Pride march in Cape Town in 1994. He asked himself, 'Why were we the first [to include a sexual orientation clause]?' And he went on: 'It was not just because of Simon, or Cecil Williams, or Edwin Cameron … It was not just a question of fairness … We have every kind of belief … If we become intolerant, we don't stand a chance. It is for us, and our freedom.' Much less awe-struck, much more pragmatic, this explanation links the Equality Clause to political necessity and a historically specific set of political needs that are entirely persuasive and far-reaching.

The simple fact is, that the entire motivation for the liberation struggle was its resistance to a history of systematised inequality that had existed and been refined for over three centuries. Our Bill of Rights recognises this by placing equality as the first item to be listed, something which is very rare in written constitutions. Through this prioritising, the very format of the Bill of Rights itself acts as a (we hope) permanent memorial to the historically-rooted motivations behind the liberation struggle and our national commitment to constitutionalism.

Rather than being a specific and baffling subject of 'awe', the Equality Clause is a logical and inevitable outcome of our commitment to a democratic and, above all, constitutional state. If, as the slogan had it, 'An injury to one is an injury to all,' then the truly baffling thing would have been a 'New South Africa' in which gay and lesbian citizens remained a criminalised sub-species.

While it is understandable that we might give daily thanks for the Clause, we should note that our newfound freedoms are not entirely reliant on it. While this might diminish our 'awe' at its advent, it does not diminish the Clause itself. It is, however, true that in *National Coalition for Gay and Lesbian Equality v Minister of Justice* (the so-called sodomy case) it is made abundantly clear that the decriminalisation of consensual sodomy between males did not rely solely on the Equality Clause. The judgment indicates that on the grounds of dignity alone or privacy alone, the offending legislation could have been struck down. So, once more, the 'awe' one feels at the inclusion of the Clause should not blind us to the larger – arguably more fundamental – pressures that impelled our experiment in constitutionalism. While these pressures diminish our awe, they also dilute our feelings of exceptionalism.

This said, we should note that our commitment to achievement of constitutionalism is new and fragile. The newfound confidence we have is perhaps muted by the knowledge that in every instance, the waiving of discriminatory legislation has been a result of costly judicial challenge, not voluntary legislative initiative. In this way, any negative fall-out that might flow from such 'moffie-friendly' developments could be directed at the courts and not the legislature. In a Southern African context, this is a much more worrying and real contradiction than the 'gap' at which Kraak niggles.

How far we are from what Kraak calls a 'safe haven' can be seen in the hostility attracted by recent court cases around co-adoption. The letters columns of the popular press were filled with hate speech. 'All of a sudden we use the term "unconstitutional" to the benefit of just about every weirdo in the community,' wrote one sage beneath a headline that screeched, 'Constitution favours miscreants.' Another, under the heading 'Unnatural environment', raged that 'And in this day and age, in this "democracy", it appears as if anything goes.' We would be ill advised to put these fulminations down to a mad fringe element. Rather, we should note the potentially awkward consequences for our constitutional democracy when it is the courts that, in the absence of significant legislative and executive support, bear the brunt of potentially unpopular decisions 'favouring' still unpopular minorities.

Kraak's own somewhat anguished search for the missing link in our constitutional history is, I would contend, touching but misplaced. Rather than search for a chimerical clue, we should join in Justice Edwin Cameron's timely caveat:

> The Constitution embodies our best hopes and our highest aspirations,
> not only for others, but for ourselves. It contains a series of binding
> promises we as South Africans have made to one another …
> If we abandon them, we abandon all hope that a civilised and
> mutually respectful society will emerge in our country.

Throughout Kraak's inquest there is an undertow of the exilic. To contradict that, we need to recognise the historically instrumental force of inequality in South Africa, and the still present bigotries that only the Constitution can effectively protect us against. It is this Constitution to which the entire process of political liberation led, and it is this document that demands every citizen's respect and commitment.

139

The moment the ANC embraced gay rights

Peter Tatchell

Peter Tatchell recalls how his exposure of ANC homophobia and his public challenge to the exiled leadership in Lusaka helped persuade the ANC to support lesbian and gay human rights. A version of this essay appears on Tatchell's website www.petertatchell.net.

As a gay teenager growing up in Melbourne, Australia, my three great passions were men, surfing and politics. All three came together in the summer of 1971, when at the age of nineteen, I went on my first anti-apartheid protest. The protest was against the all-white South African Surf Life-Saving tour. At one of my favourite beaches, Lorne, on a blistering hot morning, 40 of us lay down on the sand in a bid to stop the South African team taking their boat out of the boathouse. We succeeded, for a while, making our symbolic point – before being battered and bloodied, and then carted off by the police. So began my two decades of activism against the apartheid regime: pickets, boycotts, marches and sit-ins.

Over those long years, I kept hearing disconcerting stories about homophobic attitudes within the African National Congress – the main liberation movement and the likely governing party of a post-apartheid South Africa. At the left-wing World Youth Festival in East Berlin in 1973, which I attended as a Gay Liberation Front delegate, there were reports of the victimisation of lesbian and gay ANC members, and warnings that queers would have a tough time when the ANC came to power.

Homophobia existed at high levels in the ANC, even though there was a long history of gay people being involved in the struggle against apartheid. The gay theatre director Cecil Williams was one such person. He played a key role in aiding Nelson Mandela when he was on the run from the police in the early 1960s. To enable Mandela to carry on his underground activism and avoid detection, Williams had Mandela disguise himself as his chauffeur.

Despite the contributions of courageous lesbian and gay people such as Cecil Williams, some in the ANC still took an avowedly and unashamedly anti-gay stance.

In those days, only a handful of anti-apartheid activists dared challenge the homophobia – and sexism – of sections of the ANC leadership. There was a near-universal expectation that opposition to apartheid involved uncritical support for the liberation struggle. It was deemed betrayal to question the ANC. Criticism was unwelcome – even when it was constructive and came from friends and allies. We were told by the official Anti-Apartheid Movement that any doubts or concerns had to wait until the white supremacist system was overthrown. Most anti-apartheid activists duly obliged. I was one of them. My fear was that speaking out would give comfort and succour to the white minority regime, and undermine support for the just cause of the ANC. Although I made my concerns known behind the scenes, publicly I remained silent.

In 1987, after nearly twenty years' involvement in the anti-apartheid struggle, I felt unable to stay silent any longer. No movement for human liberation has a right to demand unconditional loyalty. Such a demand leads, inexorably, to collusion with injustice. It was, after all, the insistence on uncritical support that resulted in so many people on the Left ignoring or excusing the terrible crimes of the Stalin and Mao eras.

True loyalty sometimes involves saving friends from their own excesses and mistakes.

My worry was that unless leading members of the ANC were confronted over their homophobia, a post-apartheid, ANC-ruled South Africa might pursue the same kind of anti-gay policies that were common in other revolutionary states, such as Cuba, the Soviet Union and China.

This was not an unreasonable fear. When battling to overthrow dictatorship and fascism, most ANC-style liberation movements talked about creating a society with social justice and human rights for all. But after liberation they usually enforced a heterosexist regime that left queers just as victimised as before – if not more so. Would it be a liberation worthy of the name if a free South Africa perpetuated the homophobia of the apartheid state?

141

After trying to influence ANC attitudes privately without success, as had many other people before me, I concluded that the only way to change things was by publicly exposing the ANC's rejection of lesbian and gay human rights. My calculation was that the subsequent uproar would embarrass the ANC leadership and this might precipitate its switch to a more gay-sympathetic policy.

Accordingly, in August 1987, on hearing that ANC executive member Ruth Mompati was visiting London to promote South Africa Women's Day, I devised a plan and requested an interview.

A courageous fighter against the apartheid regime, Mompati was one of the leaders of the biggest women's demonstration in South African history. In 1956, 20 000 women marched on the Union Buildings – the seat of government in Pretoria – to protest at the extension of the pass laws to women.

Most of my interview with Mompati, which was later published in *Labour Weekly*, was about the struggle for women's emancipation. But towards the end, I raised the issue of women's sexual emancipation – in particular the human rights of lesbians and their role in the struggle against apartheid. This provoked an astonishing outburst that reconfirmed all the previous horror stories that I had heard about ANC homophobia.

'I hope that in a liberated South Africa people will live a normal life,' Mompati told me. 'I emphasise the word normal ... Tell me, are lesbians and gays normal? No, it is not normal.'

'I cannot even begin to understand why people want lesbian and gay rights. The gays have no problems. They have nice houses and plenty to eat. I don't see them suffering. No one is persecuting them ... We haven't heard about this problem in South Africa until recently. It seems to be fashionable in the West.'

When asked her reaction to the formation of gay anti-apartheid organisations inside South Africa, Mompati insisted: 'They are not doing the liberation struggle a favour by organising separately and campaigning for their rights. The [gay] issue is being brought up to take attention away from the main struggle against apartheid. These other problems can wait until later. They are red herrings.'

Mompati justified the ANC's lack of an official policy on lesbian and gay human rights with the riposte: 'We don't have a policy on flower sellers either.' While acknowledging that women have special problems and specific interests that need to be addressed by the ANC, she was adamant that 'lesbians and gays do not'.

Concerned to be fair, in case Mompati's views were unrepresentative of the

ANC's position, I contacted its London office and spoke to the liberation move-ment's chief representative in Britain, Solly Smith. He expressed similarly offensive opinions: 'We don't have a policy. Lesbian and gay rights do not arise in the ANC. We cannot be diverted from our struggle by these issues. We believe in the majority being equal. These people [lesbians and gays] are in the minority. The majority must rule.'

When asked if the ANC was opposed to discrimination against homosexuals and if an ANC-led government would repeal the anti-gay laws of the apartheid state, Smith replied: 'I have no comment on that.'

This was, to my knowledge, the first time anyone had recorded verbatim accounts of the homophobic attitudes of ANC leaders. I knew these quotes would cause the ANC grief and discomfort. But a bit of pain and short-term damage was necessary, I reasoned, in order to challenge, and perhaps over-turn, homophobia within the liberation movement.

Accordingly, my interviews with Ruth Mompati and Solly Smith were published in the London gay weekly newspaper, *Capital Gay*, on 18 September 1987, under the headline 'ANC dashes hopes for gay rights in SA.' As I expected, and hoped, Smith's and Mompati's homophobia provoked an outcry in gay and lib-eral circles.

To globalise the pressure on the ANC, I then circulated my article for republica-tion in the gay and anti-apartheid press worldwide, including South Africa. My aim was to get the ANC inundated with protests that would (hopefully) pressure it to confront the issue of homophobia and eventually to abandon its rejection of lesbian and gay equality.

My *Capital Gay* article did, thankfully, result in the ANC and the anti-apartheid movement internationally being deluged with letters of condemnation. People were appalled that a 'liberation movement' like the ANC could be so ignorant, bigoted and intolerant. The ANC leadership was hugely embarrassed.

But embarrassing the ANC was not my goal: it was merely a means to an end. My objective was to win the ANC to the cause of lesbian and gay human rights. I therefore devised a plan to offer the leadership a face-saving solution and a constructive way forward. This involved writing a private appeal to the ANC leadership in exile in Lusaka.

My letter, dated 12 October 1987, was addressed to Thabo Mbeki, then the ANC Director of Information. I chose him on the advice of exiled ANC contacts, David and Norma Kitson. They suggested he was the most liberal-minded of the ANC leaders and senior enough to be able to push for a radical rethink of official policy. My letter was challenging, but friendly and constructive. I argued, as the following extract illustrates, that support for lesbian and gay liberation was consistent with the principles of the ANC's Freedom Charter:

Dear Thabo Mbeki,

... Given that the Freedom Charter embodies the principle of civil and human rights for all South Africans, surely those rights should also apply to lesbians and gays? And surely the ANC should be committed to removing all forms of discrimination and oppression in a liberated South Africa?... To me, the fight against apartheid and the fight for lesbian and gay rights are part of the same fight for human rights.

Yours in comradeship and solidarity,
Peter Tatchell

When writing to Mbeki I also included a sheaf of my published articles about leading lesbian and gay anti-apartheid activists inside South Africa, including Simon Nkoli and Ivan Toms. Simon, a student activist, was a defendant in one of the great *causes célèbres* of the 1980s, the Delmas Treason Trial. Ivan was a doctor who had won acclaim for his work in the Crossroads shack settlement in Cape Town and was active in the campaign against conscription (he was later jailed for refusing to serve in the army of apartheid). This information about gay involvement in the struggle against apartheid was news to many members of the exiled ANC Executive, and apparently had considerable influence in swinging the vote in favour of a pro-gay stance.

My letter to Mbeki – following in the wake of adverse publicity from my *Capital Gay* article and subsequent protests – had the desired effect. Within a few weeks, the ANC leadership in exile began a major re-evaluation of its stance on gay issues. As a result of these internal debates, the ANC officially, for the first time, committed itself to support lesbian and gay human rights.

This new pro-gay rights ANC policy was publicly announced in a letter to me from Thabo Mbeki, dated 24 November 1987. He wrote:

Dear Peter,

... The ANC is indeed very firmly committed to removing all forms of discrimination and oppression in a liberated South Africa. You are correct to point this out. That commitment must surely extend to the protection of gay rights ... I would like to believe that that my colleagues, Solly Smith and Ruth Mompati, did not want to suggest in any way that a free South Africa would want to see gays discriminated against or subjected to any form of repression. As a movement, we are of the view that the sexual preferences of an individual are a private matter. We would not wish to compromise anybody's right to privacy ... and would therefore not wish to legislate or decree how people should conduct their private lives ... We would like to apologise for any misunderstanding that might have arisen over these issues ...

Yours in the common struggle,
Thabo Mbeki

Mbeki's statement was not as strong and comprehensive as many of us would have liked, nor had it been agreed by a formal policy-making conference of the ANC. But it was, nevertheless, a watershed moment. The ANC leadership was publicly aligning itself with the struggle for homosexual emancipation. A first!

At Mbeki's own request, I communicated his letter to gay and anti-apartheid movements world-wide. I also sent a copy to members of South African lesbian and gay groups, such as the long-time lesbian anti-apartheid activists, Sheila Lapinsky and Julia Nicol of the Organisation of Lesbian and Gay Activists (OLGA), based in Cape Town. In addition, I forwarded copies to members of the (UDF) – the main anti-apartheid coalition inside South Africa.

Long before me, other people had pressured the ANC to change its homophobic stance, but none of them had succeeded. It was, it seems, only the huge torrent of negative publicity generated by my *Capital Gay* article, and my challenging letter to Thabo Mbeki, that prompted the ANC's rethink. My intervention was, perhaps, merely the culmination of earlier efforts by others – the final straw that broke the camel's back. I was merely the catalyst for changes that had been in the making for a very long time. What is certain is that without the ANC and international anti-apartheid movements being flooded with letters of protest, my letter to Mbeki might have had no impact at all. Due credit must be given to the many people from all over the world, but especially gay and anti-apartheid activists within South Africa, who helped pressure the ANC.

Securing the ANC's official opposition to homophobic discrimination gave the struggle for lesbian and gay emancipation inside South Africa new legitimacy and kudos. It was instrumental in helping persuade some individuals and organisations fighting the white minority regime – both within South Africa and in other countries – to embrace lesbian and gay equality – or at least to not oppose it. By giving the cause of homosexual rights political credibility, the ANC's stance helped pave the way for the subsequent inclusion of a ban on sexual orientation discrimination in the post-apartheid Constitution.

Not long after the ANC came out for lesbian and gay rights, exiled ANC leaders based in London began work on drafting a constitution for a free and democratic South Africa. In 1989, I contacted a member of this constitutional working party, Albie Sachs, at the University of London, urging him to include in the ANC's draft Constitution a ban on discrimination based on sexual orientation. He was initially rather sceptical. So I provided a draft wording, backed up with examples of anti-discrimination statutes from various European countries, such as Denmark, France and the Netherlands. These countries had laws incorporating either comprehensive protection against discrimination or an explicit ban on discrimination on the grounds of sexuality. These concrete legal precedents apparently helped reassure Sachs, and later helped convince others in the ANC leadership, that a ban on anti-gay discrimination was feasible and practical.

A little later, I sent my own suggested draft wording – together with samples of anti-discrimination laws from other countries – to lesbian and gay groups inside South Africa (especially OLGA and GLOW – the Gay and Lesbian Organisation of the Witwatersrand). I also arranged for them to write direct to Albie Sachs in London and to lobby the anti-apartheid UDF inside South Africa.

In December 1989, on my initiative, a meeting was held in London between Sachs and an OLGA representative, Derrick Fine. They discussed OLGA's constitutional proposals face to face. This personal meeting helped to cement Sachs's backing for a constitutional clause prohibiting discrimination based on sexual orientation. His support later helped win over other key people in the ANC leadership.

After the collapse of the apartheid regime and the unbanning of the ANC in February 1990, OLGA held meetings inside South Africa with senior ANC members, including Frene Ginwala, Albie Sachs and Kader Asmal, all of whom expressed a positive attitude towards OLGA's constitutional proposals. Sachs, in particular, continued to have contact with OLGA and other lesbian and gay organisations to further develop the idea of homosexual rights as part of a broad human rights package within South Africa's new Constitution. He did, however, warn OLGA that there was 'no guarantee' that a majority in the ANC would endorse constitutional protection for lesbians and gays: an indication that sections of the liberation movement remained unsupportive or ambivalent on the issue of homosexual equality.

Undeterred, in September 1990, OLGA made an extensive submission to the ANC's Constitutional Committee, which was in charge of formulating the movement's draft Bill of Rights. This submission was supported by eleven other South African lesbian and gay organisations, including GLOW. It proposed a Bill of Rights that would 'protect the fundamental rights of all citizens' and guarantee 'equal rights for all individuals, irrespective of race, colour, gender, creed or sexual orientation'.

Simultaneously, OLGA, GLOW and other gay organisations used the ANC's endorsement of lesbian and gay equality to lobby the United Democratic Front and other anti-apartheid groups within South Africa. This lobbying helped persuade prominent campaigners in some of these groups to back the inclusion of a constitutional ban on anti-gay discrimination. These efforts had a successful outcome when, in November 1990, the publication of the ANC's draft post-apartheid Constitution included an explicit prohibition on homophobic discrimination. In addition, OLGA developed and canvassed support for a specific and comprehensive Charter of Lesbian and Gay Rights. In 1993, this proposal won the endorsement of a national conference of lesbian and gay organisations, which had been convened to forge a united campaign for constitutional protection. The push for lesbian and gay human rights was subsequently carried forward in the post-1994 period by a new umbrella organisation – the National Coalition for Gay and Lesbian Equality (NCGLE).

It is thanks to the efforts of these many far-sighted, determined and courageous lesbian and gay South Africans that constitutional rights for homosexuals were finally won, making South Africa the first country in the world to outlaw discrimination based on sexual orientation.

Peter Tatchell published his account of his interview with the ANC's Ruth Mompati in *Capital Gay* of 18 September 1987. Thabo Mbeki, as Director of Infomation for the ANC, responded in the 24 November 1987 telex. The reproductions are courtesy of Peter Tatchell and the origi- nals are in Tatchell's personal archive.

ANC dashes hopes for gay rights in SA

"Lesbians and gays aren't normal" – say ANC leaders

MEMBERS of the Anti-Apartheid Movement in Britain have privately expressed surprise and dismay following statements on lesbian and gay rights by two leading officials of the African National Congress of South Africa.

Speaking to *Capital Gay* last month, Solly Smith, the ANC's representative in Britain, said: "We don't have a policy. Lesbian and gay rights do not arise in the ANC. We cannot be diverted from our struggle by these issues. We believe in the majority being equal. Those people (lesbians and gays) are in the minority. The majority must rule."

When asked if the ANC was opposed to discrimination against gays, and if it would repeal the Botha regime's anti-gay laws after South Africa was liberated, Smith replied: "I have no comment on that."

His statement comes in the wake of earlier comments by Ruth Mompati, a leading member of the ANC national executive based in Lusaka who was recently in Britain on a speaking tour. She told *Capital Gay:* "I cannot even begin to understand why people want lesbian and gay rights. The gays

have no problems. They have nice houses and plenty to eat. I don't see them suffering. No-one is persecuting them... We haven't heard about this prob-lem in South Africa until recently. It seems to be fashion-able in the West."

When quizzed about her reac-tion to the formation of anti-apartheid gay organisations in South Africa, Mompati insisted: "They are not doing the libera-tion struggle a favour by organising separately and cam-paigning for their rights. The (gay) issue is being brought up to take attention away from the main struggle against apartheid. These other problems can wait till later. They are red herrings."

Mompati justified the ANC's lack of policy on lesbian and gay rights by stating: "We don't have a policy on flower sellers either."

Whilst she believed that women have special problems and interests which need to be addressed by the ANC, Mom-pati was adamant that "lesbians and gays do not." "We are not going to single them (gays) out for special attention and treat-ment."

Did she agree that gay people should be free from oppression? "I'm not going to comment on that," replied Mompati. On being further pressed, she stated: "I hope that in a liber-ated South Africa people will live a *normal* life. I emphasise the word *normal*... Tell me, are lesbians and gays normal? No, it is not normal. If everyone was like that, the human race would come to an end."

These statements by Smith and Mompati contrast with the more sensitive remarks made by ANC representatives to a South Afri-can student delegation in Harare in April 1986. Accord-ing to the student's written report – entitled *NUSAS Talks To The ANC* and since declared a banned publication by the Botha government – the ANC representatives said they had "no policy" on lesbian and gay rights, though they "kept an open mind on the issue." The ANC is also reported as having stated: "ANC policy grows as it confronts social questions that need to be addressed. A democ-ratic state should restructure and accommodate issues related to oppression... freedom of association is enshrined in the Freedom Charter (the ANC's declaration of principles)."

Support

Meanwhile, a number of prominent anti-apartheid lead-ers inside South Africa have recently expressed their support for lesbian and gay rights.

Earlier this year, the Chair of the Rand Gay Organisation, Siphiwe Alfred Machela, encountered problems in finalis-ing a trip to address gay organi-sations in Sweden. When Win-nie Mandela, wife of the impris-oned ANC leader Nelson Man-dela, heard about these prob-lems, she offered to help sort things out and to send a personal message to the Swedish gay movement. Additionally, she has given her backing to gays involved in the anti-apartheid struggle, including Tseko Simon Nkoli who is currently on trial with 19 others charged with treason and could face the death penalty.

Support for the gay cause has also been forthcoming from Archbishop Desmond Tutu

who has met with Siphiwe Machela and visited Tseko Nkoli during his trial, giving them both his personal blessing.

In June this year, Dr Beyers Naude, the out-going general secretary of the South African Council of Churches, stated that he welcomed the involvement of lesbians and gays in the fight against apartheid. The same month, Murphy Morobe, a leader of the main legal anti-apartheid organisation, the United Democratic Front, assured Siphiwe Machela of his support for gay rights aand expressed his satisfaction at the anti-apartheid commitment of the Rand Gay Organisation.

This week, a spokesperson for the Anti-Apartheid Movement in Britain, Karen Talbot, said: "We welcome the involvement of lesbians and gays in the Anti-Apartheid Movement. Their solidarity work is much appreciated. We also value and support the contribution that lesbian and gay activists in South Africa, such as Tseko Simon Nkoli, are making to the strug-gle against apartheid."

Peter Tatchell

* Letters of protest can be addressed to: ANC, PO Box 38, 28 Penton Street, London N1 9PR.

Ruth Mompati: "No-one is persecuting gays"

PETER TATCHELL,
45 ARROL HOUSE,
ROCKINGHAM STREET,
LONDON SE1 6QL.

DEAR PETER,

SORRY FOR THIS LATE RESPONSE TO YOUR LETTER OF OCTOBER 12 FOR
WHICH I THANK YOU MOST SINCERELY. THANKS ALSO FOR THE ENCLOSURES.
SINCE I GOT YOUR LETTER, WE HAVE RECEIVED QUITE A FEW QUERIES
ON THE MATTERS THAT YOU RAISE.

THE ANC IS INDEED VERY FIRMLY COMMITTED TO REMOVING ALL FORMS
OF DISCRIMINATION AND OPPRESSION IN A LIBERATED SOUTH AFRICA.
YOU ARE CORRECT TO POINT THIS OUT. THAT COMMITMENT MUST SURELY
EXTEND TO THE PROTECTION OF GAY RIGHTS. I WOULD LIKE TO BELIEVE
THAT MY COLLEAGUES, SOLLY SMITH A ND RUTH MOMPATI, DID NOT WANT
TO SUGGEST IN ANY WAY THAT A FREE SOUTH AFRICA WOULD WANT TO SEE
GAYS DISCRIMINATED AGAINST OR SUBJECTED TO ANY FORM OF REPRESSION.

AS A MOVEMENT, WE ARE OF THE VIEW THAT THE SEXUAL PREFERENCES
OF AN INDIVIDUAL ARE A PRIVATE MATTER. WE WOULD NOT WISH TO
COMPROMISE ANYBODY'S RIGHT TO PRIVACY BOTH NOW AND IN FUTURE,
AND WOULD THEREFORE NOT WISH TO LEGISLATE OR DECREE HOW PEOPLE
SHOULD CONDUCT THEIR PRIVATE LIVES. WE HAVE, CONSEQUENTLY,
NEVER BEEN OPPOSED TO GAY RIGHTS. THAT POSITION REMAINS
UNCHANGED.

AS YOU KNOW, WE ARE ALWAYS INTERESTED TO SEE AS MANY PEOPLE AS
POSSIBLE INVOLVED IN THE STRUGGLE AGAINST APARTHEID. WE
THEREFORE APPRECIATE THE INITIATIVES UNDERTAKEN BY GAYS TO
INVOLVE THEMSELVES AND OTHER PEOPLE IN THIS STRUGGLE. ABOUT THIS
THERE CAN BE NO QUESTION.

WE WOULD LIKE TO APOLOGISE FOR ANY MISUNDERSTANDING THAT MIGHT
HAVE ARISEN OVER THESE ISSUES AND HOPE THE FOREGOING WILL CLEAR
THE AIR. YOU ARE FREE TO USE THIS LETTER AS YOU SEE FIT.
CERTAINLY WE ARE INTERESTED THAT EVERYBODY WHO HAS EXPRESSED
CONCERN ABOUT THIS MATTER IS INFORMED OF THE POSITIONS STATED IN
THIS LETTER.

REGARDS AND BEST WISHES.

YOURS IN THE COMMON STRUGGLE,

THABO MBEKI,
LUSAKA, NOVEMBER 24, 1987.

ANCSA ZA45390

Address at Simon Nkoli's memorial service, St Mary's Cathedral, Johannesburg, December 1998

Patrick Mosiuoa ('Terror') Lekota

Simon Nkoli's co-trialist Mosiuoa 'Terror' Lekota delivered this tribute to 'Si' at Simon Nkoli's memorial service in 1998. In 1999, Lekota was to become the Minister of Defence. Gcina Malindi, another co-trialist and a close friend, was the master of ceremonies. The transcript was made from a videotape in the Idol Pictures archive.

Gcina Malindi: Comrade Terror has made time to come to this service and to share with all the people who are here who have been Si's friends and comrades. I ask Comrade Terror to come forward. I just hope that he is not going to repeat some of the jokes that he and Si used to share in prison. Some of them may be very much inappropriate.

Mosiuoa Lekota: Thank you, Mr Master of Ceremonies, and thank you, dear friends.

I must start off by extending my gratitude to the memorial committee that is putting together these arrangements, and for giving me the privilege to join tonight by way of having a direct participation in the proceedings here.

This afternoon I have travelled from KwaZulu-Natal by road and I must confess that although there is a campaign of Arrive Alive, I had no choice but to break several of the traffic rules to get here. Not because the committee had asked me to come here. I am here tonight because I do want to be here tonight. I would like to testify because I believe it is correct to one of the challenging lives of those young South Africans with whom I had the privilege over the years to share time behind bars, in the streets of the townships and the anxieties that we all we went through as we struggled to see the rise of a new democracy in our country. I say to testify to this life because I think this is one certainly unique life of all of them. With many of them the lessons that came were those that we went through in the hard times and the lonely nights in the prisons. With many of them their lessons will kind of repeat themselves but there are lessons that come and that did come with association and joint struggle with Si within the confines of prison and beyond.

I suspect that a lot of talk has been done about what kind of personality Si was, but I do want to say that he was one of the few people that I have known, even behind prison bars, who had a level of conviction and a capacity to sustain morale when all seemed to be lost. And to sustain enthusiasm for a cause which is appealing when there is company, but is extremely lonely when others are not there. For it was always easy in the early period to make some fiery speeches when there were masses and masses of people in the Johannesburg City Hall, in the Jabulani amphitheatre, in the stadium at Sharpeville, and so on. Sometimes the masses of people could drive you to make statements which you would not otherwise have made. Usually you discovered such statements when the police had you and all of the crowds were comfortable in their beds in their different homes, safe from the clutches of the security police. So you had to be very clear about the things you were about. But I found Si capable of sustaining the level of enthusiasm and commitment, ongoing work on a daily basis that was even. That didn't flag as much as it did with so many, some of whom chose to go into the witness boxes against ourselves.

Many of you know Si better than I, so I will not go into where he was born and who was his mother and other things like that. I do want to say a few things which probably have never been said and may never be said. When you were locked up in the prisons of apartheid, one of the most pressing needs especially for young men in the best years of their lives were the sexual pressures – the need to gratify these. Now of course, there are two types of people you find in jail. And I didn't discover that until when I had met Si. There are those who in the desperation of the pressures to satisfy their carnal desires lose their minds and become senseless beasts. If you are going to survive you have to break their noses for them and their teeth for them. They will violate other human beings, they will break them and destroy them forever. They will cease to be human beings. But there are ordinary men and women who are oriented in the gay orientation. For them it is not a convenience or a situation created by the desperation of the conditions of jail. This is a condition that is what nature has given to them, and they will go about their own activities without violating others. These two categories of people are different. And I must say that it wasn't until I had met Si and very serious and contentious argumentation and debates that had arisen as a result. And it was not an easy situation.

If you think that it was a discussion such as the situation is here – you have no clue. It was a serious and dangerous situation. At a time when the old apartheid regime was continuously calculating to find ways in which it could destroy and break the credibility of freedom fighters.

These issues were some of those that were most sought after – a weapon that the old regime sought to use to destroy the liberation movement. So the argumentation around these issues was taking place in an atmosphere in which it was an issue of survival at the same time. But in the end I feel bad, and I have been thinking again this afternoon how that our orientation within our communities – whether it is African, Afrikaner, English and all of the traditions one can think of – humanity has not recognised the reality and accepted the reality. And I want to state it in a moment, but before I do that, let me say this. I quite often asked myself, whilst we struggled for equality between black and white in this country, why was it that whether a watermelon was yellowish outside such as that yellow there, or greenish such as that green, is it recognised nevertheless in the judgement of the rulers of our country a watermelon? This was so easy to understand, but when a human being's colour differed from another, the rulers of our country could not come to see that this colour did not change the quality of the species from being a human being. A little later, after the discussions and the argument that I was talking about, on reflecting on these issues, one of the things that happened one day was our visitors that had brought us some fruit had brought some bananas. Now, some of these bananas were almost like twins, they were not quite twins but they were not one there, one there, they were like, you know, caught together as a twin. I did not think this is not a banana. I continued to enjoy them and towards the end of enjoying these twins of bananas, the question suddenly popped up in my mind. If Si was a gay and I enjoyed all these other comrades who were not gay – why can't I enjoy him, as what he is?

152

It helped me understand that within the broad struggle to make sure that our society recognised and accepted the humanity of all of its people, that within that broad struggle this issue was now raising a subordinate struggle, if you like. Not subordinate because it was not as important as the other. Subordinate in the sense that it was not a primary struggle at that point in time, but nevertheless that sooner or later this struggle too – of the right of the recognition of the orientation of men and women, whatever it may be – that this too was a struggle that would have to be fought sooner or later. Indeed, if it was not resolved within the broader struggle I am referring to, that somewhere in history there was a moment when its place would be claimed by that struggle as well. So subordinate struggles like the gender equality issue, subordinate in the sense that they were not the primary issue and they were seen as linked to the main one, were being waged and had to be waged.

So I testify tonight to the life of a young comrade who dared to mobilise on the issues of his time, but also had the courage and the daring ability to begin to challenge those around himself on the issues that were not urgent at that time, but important, and would have to claim central attention sooner or later. So if our Constitution today acknowledges the right of everybody, whatever their orientation, those of us who were in the Delmas Trial will be failing history if we didn't acknowledge that Simon became the leading light that raised this issue within that collective of the 22 accused on trial there. But of course his participation went beyond, the impact was to focus attention on men and women who were and understood the issue of the gay rights, but perhaps for whom the issue of the struggle for equality was not so significant – but as a result of the participation of Si within that trial, we suddenly became aware of large numbers of South Africans, black and white, who saw and understood the lead that Si was giving. That if this issue was to be resolved, the black–white question had to be resolved as the foundation building onto a Constitution that would recognise everybody.

I have a little story I must tell. I have been warned by the Chair not to say this, but this, I am sure, has never been said by anybody. In the course of the argumentations that were taking place before the issues were resolved, one of our co-accused – who supported my conservative position – when we were having visitors, spoke to one of the comrades and said, 'You know, we have this difficulty.' And was very indignant that, you know, this gay-orientated comrade was here amongst us. Now the visitor did not answer this comrade. The visitor said, 'Well, look, I would like to think about this matter,' and left. And of course you know this friend of mine came back and said, 'Look, you know, I think that we are right. Even the visitor that I had, I shared this difficulty with.' Two days later we got a message via another comrade who said, 'Well, chaps, can I talk to you confidentially?' He said, 'Well, you know, this comrade whom you trust so much and went to complain to, doesn't know how to advise you because this comrade is a gay person.' I thank you.

153

154

In these extracts from the many hundreds of letters Simon Nkoli wrote from prison, Nkoli describes his relationship with GASA and with his fellow prisoners.

The letters are in the Simon Nkoli collection at the Gay and Lesbian Archives of South Africa.

VERSEËL EERS DIE TWEE SYKLAPPE, DAN HIERDIE EEN—SEAL THE TWO SIDE FLAPS FIRST, THEN THIS ONE

SNY HIERDIE KLAP EERSTE OOP

TO OPEN CUT THIS FLAP FIRST

G.P.-S. (F-L)

G 316

OFFICIAL—AMPTELIK

Gebruik van hierdie omslag om posgeld te ontduik, is strafbaar met R.100 boete.
Penalty for private use to avoid payment of postage R100.

AAN
TO

Mr Roy Shepherd

115ᴬ Boron Street

Belgravia

2094

HOOF VAN DIE GEVANGENIS

1986-05-02-

MODDERBEE

HEAD OF THE PRISON

1986-05-05

BENONI

Simon Nkoli CHU3/85
Modderbee Prison
Private Bag X10045
Benoni 1500

INSLUITTINGS WORD NIE TOEGELAAT NIE—ENCLOSURES ARE NOT PERMITTED

2

BEGIN HIER SKRYF—START WRITING HERE

3 April 1986

Dearest Roy

I am very sorry that you sounded so unhappy something when
you write here this morning I might have not understood

155

remember what kind of music I do like? Well let me remind you, I like reggae, fussion, disco, African music and country. I remember Paul van Schaick also liked the same music as mine. Oh! that guy, where is he. You know since he left for India.

Roy is arrived back from Denmark? Is he going to make a report back to RCro. Father Don said that RCro has about 100 members already and think that is good neh. Progress on their side. I wonder what is the outcome of ICJA regarding Gaba. Ian Creek said he will write to me. He is SHRG from that has suggested that ICJA should suspend Gaba for about 2 years, or untill I am released.

What did you think of my letter which appeared in Exit, July edition. Do you think I responded well to Andrew Clark's. Well that is what he deserved from me.

am I going to do now. I think I will always have some time to get it to you.

I had just written unpleasant letter to Ann Smith - Well I have just asked her to see to it that my name should not be used so much in the press (Exit) Especially when the truth is not beeing told about it. The rest of what I said to her I will tell it to you when you come to me. when are you coming? Maybe I should stop writing now because you may come tomorrow — or I may recieve your letter tomorrow afternoon — at the moment I hadn't much to tell you — See you then.

Tell me, did you enjoy the book you were reading "Town like Alice" I guess you didn't cry as I did. I think I was imagining

2 August 1986

They really want to support me, but truth, guys I am refusing. Why? They don't have money themselves, they are the people who need support. Really. After all it will be unfair for them to support me while most of them doesn't know me. I am not a member of RHO. The people who should be supporting me are Gasa - since I was arrested while I was a member of Gasa, I think if Gasa cannot support me because I am arrested on "irrelevant" issues as they say. To RHO I should be regarded as such.

I have asked the members of Saturday Group, sorry I mean the members of RHO that they can supply me with writing, I think I should have asked them not to do anything before I can speak with Gasa people, especially Kevin Botha. I have the rights to refuse any support from RHO in protest of Gasa's thinking that I am charged on "irrelevant" issues, what is gay related matters they wanted me to be arrested, Sodomy, loitering, public violent or what? I am absolute mad to read about me being "arrested on irrelevant" issues to gay related matters.

11 August 1986

Well, Mr Petrus Mokoena has just poured me a cooldrink because he sees me falling asleep while writing. He said I must go to bed - he really feel pity for me, He told me today that he is aware that I am the only one who doesn't get visitors everyday. "Jou mother comes after such how long my son-jou must be lonely" he told me "That's why you're not getting fat"

"But I've got a friend who is coming to Gainna, Johny and I" I replied "He even writes to us"

"Oh I see" Mr Mokoena "But you must have a person dedicated to you. I do understand that you have that friend of yours that you share with your friends, they have girlfriends that are paying a special visit to them, their families are coming everyweek, why don't you have a a girlfriend as well, or don't you want them"

I nearly said I've got a boyfriend, but Mr Petrus Mokoena would not understand what do I mean, he doesn't know what I am, maybe if he suspect he doesn't say it, But I am very happy that he is concerned about me.

157

9 September 1986

Ms CE Heaton-Nicholls
PO Box 61875
2107 MARSHALLTOWN

Mr Kevan Botha
National Secretary
Gay Association of
South Africa

Dear Mr Botha

I am, as you will recall, a defence lawyer involved in the Delmas treason trial where one of the defendants is Mr Simon Nkodi. I am writing to you to place certain matters on record:

(1)   You were assiduous, you will no doubt recall, in making contact with me before your departure to the crucial meeting of the International Lesbian and Gay Association meeting in Copenhagen in July 1986. Your particular anxiety at that time was to ensure that Mr Simon Nkodi was not opposed to GASA's continued membership of the ILGA.

(2)   So anxious were you about this issue, that you even telephoned me from Copenhagen to put various questions to me about Simon's attitude on this and other issues.

(3)   You will also recall that Simon Nkodi eventually in response to your solicitations expressed his opposition to GASA's expulsion from the ILGA despite the fact that GASA and other gay organizations in South Africa had given him very little, if any, solidarity or support in his long months of detention and trial on political charges.

(4)   I have been authoritatively informed that Simon's opposition to GASA's expulsion from ILGA was a crucial factor in the eventual vote by the ILGA not to expel GASA.

(5)   This pivotal fact, however, nowhere appears in the exultant reports which appear on the front and other pages of EXIT dated July/August 1986 (number 11). Perhaps you, who presumably were the chief source of information for these delighted news reports, will be able to inform the GASA national executive as well as the editorial members and readers of EXIT why the crucial role that Simon played in the decision not to expel GASA was suppressed in the account of your Copenhagen trip.

(6)   But the real burden of my letter is something else. On page 3 of the report in the July/August EXIT it is said that you "cautioned the ILGA about aligning itself automatically with support for Simon Nkodi". You are reported to have said:

        " Amongst other charges five of murder put the case in a different category."

(7)   The clear implication of this report is that, since Simon is charged with murder, he should not be treated as a victim of political oppression or as being a prisoner of conscience. If this is so, Simon Nkodi on whose behalf I act, the gay public of South Africa and I myself deserve answers from you to the following questions:

        (i)   Are you conversant with the charge sheet in the Delmas trial?

        (ii)   Do you have any knowledge of the sort of evidence that the State has until now been able or been unable to lead in an attempt to substantiate in any way the murder charges which form part of the indictment?

(iii)   Are you aware that the State case has very nearly come to a conclusion and that virtually no evidence of any nature has been forthcoming to implicate Simon or indeed any of the other accused directly in the murder charges?

(iv)   Are you aware that, even on the basis of the allegations set out by the State in the indictment, the murder charges are substantially based on a political conspiracy by the UDF to secure the liberation of South Africa, and that no direct action of any kind leading to the deaths is alleged to have been perpetrated by any of the accused?

(v)   Are you aware, for instance, in support of the above, that three of the twenty-two accused who are nonetheless also charged with the "murders", were in fact in detention at the time the alleged murders were committed and that this shows the indirect and conspiratorial nature of the murder allegations?

160

(8)   On a personal and professional level, I find it contemptible that you made frequent efforts to contact me, as Simon's lawyer, but that not once did you make any attempt whatsoever to establish from me the significance of the "murder" charges. If you had been in any way truly concerned by the "murder" allegations against Simon, a mere enquiry from you could have elicited any or all of the information set out above.

(9)   The only reasonable inference to be drawn from your
        conduct is that you deliberately sought to
        manipulate Simon Nkodi and his legal advisers,
        notwithstanding the fact that Simon has been in
        detention without being convicted on any charges
        for very nearly two years now, but that at the same
        time you were content to smear him in your effort
        to keep GASA in the ILGA.

(10)   Had you at any stage whatever in the period when
        you were assiduously cultivating Simon's and my
        co-operation for your own political and/or social
        ends been candid enough to intimate your "concern"
        at the allegations of murder against Simon -
        instead of suppressing this until, behind Simon's
        back and in a foreign forum, you could perpetrate a
        cowardly slander on him - you would at least have
        given Simon the dignity and choice of assessing
        your own motives and methods in a proper context.
        Your deliberate suppression of your true design
        until you had artfully procured Simon's endorsement
        of the anti-explusion stance, constitutes
        despicable and disingenuous conduct.

(11)   The fundamental question which your conduct raises
        is the entitlement of those organizations
        purporting to represent South Africa's gays to
        remain accredited members of international gay
        forums. It is to my personal regret that I
        conclude that your conduct may well provide an
        argument for the consideration of GASA's continued
        membership of the ILGA.

(12)   In my personal role as a lawyer I have in the past
        represented gays who have been oppressed by the
        legal position in South Africa and have myself been

161

an unconditional protagonist of gay rights. That is still my stance. My view is, however, that gay rights are inseparable from larger questions of human liberation. In South Africa, that means that gays should not think that they can fight in isolation from other oppressed groups for their right to live in peace and dignity. This country's oppressed form part of an indivisible majority. Insular thinking and the sort of vicious pettiness which your attitude evinces do the larger cause of liberation profound harm.

(13) Your disgraceful behaviour in making the unfounded insinuations which you chose to level at Simon Nkodi at the international meeting has deeply wounded my client. On his instructions, this letter will, in the absence of a satisfactory explanation from you, be sent not only to EXIT - whose editorial board and readers, as I have said, deserve an explanation from you - but also to international organizations who may be concerned in these questions.

(14) If South Africa's gay organizations are to regard themselves as legitimately entitled to remain part of international gay forums, it would seem to me that they have to establish their credentials in the anti-apartheid struggle. The despicable conduct as an official representative of GASA creates a regrettable basis for the view that, organizationally, gay institutions in South Africa are not only averse to the progressive forces which seek to create a freer and more just society in South Africa, but may well also be the appropriate objects of expulsion attempts from overseas. If this conclusion is not justified, Simon Nkodi, I

myself and the many gays whom I know to be committed to the idea of a truly free and democratic South Africa await your early response.

Yours faithfully

Caroline Nicholls.

C E HEATON-NICHOLLS

163

These photographs are from the late Simon Nkoli's personal collection. The photographs are not annotated and the provenance is uncertain. To the best of our knowledge they are (clockwise from top right): (1) Simon Nkoli re-enacts his recent experience of imprisonment at Lee's Place, a favoured gay shebeen in Soweto, where many of the early GLOW meetings took place, circa 1988. (2) A party held for Simon Nkoli at the Barbican Studios, Johannesburg, after he was acquitted in 1988. (3) Some of the leaders of GLOW, including Linda Ncgobo

165

(seated left) and Simon Nkoli (seated centre), at Lee's
Place, circa 1988.
(4) Alfred Machela (left) and Simon Nkoli (right) at Lee's
Place, circa 1988. The photos are in the Simon Nkoli collection in the Gay and Lesbian Archives of South Africa.

Address at Simon Nkoli's memorial service, St Mary's Cathedral, Johannesburg, December 1998

Kevan Botha

In Kevan Botha's tribute at Simon Nkoli's memorial service in 1998, Botha reflects on the evolution of his personal politics since the turning point of the 1986 ILGA conference. The transcript was made from a videotape in the Idol Pictures archive.

Many tributes to Simon this afternoon celebrate his guiding example at the forefront of various frontiers of struggle. I wish to remember Simon, however, this afternoon in a very special way, a much more personal way, and reflect on the lessons that he taught me and the impact that he had on my life.

I first came to hear of Simon in 1984 when the then chairperson of GASA Rand, Jeremy Zipp, reported on the activities of what was called the Saturday Group to the Executive Committee of the Gay Association of South Africa, known as GASA. About a year later his name surfaced again, this time as a defendant in what became known as the Delmas Treason Trial. I had just been appointed as the national secretary of GASA and it fell to me to record the deliberations of National Executive Committee meetings. The minutes of those meetings record for posterity the myopic debate which followed the inevitable criticism that GASA had not issued any public statement in support of Simon and his fellow triallists. To my own discredit, the record shows that I was a keen and passionate protagonist of the idea that the fledgling GASA would be apolitical. There were, of course, voices of dissent, but the notion of a divisible, severable category of struggle against discrimination prevailed and in due course I set off for Copenhagen to defend GASA from expulsion from the International Lesbian and Gay Association.

In the days preceding my departure, with growing international outrage brewing, I received word from Simon in prison that he did not support the expulsion of GASA. Blinkered and idealistic, and with my cosseted view of justice in South Africa, I crafted an argument that distinguished the charge of murder that Simon faced [from] the political expediency of the government of the time. Naïve, but argued with passion, it was a defence that initially won in Copenhagen but lost in the arena of international condemnation that followed. It is an argument, out of the many arguments in my life that I have made, of which I am least proud. It was a specious argument that required profound contrition and apology, and I was pleased in my life and while Simon was alive to have done so. Throughout these turbulent times, however, Simon remained in prison, silenced by decree and the reality of incarceration.

It was at that time, and in the face of universal criticism, that I received a call from Edwin Cameron. It was a defining moment in my life and challenged my view that the apartheid judiciary could be relied upon or even trusted to deliver justice. At the same time, with Simon's help, it forced me to confront the reality of the deprivation that prevailed in our country and the gross indignity that was the lot of the majority of my fellow South Africans. For me, it was a formative political awakening – a period of insight and reappraisal. The magnitude of my own arrogance at the time and the inexcusable disregard of the organised white lesbian and gay movement finally dawned on me.

Throughout all those events, Simon displayed an inner serenity and magnanimity of spirit that was a forerunner of the reconciliation that would follow the creation of a democratic order more recently. In all that time that followed, Simon accepted with grace and forgiveness the immense personal and emotional suffering that I inflicted on him, on Roy, on his family and his friends. For me, Simon and the events of [1986] would serve as a point of personal hubris. Thereafter, I would never again be able to claim ignorance. It was for me my personal turning point. My personal understanding of the interconnectedness between all forms of discrimination allowed me to argue those points with insight in the constitution-making process in the 1990s. In my personal growth and education, Simon was both mentor and teacher. For that he deserves my sincerest appreciation and gratitude. In the moulding of my life's experiences, Simon will always be able to claim a special place. Simon, comrade in struggle, friend, gentle teacher, we were both fallible, our lives touched each other, but I had mine enriched by that experience. When the time comes for the recording of the contributions of the millions of nameless South Africans who reached out without bitterness to their intransigent white compatriots, your name will be entered with admiration and pride. Hambe kahle, Comrade, rest peacefully.

167

Zackie Achmat sketches the life and achievements of Simon Nkoli in this obituary, published in issue 4, June 1999, of *Equality*, the National Coalition for Gay and Lesbian Equality's newsletter. The full set of *Equality* newsletters is in the National Coalition for Gay and Lesbian Equality collection in the Gay and Lesbian Archives of South Africa.

WE MOURN

SIMON TSEKO NKOLI

GLO

By Zackie Achmat

Photograph by Gordon Rainsford

On the eve of 1998 World AIDS Day, 30 November 1998, South Africa lost a freedom fighter, leader and activist to HIV/AIDS. Simon Tseko Nkoli, a founder and leader of the lesbian and gay movement, had died.

The Gay and Lesbian Organisation of the Witwatersrand (GLOW) mourns and pays tribute to its founder and honorary life-president, Simon Tseko Nkoli. GLOW is joined by the National Coalition for Gay and Lesbian Equality, all its affiliates, and many thousands of lesbian and gay people throughout Southern Africa. We say *Hamba Kahle*, Comrade.

Simon Tseko Nkoli was born on 26 November 1957 in Phiri, Soweto. The Nkoli family later moved to Bophelong in the Vaal. In his early years, Si (as he was known to his friends) was confronted by apartheid, poverty and pass laws. As a young child, Simon hid his parents, Mrs. Elizabeth and the late Mr. Elias Nkoli, from the South African Police because they were regarded as "illegal" squatters. These memories were to guide him in the struggle for national liberation and sexual freedom.

The activism, heroism and energy of the youth movement were central to Simon Nkoli's political awareness and leadership. Simon attended a Catholic school and like many other youth of his generation, he joined the Young Christian Students (YCS). In 1976, when the police gunned down hundreds of children in the name of Afrikaans and apartheid, Simon became a student activist and leader then, only 18 years old. He was often questioned and harassed by the Security Police.

In 1979, Simon Nkoli joined the Congress of South African Students (COSAS) and became the general-secretary of the Vaal Triangle. At that time, COSAS was leading high school students throughout South Africa in our battle against apartheid education. COSAS campaigned for textbooks and teachers, and made students aware of the struggle for liberation. Here Simon learnt that the day-to-day issues of poor people are as important as the bigger demands for liberation. In 1982, Simon played a key role in the formation of Youth Congresses in both Soweto and the Vaal.

Simon Nkoli was an active member of the United Democratic Front (UDF) in the 1980s. As with many activists of his generation, he supported and later join African National Congress (ANC)-when it was dang and required courage to do so. He remained a mem the ANC until his death.

VAAL UPRISING

In the context of a National Party government an Botha attempting to use black local councillors as apa collaborators, Simon helped to establish the Vaal Association. In response to increased rents and attac the living standards of the poor, residents orga stayaways and consumer and rent boycotts. Simon F organise and support these struggles - for this he w suffer detention, torture and imprisonment.

DELMAS TREASON TRIAL

In 1984, Simon Tseko Nkoli joined 21 fellow comrac the Delmas Treason Trial. His co-accused included and ANC leaders Terror Lekota, Popo Molefe, Manthata, Gcina Malindi and Moss Chikane. 1 comrades spent more than 4 years on trial for their Some were then imprisoned.

During their detention, Simon Nkoli faced another which changed the face of lesbian and gay politi Southern Africa-he came out as a gay man. During months of debate and discussion with his comrades lawyers, Simon convinced these senior UDF and leaders that lesbian and gay people faced discrimin: He confronted and destroyed the myth that holds tha unAfrican to be gay. His friends like Gcina M: defended his record as an anti-apartheid activist.

Across the world, lesbian and gay people rallied to support of Simon Nkoli and the Delmas Treason Trialis South Africa, the white-led gay and lesbian move disowned Simon Nkoli and the struggle against apart Simon Nkoli's courageous stand at the Delmas Tre Trial left us a legacy. He defended lesbian and equality as part of the struggle against apartheid an human dignity. He gave all progressive activists, especially African and Coloured activists, the courac come out within the liberation movements. The growth lesbian and gay movement on the continent of Africa much to our gay martyrs-Simon Tseko Nkoli, Linda Ng and British Gcxabai.

E PARADE

n Nkoli and his GLOW comrades organised and led
rst three lesbian and gay Pride Marches in Southern
. The streets of Johannesburg resounded in 1990 with
n's voice as he led the chants-"Out of Closets - into the
ts" and "Not the Church, Not the State - We Ourselves
de Our Fate". Simon fused the struggles of lesbian and
people in Southern Africa with the international
ment for equality. The Pride March is a monument to
n Nkoli's belief that lesbian and gay people have to
up and defend our rights.

W

the Delmas Treason Trial a new tradition emerged.
n Nkoli and his comrades founded GLOW as the first
black township based organisation of lesbian and gay
e. GLOW was non-racial and supported the African
nal Congress. As part of the democratic movement
under Simon's leadership, GLOW condemned the
phobic defence used in the trial of Comrade Winnie
ela. GLOW became the home of youth who were
ted and despised in our communities. It became the
for ABIGALE, PEGLO and other black-led township
organisations.

AIDS

w front opened up. Justice Edwin Cameron, then a
n rights activist and lawyer, warned that HIV/AIDS
become the new apartheid. As the epidemic attacked
ay communities of South Africa, in a time when the
nal Party government neglected gay men and black
le in the HIV/AIDS epidemic, lesbian and gay
nunities and activists mobilised. Simon Nkoli, Peter
e, Alfred Machela and other comrades mobilised
ship AIDS Project was born.

wing the example of GASA - 6010, OLGA and the
ational lesbian and gay movement, Simon and his
ades conducted safer sex workshops, circulated
rials, and campaigned for treatment. The first South
n court case dealing with issues of privacy and
dentiality in the context of HIV/AIDS saw Simon Nkoli
his comrades in GLOW supporting the late Barry
eary, a gay white man living with HIV/AIDS.

n Nkoli lived with HIV/AIDS for more than 12 years. As
many people, he faced racial oppression, homophobia
now, AIDS-phobia. But after many years, Simon took
nother burden-deciding to live openly with HIV/AIDS.
e are more than 3 million people in our country with
AIDS, and Simon Nkoli was one of the very few who
"HIV is a virus-not a shame". In this struggle, he was
orted by many people. But his partner and lover,
erick Sharp; his friends and comrades, Peter
lahledi, Paul Mokgethi, Yoyo Kani and Peter Mosime,
rve a special mention.

SALUTE SIMON TSEKO NKOLI

n Nkoli was a founder member of the National
ition for Gay and Lesbian Equality and he lived to see
rights of lesbian and gay people enshrined in the
Constitution and in law. He was a board member of the
International Lesbian and Gay Association (ILGA) and was
instrumental in securing South Africa as the host country of
the 1999 ILGA World Conference. Simon was honoured in
the Netherlands, Canada, Britain, Norway, Australia and the
United States. He had friends and comrades in many
African countries.

Simon was generous and funny. His coming out in the
Delmas Treason Trial gave inspiration to many lesbian and
gay people. His stand encouraged us to take our future into
our own hands.

The late Simon Tseko Nkoli

Today, we say rest in peace Comrade Simon Tseko Nkoli. In
Africa, you have created an army to fight oppression and
injustice. We will defend your legacy and the equality of all
people with HIV/AIDS.

To Simon's partner, Roderick; Mrs. Elizabeth Nkoli, his
sisters Mamoipone and Maputso, his brother Oupa, and his
family; Peter Mohlahledi and all his friends-we mourn your
tremendous loss. Simon Tseko Nkoli was your son and
friend and our leader. He was a son of Africa.

This cartoon appeared in the 25 August 1985 edition of *Rapport*, an Afrikaans newspaper. Roughly translated it says: 'The SA Institute for Medical Research is investigating the possibility that AIDS is transmitted by insects or other animals ... How did you get AIDS? A poof-adder bit me ... Hey, what do you want to test here with that arse-o-meter!' The cartoon was cut out and stuck into the personal album of one of the first people known to have died from AIDS-related causes in South Africa. The album is in the Triangle Project collection in the Gay and Lesbian Archives of South Africa.

170

Part 2

The Constitution

Fragments from the archives II **Graeme Reid**

ARCHIVE: Presentation to GLOW Action Committee and SHOC workshop **Edwin Cameron**

ESSAY: Engendering gay and lesbian rights: The Equality Clause in the South African Constitution **Jacklyn Cock**

ARCHIVE: Submission to the Convention for a Democratic South Africa **The Equality Foundation**

ARCHIVE: 'We must claim our citizenship' **National Coalition for Gay and Lesbian Equality**

The Equality Clause

ARCHIVE: Public letter to the Constitutional Assembly **Archbishop Desmond Tutu**

Fragments from the archives II

Graeme Reid

1991   Presentation to GLOW Action Committee and SHOC workshop
Edwin Cameron

1993   Submission to the Convention for a Democratic South Africa
The Equality Foundation

1995   Report 'We Must Claim Our Citizenship' **National Coalition for Gay
and Lesbian Equality**

1995   Letter to the Constitutional Assembly **Archbishop Desmond Tutu**

2004   Cake 'Happy 10 Years of Gay Democracy'. **Gay and Lesbian
Organisation of Mpumalanga (GLOM)**

The archival material in Part 2 relates to the period of constitutional negotiations in South Africa. Edwin Cameron's presentation and the National Coalition for Gay and Lesbian Equality's report give insight into the internal workings of gay and lesbian organisations. The former was part of an internal organisational workshop and the latter was initially prepared as a report for affiliate organisations. Neither of these pieces was intended for general consumption but both have entered the public domain through the archive. In contrast, the Equality Foundation's submission to the Convention for a Democratic South Africa (CODESA) and Archbishop Desmond Tutu's letter to the Constitutional Assembly were part of the process of public participation in making the Constitution.

When Edwin Cameron addressed the Gay and Lesbian Organisation of the Witwatersrand (GLOW) and the Society for Homosexuals on Campus (SHOC) workshop 'Lesbian and Gay Rights are Human Rights' in March 1991, the African National Congress (ANC) had recently released its draft Bill of Rights which specifically safeguarded individuals against discrimination on the grounds of 'sexual orientation'. At the same time Winnie Mandela was being tried on charges of kidnapping and assault in a high-profile case that invoked a homophobic defence and was witness to anti-gay protests outside the court. Just three days prior to the workshop, a public letter from GLOW to the National Executive Committee of the ANC questioning the ANC's commitment to the cause of gay and lesbian equality had been published in the South African press. Aspirations and expectations ran high amongst activists working in gay and lesbian organisations, where emotion sometimes trumped strategy. Various draft 'charters' and 'programmes of action' were drawn up in Cape Town and Johannesburg outlining demands for full citizenship, including the right to marry. The critical issue at the workshop was how far the gay and lesbian community should go in articulating demands for inclusive citizenship. In his presentation, Cameron endorsed the sentiment of idealism, but not the strategy. He sounded a note of cautious optimism and persuaded the meeting to adopt a more strategic approach to the constitution-making process that would not alienate potential allies. He observed that lawyers are 'temperamentally conservative' and 'tactically conservative', and it was Cameron's own temperament and sense of tactics that were deeply influential throughout the constitution-making process, which began at CODESA and culminated in the adoption of the South African Constitution in 1996.

Throughout the constitution-making process, the crux of the matter was – should a blanket Equality Clause be accepted, or should specific characteristics, including sexual orientation, be enumerated? In the former, the interpretation of the Bill of Rights would always be at the discretion of the courts, while the latter allowed no such ambiguity. The Equality Foundation appointed Kevan Botha as a consultant to represent gay and lesbian interests at CODESA. Working closely with Cameron, Botha made various submissions arguing in favour of an enumerated clause.

175

Representatives from gay and lesbian organisations from across the country established the National Coalition for Gay and Lesbian Equality (NCGLE) in 1994, the same year in which South Africa's first democratic elections were held. The NCGLE was an umbrella body composed of affiliate organisations represented on an interim Executive Committee through regional structures. At its peak it boasted some 78 affiliates. The NCGLE self-consciously modelled itself on other successful one-issue political campaigns – the End Conscription Campaign in particular. Its primary goal was straightforward – to ensure that the words 'sexual orientation' remained in the final Constitution. The NCGLE would then embark on a systematic programme of incremental law reform, along the lines of the programme of action outlined by Cameron at the GLOW workshop and elaborated on at the inaugural meeting of the NCGLE. This programme became known as 'Edwin's laundry list'. The list consisted of the most winnable objectives, such as securing an equal age consent for gay and straight youth and scrapping the sodomy laws, followed by more controversial issues such as same-sex partnerships, marriage and adoption. The role of the NCGLE was to co-ordinate the lobbying process and generate a coherent voice from a hitherto relatively weak and fractious gay and lesbian community. Implicit in the NCGLE's 1995 report, entitled 'We Must Claim Our Citizenship', are the tensions between activism and tactics, between professional suit-and-tie lobbying and the ideal of mass mobilisation. The report was drafted by Zackie Achmat, a leading figure in the NCGLE.

The NCGLE, however, represented a minority interest in the constitution-making process and was reluctant to respond to the call of the Constitutional Assembly for public submissions in the form of letters. The concern was that this would become a game of numbers between those in favour of, and those opposed to, equality on the basis of 'sexual orientation'. The NCGLE could not compete with an orchestrated campaign by conservative religious congregations, for example. This concern was backed up by market research commissioned by the NCGLE, which demonstrated that the majority of South Africans were not in favour of gay and lesbian equality. (The NCGLE put an embargo on the research.) Instead of calling for public submissions, the NCGLE solicited letters from affiliate organisations, and from high-profile individuals, and then submitted them close to the Constitutional Assembly's deadline. The letter from Archbishop Desmond Tutu was particularly important. Not only did he support the inclusion of a sexual orientation clause, he also went further than the most liberal-minded Anglicans by asserting a 'fundamental human right to a sexual life, whether heterosexual or homosexual'. A far cry from the more familiar church stance: 'love the sinner, hate the sin'.

The photograph of the cake 'Happy 10 Years of Gay Democracy' takes us ahead to 2004, when the small gay and lesbian community of Wesselton, Mpumalanga, organised a beauty pageant to celebrate ten years of democracy in South Africa. Pageant organiser Bafana Mhlanga's concept for the cake was a rainbow depicting gays involved in the struggle for democracy on one side and emancipated gays on the other, divided by an image of the new South African flag. The local confectioners came up with this more modest interpretation, conveying the sense of rainbow through the creative use of icing. In this context, 'rainbow' alludes to the phrase first coined by Archbishop Desmond Tutu, 'the rainbow people of God', which has become the pre-eminent metaphor for the new South Africa's 'rainbow nation'. And 'rainbow' also refers to the international symbol of gay solidarity, the rainbow flag.

Presentation to GLOW Action Committee and SHOC workshop

Edwin Cameron

As part of a campaign initiated by the Organisation of Lesbian and Gay Activists (OLGA) to formulate a Charter of Lesbian and Gay Rights, the Gay and Lesbian Organisation of the Witwatersrand (GLOW) and the Society for Homosexuals on Campus (SHOC) – a student organisation based at the University of the Witwatersrand (Wits) – hosted two consecutive workshops entitled 'Lesbian and Gay Rights are Human Rights'. In this extract from the workshop held at Wits on 16 March 1991, prominent activist-lawyer Edwin Cameron outlines his perspective on the constitution-making process. The audiotape and transcript are in the Gay and Lesbian Organisation of the Witwatersrand collection in the Gay and Lesbian Archives of South Africa.

Introduction by workshop chairperson Kim Berman

Lesbian and gay rights are human rights. This is the 16th of March, Saturday at 2 p.m. at Wits, SHB6 [Senate House Basement 6].

On behalf of the GLOW Action Committee and SHOC I would like to welcome you all to the first of our series of workshops entitled 'Lesbian and Gay Rights are Human Rights'. This is going to be the first in the series to begin the process of discussion around forming a lesbian and gay charter.

Recent events in the news highlight the extreme urgency and necessity for the lesbian and gay community to start mobilising and campaigning to secure our rights in the present and future of our country. The vicious homophobia that has emerged out of the so-called Winnie Mandela Trial is unacceptable and a breach of our human rights.

Another news item that is topical is, of course, the drive to criminalise homosexuality in Britain. And this can happen because a lesbian and gay rights charter does not exist in that constitution.

Two days ago Radio 702, in a programme, broadcast public opinion about homosexuality that was terrifying in its ignorance and hatred. One person demanded that all gays should be gassed. Another said that they should be shot. And others, in their great liberal tolerance, said that we should just leave them alone as they are quite a happy bunch.

So we have a lot of work to do. The panellists of today's workshop will start the process of providing a context and direction in recognising and establishing our human rights. We hope that the discussions following will produce resolutions and objectives in carrying this process forward.

As an introduction to today's proceedings I'd like to quote Comrade Albie Sachs from his book, *Protecting Human Rights in the New South Africa*, which, also, I'd like to refer to you as a text that's very useful in writing up our own charter.

He states:

> No one gives us rights, we win them in struggle. They exist in our hearts before they exist on paper. We are not used to the idea of rights, certainly not of constitutional rights. Our debates are about power rather than rights. We speak about human rights only in terms of how they are violated and not in terms of how they can affirm and legitimise a new society.

Today we are here to decide just what kind of action we as the lesbian and gay community need to take to shape and protect our own future. We need to take that indignation we feel in our hearts – that by the state's decree we are criminals and the uninformed public and media present us as sexual abusers or perverts – we need to take that and transfer it onto paper in the form of a lesbian and gay charter.

Are we just hoping that we will be included in the Bill of Rights? Are we supposed to just accept gratefully and silently crumbs handed down to us? We, the lesbian and gay community, have to take our future into our own hands. We welcome solidarity and support from progressive organisations, but this is our struggle and we demand that lesbian and gay rights be included as policy in a democratic, non-racial, non-sexist, non-heterosexist, non-homophobic new South Africa.

So I'd like to start introducing the panellists. Our first panellist is Edwin Cameron and it is a pleasure and an honour to welcome Edwin as a special friend and protector of gay rights, and friend to GLOW, a gay rights organisation in South Africa. He's a human rights lawyer and he's based at Wits. He works in conscientious objection, AIDS and gay rights.

After him I'll introduce the others.

Presentation by Edwin Cameron

Thanks very much, Kim.

I want to be quite provocative this afternoon because there's a lot of ferment in the gay community internationally about how our human rights should be given expression. And what I want to say this afternoon might be opposed by some of you, but the viewpoint that I want to give is that we should probably be quite conservative in how we go about trying to achieve our rights. That's the theme of my talk.

I'm going to start off by saying what the ideal is, and I'm going to stick strictly to my fifteen minutes. Then, in the perfect society, how this ideal could be implemented. Then I'm going to come back to practicalities, how the ideal is a tension with the practical in South Africa. And then I'm going to suggest a practical programme, in conclusion, for us.

If we start with my first point, what is it that we really want, what would be the ideal position as regards gays' and lesbians' human rights, I think what we really want is a society in which all forms of irrational discrimination are not only outlawed, but are non-existent. So the fact of skin colour or disability or medical status or sexual orientation would be irrelevant, both socially and in terms of governmental actions. If that were the case, we'd have a society in which gay and lesbian affiliation or orientation would be seen as a natural variance of human expression. That's what we really want.

Then, if we look at how that ideal would be embodied in the perfect society, there would be various things that one could this afternoon take up in a lesbian and gay charter. One would want, first of all, remedial legislation. You demand that anti-hate legislation be passed. And there are various charters which Donné and Terry gave to me, from [countries] across the world which have such charters, that you're not allowed to incite hatred or spread ignorance or lies about certain groups.

There's a whole debate about that in South Africa as regards race. Should you prevent racist speech or should it be part of free speech and only be prevented when it incites people to violence? The same debate is taking place in gay groups internationally about anti-gay hatred, anti-lesbian hatred. In the ideal society you'd have anti-hate legislation. You'd also have legislation either in the Bill of Rights or in a different sort of law or statute, which expressly prohibits discrimination on any grounds against gay people, whether in tenancies, education, public facilities. So you have legislation on the one hand.

Secondly, in the ideal society and what we could demand this afternoon in the gay and lesbian charter. Secondly, you'd have governmental action and enforcement. You'd say it's not good enough that the government outlaws things, the government has actually got to do things. No, not good enough that the government says that black people can now buy land. You actually need a government-implemented land programme to redress inequities.

So you'd demand also in a gay and lesbian charter that the government should address discrimination. In fact, the ANC draft Constitution is very interesting

181

because it contains a clause, clause 14, which deals with positive action. Clause 14 is positive action. It says that:

> The state shall observe the principles of non-racialism and non-sexism and encourage the same in all public and private bodies.

It says:

> All benefits conferred and entitlements granted by the state shall be distributed on a non-racist, non-sexist basis.

One would argue there that non-sexist includes what Kim was talking about, non-heterosexist.

Then there's an article 13 in the ANC's Constitution which refers to affirmative action, and that clause allows the government to take action in favour of men and women who in the past have been disadvantaged by discrimination. And we'd say it's quite evident that gay people in South Africa, not just affluent white middle-class gays, but gay people, the whole body of gay people in South Africa, of whom only 18 or 20 per cent are affluent, middle-class and white, that they have been discriminated against, and you demand governmental action to remedy it.

Thirdly, in an ideal society, if we were going for that ideal that I've articulated, we'd demand a change in public consciousness. We'd say it's unacceptable that advertising and public entertainment and public conceptions of sexuality and of togetherness and of emotional bonding represent only heterosexuality. We'd demand that through the media, through schools, through advertising, that that should be changed.

182

That is the one extreme of what we could put together this afternoon and that's what I'm arguing against. That's what I'm saying we shouldn't do. I'm saying we shouldn't go so far this afternoon. Let us take a step back from the statement of the ideal and the statement of how we could really implement the ideal. Let's take a step back and look at where we really are in South Africa.

Firstly, we see that our laws are in a terrible position in South Africa. We see firstly that there's a differential age of consent. For lesbians and for gay men, the age of consent is nineteen,[1] which is unjustifiable. It's wrong, it's unjustifiable. It leads to frightening results, causing great misery for people. You have people who interact with people who are eighteen or seventeen, where there's clearly an informed sexual consent, and these people are then stigmatised criminally.

Secondly, there are specific discriminatory offences, 'sodomy', 'unnatural sexual offences'. The idea of men at a party: there's a statutory offence that any act calculated to cause sexual gratification or stimulate the sexual response committed where more than two men are present, is an offence. So kissing or even holding hands, depending how far you go, could be an offence.

We see that there's job discrimination. I've been waiting for seven or eight years now for the right case. Mostly one doesn't hear of the cases because the people who are victimised are the people who are not assertive, the people who aren't here this afternoon, who don't go to gay parties or socialise with gay people. The victims of discrimination in our country are mostly those who are most vulnerable to it. It's a vicious circle. It's a self-confirming phenomenon where the sort of person who's going to get denied a promotion or get the sack or get transferred because he or she is a gay or lesbian, is likely to be the person who's going to accept it, is going to feel worse about it and be less likely to complain about it.

We see that there's discrimination in public resources. One example is that if you've contracted AIDS from a blood transfusion, you get given provincial council-supported AZT. You're not given that if you're gay. It's irrational, it's outrageous, it's indefensible. There should be no discrimination in the provision of public resources when it comes to sick people.

1. As opposed to a heterosexual age of consent of sixteen years of age.

We see that in custody cases there's a constant spectre hanging over mostly gay mothers, but also used against gay fathers. It's a terrifying spectre. I get phoned almost every week by the Gay Advice Bureau. Someone's just phoned them, there's a divorce hanging, the husband or the wife has said, 'I'm going to raise the fact that you're gay or a lesbian', when custody or when visitation rights are an issue.

We see that there are various other disabilities: tenancies, we see cohabitation, inheritance. In countless ways we are stigmatised and oppressed and discriminated against because we're gay.

Secondly, the present state of the debate in South Africa is very interesting. Kim, in her introduction, mentioned the whole thing around the Winnie trial. I've spoken to various of my fellow members at GLOW this week and we've all emphasised that the right to a fair trial is sacrosanct and that everything that's reasonably relevant to a fair trial is also sacrosanct.

So if, subjectively, this person believed that she was saving those boys because of something that she was opposed to, whether it was movies or comics or gayness, those allegations must be aired. But there's no doubt whatsoever that the public stigma surrounding homosexuality has also been invoked. It's been invoked as an attempt to detract from the horrendity of what might have happened if those allegations are true. And that is a frightening thing, that at this point in the public debate, as Kim has pointed out, that that should have been invoked.

On the other hand, we have a very exciting development. We have the fact that in the ANC draft Constitution, sexual orientation is specifically outlawed as a basis for discriminating against people. Under article 7, where there's a reference to gender rights, article 7.2 says that:

184

> Discrimination on the grounds of gender, single parenthood, legitimacy of birth or sexual orientation shall be unlawful.

That's specifically under Gender. Under the first article, article 1.1, it says:

All South Africans are born free and equal in dignity and rights.

Article 1.2 says:

No individual or group shall receive privileges or be subjected to discrimination, domination or abuse on the grounds of race, colour, language, gender, creed, political or other opinion, birth or other status.

They leave sexual orientation out of article 1, but then include it specifically later under article 7, which, for the lawyers, is just a dream because one can go and argue that gender is mentioned in article 1 and the heading of article 7 is Gender, so the drafters must have intended to include sexual orientation under Gender and under Sexism.

Lovely lawyer's arguments about it, but the point is that the ANC's Constitution Legal Committee was incredibly courageous in including it. It wasn't without some debate, but there are people on that committee, notably Albie Sachs, Arthur Chaskalson, Fink Haysom, Zola Skweyiya, Penuell Meduna, who are sympathetic to the idea of gay rights. And I'm anxious that at this point we shouldn't send off letters or do anything that's going to make their position more difficult. If this Constitution were to become law, it would be the first fundamental law in the world which actually outlaws discrimination on the grounds of sexual orientation.

So I know that our feelings in GLOW and in SHOC are high, but I think it's important not to kowtow to discrimination, but to take careful strategic and tactical decisions so that we don't send off a letter that says we now doubt the ANC's commitment to gay rights. On the contrary, we should say this should be a time of affirmation of gay rights as it is contained in this Constitution.

185

So the public debate at the moment is fractured and now we've got to decide. And the last section I want to address is, what practical programme can we adopt? And what I've said to you at the outset, what I know is controversial, what I know you may differ from me profoundly about, is that I don't believe that we should be Utopian in our demands. We should be Utopian in our thinking but not Utopian in our demands. Utopian in our thinking in that we should state the principle. The principle is a society free from all forms of irrational and unjustified discrimination. Society in which no importance is attached to sexual orientation, as little as to irrelevant aspects of race or culture. There are relevant aspects of race or culture. One can be proud and constructive about one's culture and about being gay and about being heterosexual, but irrational and irrelevant attachment to those features would be outlawed.

So we must state the principle and our principle must be Utopian. We must demand what we want in the principle, but when it comes to defining our immediate targets, I believe that we must be much more tactically and strategically minded.

Now, one of the senior members of the ANC Constitution Legal Committee saw a comment in the press which came from a member of our sister organisation in Cape Town, OLGA, which said that because article 7 of the ANC draft Constitution outlaws discrimination on the basis of gender orientation, there should therefore be marriage. Now this person is a very liberal person. It's a well-known liberal lawyer and he was quite disturbed by this. He said it's going to make it very difficult to retain this clause, because the moment the general public or informed constitutional lawyers, many of whom are conservative like me – I think most lawyers are temperamentally conservative, they're tactically conservative – when they hear that this is what this clause implies – well, then, we've got to drop it.

So it's a difficult issue we've got to decide this afternoon. I would say that we should draft the principles and then select specific targets like uniform age of consent. Select specific targets – that's how all the effective progressive organisations over the past 30 and 40 years have worked. If you look at the successful organisations, anti-apartheid organisations, look at ECC and the Black

Sash, look at the UDF campaigns, look at COSATU's living wage campaign: you target an issue and you build your campaign around it. The issue must be attainable, it must be morally foolproof, and then you target a campaign around it.

Age of consent, abolition of criminal offences, anti-hate and ignorance cam- paign, there are specific targetable issues that we can adopt this afternoon, that we can say, this is what we want, state the principle. But my own view would be that to adopt a wide-ranging gay and lesbian charter which includes a demand for an Office of Gay Affairs or for uniform custody rights or for gay marriages, I believe that that would be a mistake. That is my view and I'd like to hear every one else's as well.

Thank you.

Engendering gay and lesbian rights:
The Equality Clause in the South African Constitution

Jacklyn Cock

Writing in 2001, five years after the Equality Clause was enshrined in the South African Constitution, Jacklyn Cock tracks the origins of the Equality Clause and examines its impact, concluding that for the gay rights movement to become a transformative force, it must widen its focus on the justice of rights to include the justice of redistribution. The essay was previously published in *Women's Studies International Forum* (26:1), 2003.

Introduction

The 'gay rights clause' in the South African post-apartheid Constitution,[1] explicitly prohibiting discrimination on the basis of sexual orientation, was the first of its kind in the world. However, it represents a paradox, given the commitment of the post-apartheid state to mass participation in policy formulation and the high level of homophobia in South Africa. This essay explores this paradox through an examination of the gay rights clause. The essay falls into two parts, which explore, firstly, the origins of the clause and, secondly, its impact. The argument is based on interviews with eight key informants[2] chosen because of their expertise in the origins and impact of the gay rights clause, as well as participant observation in the movement for gay and lesbian rights over the past five years, and on secondary and primary sources, including from the Gay and Lesbian Archives of South Africa housed at the University of the Witwatersrand.

188

The inclusion of the gay rights clause in the final post-apartheid Constitution was largely due to the ability of a male-dominated gay rights movement to form strategic alliances with the anti-apartheid struggle, to mobilise the master

---

1. This refers to the Equality Clause in the Bill of Rights.
2. Key informants included:
   Jabu Dube – 9 March 2001
   Kevan Botha – 8 March 2001
   Graeme Reid – 22 May 2000
   Sharon Cooper – 12 June 2001
   Kathleen Satchwell – 3 April 2001.

narrative of equality and non-discrimination and to lobby effectively during the constitution-making process. The clause has had important, but limited, effects. Homophobia is being increasingly challenged, but not by a representative or mass-based movement. The gay rights movement was never a cohesive phenomenon with a strong, collective voice. Instead, the particular fragmented forms that sexual politics have taken in the last 50 years of South African history reflect the complex interplay of sexual identity with the politics of race, class and gender. The essay demonstrates that the transformative capacity of the gay rights movement in South Africa is limited by its socially conservative and male-dominated nature. The shift necessary for it to become transformative involves expanding the focus from justice as rights to include redistribution.

The origins of the gay rights clause

An insurgent political climate

Any explanation of the clause must be rooted in the insurgent climate of South Africa in the early 1990s. A marked cultural effervescence involved a re-configuration of the discourse on equality. This converged with the discourse on sexual rights promoted by a powerful women's movement and Western ideals of human rights. There was no single and simple script at work. In addition, the discourse of diversity, the celebration of difference and, especially, the right to freedom of sexual orientation were defended as part of the challenge of building a diverse, pluralistic society. The 'rainbow' emerged as (and remains) a strong collectivist and inclusive symbol defining unity among the diverse peoples of South Africa, and a source of national pride.

The gay rights movement was able to mobilise these discourses very effectively. In addition, the movement made connections with the anti-apartheid struggle, and particularly the African National Congress in exile in London and Lusaka. It also made contact with key actors in the political negotiations and was able to offer expert participation in the lobbying process which produced the final Constitution.

According to Graeme Reid, 'activists managed to make gay rights part of a much broader political project' (Interview, 2000). This 'broader political project' argued for social justice and opposed all forms of discrimination, but was very loosely defined. And the unity of the gay rights movement as a powerful, collective actor should not be overemphasised. It will be shown below that the movement was fragmented, splintered politically and divided along race, gender, class and ideological lines. While male-dominated, it engaged in some very effective initiatives, which can be periodised in two stages: coalition-building between 1987 and 1990 and effective lobbying between 1990 and 1994.

Coalition-building with the African National Congress 1987–1990

During the period 1987 to 1990 the gay rights movement expanded and was able to place gay issues on the agenda of the anti-apartheid struggle, both in South Africa and abroad. It achieved this by targeting the leading organisations in the Struggle, the African National Congress (ANC) in exile and the United Democratic Front (UDF) inside the country.

In this process the efforts of two men are especially important – Peter Tatchell in London and Simon Nkoli in South Africa. They were the 'carriers' of the connection between gay rights and the anti-apartheid struggle through mobilising an expanded conception of liberation.

Until the late 1980s the ANC had no policy on sexual orientation and senior officials dismissed gay issues as irrelevant. The catalyst was a particularly dismissive statement by a member of the National Executive Committee of the ANC, Ruth Mompati, in 1987. 'I cannot even begin to understand why people want lesbian and gay rights. The gays have no problems. They have nice homes and plenty to eat. I don't see them suffering. No one is persecuting them. We haven't heard about this problem in South Africa until recently. It seems to be fashionable in the West.' She saw the gay issue as a 'red herring' detracting attention from the main struggle against apartheid, and justified the ANC's lack of policy on lesbian and gay rights by stating, 'We don't have a policy on flower sellers either.' In her view, lesbians and gays are 'not normal. If everyone was like that, the human race would come to an end' (in Tatchell, 1987).

Peter Tatchell, an anti-apartheid campaigner in Britain, publicised the statement and petitioned the then ANC Director of Information, Thabo Mbeki, who issued a retraction on behalf of the ANC. Five years later, at its policy conference in 1992, the ANC formally recognised gay and lesbian rights.

Ironically, while Ruth Mompati's statement was a catalyst in forging a strategic alliance between the gay rights movement inside South Africa and the ANC abroad, the detention of Simon Nkoli was the catalyst in forging a strategic alliance between the gay rights movement and the anti-apartheid struggle within South Africa, led by the UDF. The UDF, formed in 1983, was the country's leading internal anti-apartheid organisation, with 600 affiliated bodies.

Coalition-building with the United Democratic Front 1985–1990

In 1985 Simon Nkoli, one of the Gay Association of South Africa (GASA)'s few black members, went on trial with 21 others, charged with 'high treason', following the mass protests in the black townships of the Vaal Triangle region south-west of Johannesburg in 1983 and 1984. After his acquittal after nearly three years' imprisonment, Nkoli became chairperson of the Gay and Lesbian Organisation of the Witwatersrand (GLOW). GLOW saw themselves as part of the broad movement against apartheid. The only openly gay person among the Delmas treason trialists, Nkoli always emphasised that the battles against homophobia and racism were inseparable. In his speech at the first Gay and Lesbian Pride March, organised by GLOW in 1990, he said, 'I'm fighting for the abolition of apartheid. And I fight for the right of freedom of sexual orientation. These are inextricably linked with each other. I cannot be free as a black man if I am not free as a gay man' (in Luirink, 1998:5).

This assertion of a linkage shifted the attitudes of key political actors. According to Graeme Reid, 'Simon Nkoli's detention was a watershed in gay politics here. He represented that engagement between the gay movement and the broader liberation struggle' (Interview, 2000).

The conservative nature of GASA

However, any alliance between the gay movement and the anti-apartheid Struggle was complicated by the reactionary nature of the most prominent gay rights organisation in South Africa at the time, GASA, which was largely white, middle-class and male. 'It had a very white, male, view of what constituted politics' (Kevan Botha, Interview, 2001). Nkoli said, 'It is largely because of the consistent support of the British lesbian and gay movement that I survived the terrible days and nights I spent in prison ... I have had no support from GASA since the moment of my arrest' (in Capital Gay, 9.10.1987).

GASA's 'apolitical stance' meant non-alignment in broader South African politics and, 'secondly, following a moderate, non-confrontational and accommo-

191

dationist strategy' (Gevisser, 1994:51). Other accounts view GASA as 'apartheid-friendly' and patriarchal (Luirink, 1998:21). GASA constituted a 'very male world, and they [women] did not feel welcome' (Ann Smith, a GASA president, in Gevisser, 1994:50). Furthermore, the organisation refused to show solidarity with a group of lesbians fired in 1983 by their employer (Luirink, 1998:21). Ultimately the failure to link the struggle for gay equality with the struggle against apartheid was fatal for GASA, which was suspended from the International Lesbian and Gay Association (ILGA) in 1987.

These political differences demonstrate the splintered nature of the gay rights movement in South Africa at the time. As Graeme Reid states, 'It was not a strong and unified movement' (Interview, 2000). However, it was changing; as Gevisser (1994) demonstrates, there was a major shift from the conservative or apolitical gay movement of the 1980s to the liberationist gay movement of the 1990s, which took as its starting point the need to fold lesbian and gay issues into the agenda of the anti-apartheid struggle. It was able to lobby very effectively during the 1990 to 1994 period in South Africa's transition to democracy.

Public participation in the constitutional process 1990–1994

Sexual orientation was included in the equality provision of the draft/interim post-apartheid Constitution, thus providing protection against discrimination for gays and lesbians, making South Africa the first country in the world to do so. This came to be known as the gay rights clause and it emerged from the complex negotiations which marked South Africa's transition to democracy between 1990 and 1994. These protracted multi-party negotiations led to the interim Constitution and the first democratic elections.

192

The policy process surrounding the Constitution was structured around input from the public. The process was planned as participatory, consultative and representative. The participative process meant that during 1995 the Constitutional Assembly received submissions, written and oral, from all sectors of society, on the draft Constitution. This provided crucial political space, which the National Coalition for Gay and Lesbian Equality (NCGLE) used to mobilise.

Effective lobbying by the National Coalition for Gay and Lesbian Equality

The NCGLE was formed in 1994 specifically to coordinate the lobbying efforts to retain the gay rights clause in the draft South African Constitution, and became a powerful structure representing 78 member organisations.

The key actors in this process were men who used power strategically in the policy process of the Constitutional Assembly. Part of the NCGLE's success was its single-issue focus. In this respect it was similar to the Law Reform Movement of 1968, which was narrowly defined around a single issue, preventing proposed changes to the Immorality Act which would criminalise male homosexuality. Another key to success was the accommodationist tone of the gay rights movement at the time. According to Graeme Reid, 'It was important that the coalition wouldn't speak about gay rights, only about equality' (Interview, 2000).

The master narrative of equality was equated with non-discrimination. According to Botha and Cameron, this had a strong appeal. They argued that the constitutional protection of gays 'is no doubt the product of our peculiar history, where institutionalised discrimination against people on the ground of race was perfected through the legal system. The racial legacy has given the majority of South Africans a repugnance for the use of legal processes for irrational discrimination' (Botha and Cameron, 1997:37).

One of the most influential submissions to the Constitutional Assembly from the NCGLE emphasised two themes. The first was equality and the uniformity of all forms of discrimination: the submission stressed that 'equality and non-discrimination are the fundamental and overriding principles of the Interim Constitution', and furthermore, discrimination against gays and lesbians 'displays the same basic features as discrimination on the grounds of race and gender'. The second significant theme was the argument that sexual orientation is fixed, immutable, and therefore part of the natural order. 'Sexual orientation is immutable – in that the individual cannot change it.' This was supported by 'scientific evidence'. Thus, 'Sexual orientation is an ineradicable part of human identity. Compelling historical, scientific and medical evidence shows that homosexual orientation is a natural phenomenon' (National Coalition for Gay and Lesbian Equality, 1995:8).

193

Part of the success of this submission was this accommodationist tone – reformist rather than revolutionary, it did not present a substantial threat to prevailing gender relations or patriarchal power.

Opposition to the inclusion of the gay rights clause

While in South Africa in the 1990s the master narrative of equality was powerful, there were also competing ideological elements involving notions of 'African tradition', 'Christianity' and 'normalcy'. These notions were claimed by the African Christian Democratic Party (ACDP), which lobbied very hard for the removal of the gay rights clause from the final Constitution. However, there were 'a total of 7 032 submissions from gay, lesbian and sympathetic persons and about 13 000 signatures on petitions. In comparison there were only 564 submissions against the inclusion of sexual orientation' (Kevan Botha, in *Equality,* no 3, 1996:2).

The main source of opposition to the clause, the ACDP, won only 88 104 votes out of the 32 million cast in the 1994 election. They subsequently claimed that the inclusion of the gay rights clause was 'undemocratic' (Rev. Kenneth Meshoe, ACDP leader, in SABC-TV interview, 29.5.1996). The same point was made by the then Western Cape Premier, Peter Marais, who attacked the clause by saying that Christians must choose between the Constitution and the Bible, because the former was 'written by communists under the disguise of democracy' (in *Mail and Guardian*, 22.12.2002). In reality, public participation generally in the constitutional process was limited. The process was an expert-dominated one, in which participation was shallow and public voices had limited impact.

The homophobic nature of that public is illustrated by a survey of 2 163 respondents drawn from all races and regions of South Africa in 1995. On an attitude index over eight questions posed to respondents, 48 per cent of the public was rated as anti-gay. The survey found that 44 per cent of respondents were against giving homosexuals equal rights in the Constitution. A total of 64 per cent were opposed to giving homosexuals who live together permanently the same rights as married people. An even larger number of 68 per cent opposed letting homosexuals adopt children (Charney, 1995:7).

This was the context in which the gay rights clause was achieved. Fortunately, the dominant notion of democracy was rooted in a conception of rights rather than a simple majoritarianism. In 1996, when the Constitution – including the gay rights clause – was adopted by parliament, the NCGLE shifted its focus to the implementation of the rights in the Constitution and to supporting the gay movement throughout Southern Africa.

The impact of the gay rights clause

The clause was the product of a reconfiguration of the discourse on equality, a reconfiguration that was driven by the gay rights movement. However, there are contrasting views on the significance of the clause for gays and lesbians. Graeme Reid states, 'The clause is very important ... it promotes a sense of citizenship' (Interview, 2000). Kevan Botha maintains that 'The clause is meaningless unless you're "out". In order to claim the rights you have to acknowledge and own the identity of being gay' (Interview, 2001). Sharon Cooper, editor of Womyn, argues that the clause 'has had no impact on the masses. It's brilliant legislation but meaningless to people without jobs. The law is a luxury, it only works for rich, white people' (Interview, 2001). Edwin Cameron maintained that since the gay rights clause there has been 'a major shift in intellectual and cultural circles in accepting homosexuality, and beyond these circles, the issue of equity is being taken seriously by the government for the first time' (in Daniels, 1998:9).

Much of the action to establish full equality on the basis of the gay rights clause has involved legal efforts to recognise the validity of homosexual family relationships, and to secure the recognition of gay relationships in the courts on domestic issues such as the parental rights of same-sex partners and their access to benefits. In contrast to the male-dominated nature of the gay rights movement in South Africa before 1994, lesbians are playing a prominent role in these attempts.

195

A basis for legal action

The first recognition of same-sex relationships in South African law was the Special Pension Fund Act, designed to assist veterans from the liberation struggle in 1996/7. According to Kevan Botha, this was due to the lobbying efforts of 'the many lesbian women in MK [the armed wing of the ANC]' (Interview, 2001). An important example of lesbian action occurred in 1998 when the Pretoria High Court ruled in favour of a lesbian police captain who wished to register her partner of eleven years on her medical aid. This judgment, which overturned the refusal of the police service medical scheme, was hailed by the NGCLE as 'historical' and 'a victory for equality, dignity and justice for all people in South Africa' (in *Sunday Independent,* 8.2.1998).

There have been other significant gains. A Pretoria High Court judge ruled in 2000 that a schoolgirl could live with her lesbian mother (*Sunday Times,* 27.8.2000). In 2000 the Pension Fund Adjudicator ruled that pension funds which excluded same-sex partners from benefits were unconstitutional.

In 2001 a Pretoria High Court judge ruled that the Child Care Act and the Guardianship Act, which prevented a lesbian couple from jointly adopting their two children, were unconstitutional. He ruled that the legislation should be amended to include same-sex life partners. This is important in view of the projected three million AIDS orphans in South Africa by 2010. In a second ruling, the judge decided in favour of a lesbian in a fourteen-year cohabiting relationship who sought to have the conditions of the Judges' Remuneration Act made applicable to her domestic partner. This would involve benefits such as pension, medical aid and a subsistence allowance.

A number of cases, including the two cited above, have been brought to the ultimate legal authority, the Constitutional Court. For example, in 1999 the Constitutional Court ruled that laws relating to sodomy in various pieces of legislation were unconstitutional and invalid. In his separate concurring judgment, Judge Sachs argued that 'the violation of equality by the anti-sodomy laws is all the more egregious because the offences also violate the right to privacy by touching the deep, invisible and intimate side of people's lives.' In his view, the Constitution requires that the law and public institutions 'acknowledge the variability of human beings and affirm the equal respect and concern that should be shown to all as they are ... The decision of the Court should thus be seen as part of a growing acceptance of difference in an increasingly open and pluralistic South Africa' (www.concourt.gov.za).

Another case won by the NCGLE on behalf of several same-sex partners, both male and female, before the Constitutional Court in 1999, involved the right of same-sex partners to South African residence as spouses.

Clearly a strong legal framework has been established. This is also evident in the Labour Relations Act of 1995, which states that discrimination on the basis of sexual orientation is an unfair labour practice. Examples of such discrimination include: not being hired because you are gay or lesbian, losing your job because of your sexual orientation, refusal by the employer to include your partner in employment benefits such as medical aid, pension, housing benefits, life insurance, bursaries, provident fund and other employment benefits, abuse and harassment at work by other employees because of your sexual orientation, denial of leave when your partner is sick or dies. Another victory is the Employment Equity Bill, which defines 'family responsibility' to include gay and lesbian relationships.

The cases brought by the NCGLE have involved 'clever sequencing. We started with the sodomy law. That was the basis for a lot of the discrimination in law. But it was seen as a male issue, as an issue that women couldn't relate to. After that we took up the immigration matter which opened up access for all couples, then pension and custody cases ... cases all leading up to marriage' (Kevan Botha, Interview, 2001).

Probably the most controversial issue relates to same-sex marriages.[3] Kevan Botha maintains that 'Gay marriage is the big issue we have to address' (Interview, 2001). A white lesbian couple who took part in a marriage ceremony in 2000 have vowed to take it to the Constitutional Court to make their union legal. '... we'll fight not only for ourselves but for the many other gay and lesbian couples whose marriages are not recognised in this country' (in *Star*, 15.3.2000).

In many other societies around the globe, gay men and lesbians are struggling for this kind of recognition and right. 'As the new millenium begins, struggles by non-heterosexuals to secure equal recognition and rights for the new family relationships they are now creating represent some of the most dramatic and fiercely contested developments in Western family patterns' (Stacey and Biblarz, 2001:159). The struggles are intense because existing marriage and family policies 'encode Western culture's most profoundly held convictions about gender, sexuality and parenthood' (Stacey and Biblarz, 2001:160).

197

However, it is debatable how transformative these efforts are. All the legal actions described above reflect racialised class privilege. All promote an image

3. Other societies are changing marriage laws. In December 2000 The Netherlands gave final approval to groundbreaking laws allowing same-sex couples to marry in a civil ceremony and adopt children. Dutch law has recognised registered partnership of gay couples since 1998 but those couples did not have the same rights as heterosexual couples with regard to adopting children. Only one partner had full parental rights (*New York Times* 20.12.2000 'Same-sex couples can now wed in a civil ceremony for the first time anywhere in the world').

of neatly couple-ist, 'almost normal', domesticated gays and lesbians. Castells maintains that the legal recognition of same-sex marriages means 'a funda-mental breach has been opened in the institutional scaffolding constructed to control desire' (Castells, 1997:220). However, American gay playwright Tony Kushner argues that 'Openly queer GIs [soldiers in the US army] and same-sex confectionery couples on wedding cakes won't be enough' (in *The Nation*, 7.4.1994). His argument is that gay men and lesbians are more than 'hetero-sexuals with a difference'. The crucial question relates to whether the full reali-sation of gay rights implies the transformation of fundamental societal institu-tions such as marriage and the military.

Gay rights and the transformation of the South African military

The difficulty in establishing substantive, as opposed to purely formal or abstract, equality may be illustrated with reference to a specific South African institution, the military. The apartheid army, the South African Defence Force (SADF), enforced particularly rigid gender identities and was particularly abusive to homosexuals (Krouse, 1994; Cock, 1991). While gays were not excluded they were subjected to 'a form of hidden terrorism which permeates every ech-elon of the military environment' (Krouse, 1994:211). This 'terrorism' is evi-dent in how an unknown number of gays and lesbians in the SADF between 1969 and 1980 were subjected to electric shock treatment and sex-change operations.

In 1969 a psychiatric unit was established by the South African Medical Services at 1 Military hospital, Voortrekkerhoogte. 'Within the military, homo-sexuality was seen as a "disease", requiring medical treatment rather than grounds for exemption from conscription. Conscripts who were suspected of being gay were encouraged to "confess" their deviance and submit for treat-ment – electric shock aversion therapy – in the psychiatric unit ... Some gay conscripts and drug abusers were given the "choice" of going to Greefswald, a notorious labour camp on the then Transvaal border, or submitting to electric shock aversion therapy' (Van Zyl et al, 1999:v).

Such 'therapy' was applied to lesbians as well as gay men. 'Trudie Grobler, an intern psychologist in the psychiatric unit at 1 Military Hospital, was forced to observe an aversion therapy session under guidance of the psychiatrist. A woman was subjected to such severe shocks that her shoes flew off her feet' (Van Zyl et al, 1999:73). Grobler is quoted as saying, 'I know that he [Dr

Aubrey Levine, a colonel in the SADF] did aversion therapy with gay men ... You know that he showed the gay boys men and then shocked them. Then he showed them women. I presume that the same strength, method and everything was given to the woman. It was traumatic. I could not believe how her body could handle it' (Van Zyl et al, 1999:73).

Such practices belong to the apartheid era and all discrimination against gays and lesbians in the post-apartheid army is illegal. However, negative attitudes persist. A recent survey of attitudes within the new army, the South African National Defence Force (SANDF), reported that only one quarter of the almost 3 000 persons surveyed felt good about the integration of gays and lesbians in the military. Almost a third (30,6 per cent) did not want to share mess facilities with gays and lesbians. Almost half (46,9 per cent, and 49,3 per cent of the African respondents) felt that the integration of gays and lesbians would lead to a loss of military effectiveness. Almost a third (31,0 per cent) felt that gays and lesbians were 'morally weaker' than heterosexual people. The largest racial category in the sample were Africans, totalling 52,8 per cent (Department of Defence, 2000:2).

One informant who is a lesbian and a colonel in the SANDF described an intense social isolation. 'I can't afford to have any intimate relationships. If it were known that I was gay, I wouldn't be able to do my work, I wouldn't get anywhere' (Informant 3, Interview, 2000).

As gay activist Zackie Achmat said recently, 'In South Africa we have a really good legal framework; what we need now is a change in our social understandings, our attitudes' (in SABC-TV interviews, 31.1.2001). Such social understandings may change following a recent ruling that same-sex partners of members of the SANDF will in future have the same benefits as spouses. Regulations amending the definition of 'marital status' and 'spouse' to include partners in permanent life partnerships have been published in the Government Gazette (Streek, 2002:12). The amendments bring the defence regulations in line with the gay rights clause of the Constitution and follow the Judges' Remuneration Act cited above.

199

Continuing social discrimination

Despite the inclusion of the gay rights clause in the post-apartheid Constitution, homophobia is intense and widespread in post-apartheid South

Africa. Gays and lesbians continue to be denied cultural recognition and are subject to shaming, harassment, discrimination and violence. Violence against women is increasing and there is a particularly vicious edge to some lesbian attacks. For instance, in December 1996, a fourteen-year old girl from Carletonville was assaulted by a man who told her that she should go and fetch her mother and their lesbian friends. He said, 'they were trying to be men and he was going to beat them up like men'. He went on to say that 'I am going to wipe out all the lesbians in Carletonville'. When the mother tried to lay charges at the local police station she was told by the sergeant in charge, 'If I ever see you lesbians in this police station, I will kick you so hard under your arses that you will not find your way back to Carletonville. You are sick people and you disgust us' (NCGLE press statement, 1997).

According to one source, 'The "Jackrollers" [a notorious Soweto gang] go particularly for lesbians and when they catch one they say, "We'll put you right." So it is really dangerous for a young woman living in the townships to be open as a lesbian'. The same informant said, 'The Constitution protects us, but only on paper' (Informant 4, Interview, 2001). Because of this constitutional protection for gay rights, South Africa has been termed 'a satanic state'.

In 1999 a gay bar in Cape Town was the target of a bomb attack in which six people were injured. In a television interview Safety and Security Minister Steve Tshwete said that the vigilante group People Against Gangsterism and Drugs (PAGAD) was behind the recent spate of urban terrorism in Cape Town and was against the post-apartheid state. They saw it as a satanic state because of the state's support for abortion and gay rights (SABC-TV, 11.9.2000). As Luirink writes, both PAGAD and the ACDP 'link up perfectly in their agitation around still broadly popular prejudices that exist across a wide spectrum of communities' (Luirink, 1998:145). These negative attitudes and practices have been legitimised by statements from African leaders, including the presidents of Namibia, Zambia, Kenya and Uganda, who have characterised homosexuality as 'unnatural', 'unAfrican' and a Western import.

Homosexuality as 'unAfrican'

A particularly hostile set of attitudinal constraints cohere around the notion that homosexuality is 'unAfrican'. This has been most crudely stated by the president of Zimbabwe, Robert Mugabe, who in mid-1995 declared that 'gays are perverts and their behaviour is worse than that of pigs' (in Luirink, 1998:iii). He said, 'They are lower than dogs and pigs, for these animals don't know homosexual behaviour' (in Luirink, 1998:51). According to Luirink, he then encouraged the population 'to take the law into its own hands, to arrest homosexuals, to report and deport them,' saying that homosexuality was 'unAfrican and in conflict with black culture' (in Luirink, 1998:51). 'Lesbianism is not part of Zimbabwean culture', he claimed (in *Star,* 24.4.1998).

A letter to the Johannesburg newspaper, the *Star*, praised Mugabe because 'he espouses and cherishes our traditions and customs. Homosexuality is an aberration to all thinking Africans and indeed to most of civilised mankind. Homosexuals are regarded as an abominable species, which must be punished and locked up, even in the United Kingdom.' The letter ends, 'Viva Robert Mugabe ... who defends our continent from satanists, sodomists and faggots' (in *Star,* 21.8.1995). According to one view, 'Mugabe is right in one sense when he accuses Westerners of thrusting a phenomenon onto Africa. It is not homosexuality as such that has been imported, but rather a set of far more open and visible expressions of it – a supposed liberation that has developed over some time in the West' (Luirink, 1998:vi).

The implication is that what has been 'imported from the West' is not homo-sexual behaviour but a homosexual identity. Among the many European myths about Africa, the myth that homosexuality is absent from African societies is one of the strongest. Murray and Roscoe (1998) expose this myth, and demonstrate that gay and lesbian sexuality is both indigenous and traditional to some 50 African societies. What is clear is that while same-sex behaviour is both widespread and diverse, the identities of 'gay' and 'lesbian' are not. Murray and Roscoe show that while homosexual behaviour is probably univer-sal, homosexual relationships, roles and identities are not. This raises difficult questions when the strength of the modern gay rights movement is precisely the assertion of a public gay identity.

201

The cohesion and transformative capacity of the gay rights movement

A crucial question concerns the impact of the gay rights clause on the gay rights movement. Has it operated to strengthen the coherence and transforma-tive capacity of the movement? Has it provided a basis for individuals to assert a gay identity and claim rights?

The cornerstone of contemporary sexual politics is the assertion of a gay identity that can be claimed and celebrated. Castells argues that the issue of self-definition is crucial. In the network society identity is no longer defined by what people do but by their self-identity – what they believe they are. Castells argues that 'gayness and lesbianism cannot be defined as sexual preferences. They are fundamentally identities ... they do not originate from some form of biological determination ... but are culturally, socially and politically constructed' (Castells, 1997:206). This contrasts sharply with the NCGLE submission on the biologically fixed and inevitable nature of homosexuality, which reduces it to a condition rather than a choice.

Gay and lesbian identities

This notion of gayness and lesbianism as 'identities' involving choices is politically dangerous and can be expected to provoke strong reactions. The American sociologist Alan Wolfe found that 'middle-class Americans most hostile to homosexuality were most willing to see it as a conscious choice ... Make something a natural condition and Americans are quick to empathise. Make it a choice and people feel that they have the similar choice in condemning it' (in *New York Times*, 2.8.1998).

There are two forms of essentialism involved in contemporary sexual politics. A biological essentialism that asserts homosexuality as an intrinsic condition is not the only problematic form this takes. There is also a form of political essentialism which asserts that the homosexual identity 'trumps' all other identities and claims that homosexuality necessarily implies an intrinsic commitment to a revolutionary and transformative agenda. This is clearly not the case. The complicated terrain of sexual politics in South Africa demonstrates the competing force of multiple identities and that gay and lesbian people can be deeply conservative, exploitative and racist. This context differs sharply from that of a rigid and exclusive identity politics.

Multiple identities in an African context

The assertion of a public gay identity is particularly problematic in an African context. To illustrate, Kendall found that the notion of 'lesbian' was not helpful in understanding female–female relationships in Basotho society. She found widespread, apparently normative, erotic relationships among Basotho women, but this (including instances of cunnilingus) was not defined as sexual, and not a single Mosotho – to Kendall's knowledge – defined herself as a lesbian. Kendall concludes that 'love between women is as natural to Southern Africa as the soil itself, but that homophobia is a Western import' (Kendall, 1998:224). She emphasises that Basotho society has not constructed a social category 'lesbian'. Basotho women define sexual activity in such a way that makes lesbianism linguistically inconceivable. As one informant told Kendall, 'You can't have sex unless somebody has a koai [penis].' Kendall comments, 'Lillian Faderman's observation that "a narrower interpretation of what constitutes erotism permitted a broader expression of erotic behaviour (in the eighteenth century) since it was not considered inconsistent with virtue" makes sense here … No koai, no sex means that women's ways of expressing love, passion or joy in each other are neither immoral nor suspect' (Kendall, 1998:233). 'The need for legitimacy only arises in cultures (like my own) in which love between women has been pathologised or made illegitimate' (Kendall, 1998:237). This implies a very different form of sexual politics to that of 'the North'.

By the 1990s there were organisations of lesbians and gay men in many black townships throughout Southern Africa. But there has been a frequent clash of different discordant identities, and racial differences cut across a unifying gay identity. For example, one informant reported, 'in the end I only feel at home with women, with black lesbian women specifically. I don't feel at all at ease with white lesbians' (in Luirink, 1998:71).

Black lesbians experience a particular oppression. Luirink describes an interview with Tiny Machida, 28 years old and chairperson of GALZ (Gays and Lesbians of Zimbabwe), who experienced conflict with her family over her sexuality. Her father threw her out of the house when he found her in bed with a girlfriend, and she lived on the streets for over a year. She explained her parents' response in terms of 'it is their culture'. 'As in the case of Simon Nkoli, Tina Machida's family dragged her from one *nyanga* to the next. The one burnt stones to steam out evil spirits, another prescribed medicinal herbs. A third pushed her in a dam to wash "it" off' (Luirink, 1998:89, 70).

Vimbela illustrates the penalties which traditional African society can impose on lesbians. She describes a public whipping ordered by a Transkeian chief: 'I don't remember how many … lashings I received; all I remember is crying and screaming with pain as the whole village jeered at me.' She describes having 'very little contact with white gays' (Vimbela, 1994:194, 196).

For Thembi Mandla the major problem for black lesbians is African culture and tradition. 'A woman is expected to conform and is silenced into a wife-and-mother role ... White lesbians do not face the same problems. They do not have to grapple with African culture.' Mandla said black lesbians also face problems with straight black men. 'Their manhood is threatened and they are scared we might take their women' (in Daniels, 1997:17).

Several key informants emphasised these racial differences in the gay and lesbian experience in South Africa. For instance, 'Racism is huge. Black and white lesbians know nothing about each other. There is no social space for black and white lesbians to chill' (Sharon Cooper, Interview, 2001). It would seem that a lesbian 'identity' takes very different forms, with many white middle-class women still 'closeted', younger white lesbians claiming bisexuality in a 'rave' culture that is saturated with drugs and 'clubbing', and a black lesbian culture that involves rigid role-playing and distinctions between 'butch' and 'femme'.

The latter is illustrated by the social dynamics in the Namibian township of Katutura, where a lesbian football team – the Rainbow Warriors – has been formed. Members wear men's clothes, openly try to pick up women and visit gay-friendly shebeens. They call themselves the 'lesbian men', their partners are 'the ladies'. The strict roles are of great importance for this group. A woman cannot love another woman, so she becomes a 'man' (Maurick, 1999:29). They even wear men's underwear and aftershave.

Social cleavages

A public gay culture is slowly emerging in Southern Africa, but reflects these deep social cleavages. According to one informant, 'The Johannesburg clubs like Stardust are racially mixed but white-dominated. Some clubs are racist and discriminate against blacks, they turn them away. Also they discriminate in class terms. Heartland has a R200 membership fee and you're only allowed in if you're a member ... Also women do not always feel welcome. At the Skyline in Hillbrow women were not allowed in, whether they were lesbians or not' (Informant 4, Interview, 2001).

But there are other indications of a more inclusive, public and assertive gay identity emerging in scattered and embryonic forms. A Gay and Lesbian Pride Parade has taken place in Johannesburg every year since 1990. Its numbers and increasing representativeness chart the increasingly visible, assertive and public presence of the movement. The 12th Gay and Lesbian Pride Event that took place in Johannesburg in October 2001 involved some 25 000 people, according to the organisers. This is in strong contrast to the first march in 1990, organised by GLOW, when 800 marchers were provided with paper bags to put over their heads (De Waal, 1999).

The challenge is to define a lesbian and gay identity as an inclusive African identity. As Cameron and Gevisser write, 'there is no single, essential gay identity in South Africa. What has passed for "the gay experience" has often been that of white, middle-class, urban men' (Cameron and Gevisser, 1994:3). The divisions of gender, race and class which still scar South African society militate against any powerful, representative gay and lesbian movement developing. These social cleavages mean that there is no 'common experience of sexual oppression', as Jara and Lapinsky claim (1988:1).

Furthermore, the post-apartheid state's commitment to gay and lesbian rights could be shallow. 'While South African lesbians and gays have achieved unprecedented political recognition and legal protection, the rationale for these developments appears to draw more on Western ideals of social justice and human rights than on claims about traditional acceptance and social roles for same-sex patterns' (Murray and Roscoe, 1998:278). However, the same could be said of many of the policy innovations of the post-apartheid state, for example those relating to gender equality.

Also, there is uncertainty about the strength of the commitment to gay and lesbian rights within the ANC. While Nelson Mandela has emphasised that 'Equality is for everybody', Winnie Mandela played on township homophobia as part of her defence when she was accused of kidnapping a young African boy. She maintained that it was a 'rescue attempt' from a white priest accused of having sexually abused a number of African boys. A banner outside her trial in 1991 stated that 'Homosex is not in black culture'. So, 'The status of gay and lesbian issues in the broader movement for democracy remains tenuous: gay issues continue to be seen as both frivolous and "unAfrican"' (Cameron and Gevisser, 1994:4). It could be that since Cameron and Gevisser wrote, the criticism has strengthened as a response to the assertion of a public, chosen, gay identity.

Conclusion

Writing five years after the gay rights clause, it seems clear that its most lasting impact should be strengthening the capacity of the gay rights movement to promote both formal and substantive equality, and to claim diversity of sexual orientation as part of South Africa's 'Rainbow Nation'. Most informants agreed on the significance of the clause and the important role the NCGLE played in its achievement. However, the NCGLE is now disbanded and, overall, informants were divided on the status of the gay rights movement. 'No, in South Africa the gay rights movement, perhaps not even a movement, just a set of initiatives, was and is socially conservative' (Informant 5, Interview, 2001). 'The lesbians are the radicals now. The boys are leaving the struggle. They're an elite living privileged lives within the structures of patriarchalism. The people protecting the Equality Clause are a handful of under-resourced people, mainly lesbians' (Sharon Cooper, Interview, 2001). Another informant maintained that 'It is the lack of a historical perspective and an insistence on a rigid, inappropriate identity politics that is weakening the gay rights movement and threatening the gains that have been made' (Key informant 8, Interview, 2001).

Informants were also divided on the transformative capacity of the movement. Transformation involves addressing the deep structures which maintain inequality. This has two aspects: recognition and redistribution. While redistribution involves changing access to income, power and resources, recognition involves 'upwardly revaluing disrespected identities and the cultural products of maligned groups' (Fraser, 1997:15). These two aspects have yet to be integrated into a comprehensive political project in South Africa.

The assertion of rights involves expanding conceptions of humanity and citizenship. In this respect Kevan Botha maintains that 'the claiming of a new identity, based on justice and rights, is what defines empowerment ... Gay rights is empowering. It involves the claim to full citizenship and full moral standing' (Interview, 2001). But the justice of rights must be linked to the justice of redistribution. 'The majority of gay people in South Africa are poor. They remain marginalised from the social and economic mainstream and live outside of the emerging gay rights movement' (Jara and Lapinsky, 1998:8). 'At the moment we see a Western rave culture. This is not the case for the majority of lesbians and gays in South Africa. Here the majority are poor, black and female. And their issues are not addressed by the lesbian and gay movement' (Mazibuko Jara, in *Mail and Guardian,* 17.9.1999).

Many informants stressed the radical shift in sexual politics in South Africa in recent years, from the largely white, 'apolitical' and accommodationist single-issue politics to an assertion of gay rights as human rights. This human rights discourse is strongly connected to a feminist discourse on sexual freedom, but it can be mobilised to promote an assimilationist politics. The emphasis on individual rights for gay men and lesbians to be 'just the same' as heterosexuals in terms of the rights to marriage, medical benefits, child custody and military service, is socially very conservative. As Tony Kushner (1994:4, 5) writes, 'it is entirely conceivable that we will one day live miserably in a thoroughly ravaged world in which lesbians and gay men can marry and serve openly in the army and that's it'. His concern is that 'Capitalism, after all, can absorb a lot. Poverty, war, alienation, environmental destruction, unequal development, the fetishisation of violence – these things are key to the successful functioning of the free market. Homophobia is not; the system could certainly accommodate demands for equal rights for homosexuals without danger to itself'.

At the end of the day the challenge is for the gay rights movement to move beyond a socially conservative and surface homogenisation to promote a revolutionary agenda. To do so means fighting for equality while resisting the notion that equality equals sameness, as well as connecting the justice of rights to the justice of redistribution.

This assertion of difference is central to the new Left that is emerging globally, with its animating notions of human potential and social justice. It is a reinvention of the Left that involves new formations in place of traditional communist parties and emphasis on the factory floor. The new Left activism includes historically oppressed groups such as gay and lesbian activists as well as feminists and environmentalists.

The reinvented Left emphasises the realisation of human potential and the diverse ways involved in such realisation. Where the old, traditional Left asserted class relations, control of the factory or the state, the new, reinvented Left promotes wider individual possibilities such as the expression of indigenous cultures and languages as well as the expression of sexuality. In practical terms, this implies a form of 'coalition' or 'alliance' politics that is structured on the recognition of difference.

The gay rights movement in South Africa is a model of this, and contains the promise of a cohesive and transformative sexual politics. It is one aspect of

South Africa as a post-colonial society that is reinventing itself. However, the gains of the movement are fragile and in danger of being swamped by other issues such as AIDS and poverty.

Works cited

Botha, Kevan (1996). 'Profile.' *Equality*, 3.

Botha, Kevan and Cameron, Edwin (1997). 'South Africa' in West, Donald and Green, Richard (eds). *Socio-Legal Control of Homosexuality: A Multinational Comparison.* New York: Plenum.

Cameron, Edwin and Gevisser, Mark (eds) (1994). *Defiant Desire: Gay and Lesbian Lives in South Africa.* Johannesburg: Ravan Press.

Cameron, Edwin (1997). 'Sexual orientation and the Constitution: a test case for human rights.' *South African Law Journal*, 450, 472.

Castells, Manuel (1997). *The Power of Identity.* Massachusetts: Blackwells.

Centre for Development and Enterprise (1999). *Policy Analysis.* Johannesburg: Centre for Development and Enterprise.

Charney, Craig (1995). 'Between ignorance and tolerance: South African public attitudes on issues concerning gays, lesbians and AIDS.' Unpublished report, Johannesburg: AIDS Law Project, Wits.

Cock, Jacklyn (1991). *Colonels and Cadres. War and Gender in South Africa.* Cape Town: Oxford University Press.

Daniels, Glenda (1997). 'Slow coming out for black lesbians.' *The Star*, 20.11.1997.

Daniels, Glenda (1998). 'Straight talking.' *The Star*, 3.4.1998.

Department of Defence (2000). 'Result of the Study on the Integration of Gays and Lesbians in the DOD.' Unpublished paper.

De Waal, Shaun (1999). 'Marching from fear to fun.' *Mail & Guardian*, 17.8.1999.

Fine, Derek and Nicol, Julia (1994). 'The lavender lobby: working for lesbian and gay rights within the liberation movement' in Cameron, Edwin and Gevisser, Mark (eds). *Defiant Desire: Gay and Lesbian Lives in South Africa.* Johannesburg: Ravan Press.

Fraser, Nancy (1997). *Justice Interruptus: Critical Reflections on the 'Postsocialist' Condition.* New York: Routledge.

Gevisser, Mark. 1994. 'A different fight for freedom' in Cameron, Edwin and Gevisser, Mark (eds). *Defiant Desire: Gay and Lesbian Lives in South Africa.* Johannesburg: Ravan Press.

Jara, Mazibuko and Lapinsky, Sheila (1998). 'Forging a representative gay liberation movement in South Africa.' *Development Update*, 2: 2.

Kendall, Jane (1998). 'When a woman loves a woman in Lesotho' in Murray, Stephen and Roscoe, Will (eds). *Boy–Wives and Female Husbands: Studies of African Homosexualities*. New York: St Martin's Press.

Krouse, Matthew (1994). 'The Arista Sisters, September 1984: a personal account of army drag' in Cameron, Edwin and Gevisser, Mark (eds). *Defiant Desire: Gay and Lesbian Lives in South Africa*. Johannesburg: Ravan Press.

Kushner, Tony (1994). 'Gay rights in the US.' *The Nation*, 19.4.1994.

Luirink, Bart (1998). *Moffies: Gay Life in Southern Africa*. Cape Town: David Philip.

Maurick, Madeline (1999). 'Lesbian life in a Namibian town.' *Mail & Guardian*, 17.9.1999.

Meshoe, Kenneth (1996). South African Broadcasting Corporation, interview, 29 May.

Murray, Stephen and Roscoe, Will (eds) (1998). *Boy–Wives and Female Husbands. Studies of African Homosexualities*. New York: St Martin's Press.

National Coalition for Gay and Lesbian Equality (1995). Submission to the Constitutional Assembly.

Nkoli, Simon (1987). 'Gay rights in apartheid South Africa.'*Capital Gay*, 9.10.1987.

Stacey, Judith and Biblarz, Timothy (2001). '(How) does the sexual orientation of parents matter?' *American Sociological Review*, 66.

Streek, Barry (2002). 'Equal rights for gay soldiers', *Mail & Guardian* 11.1.2002.

Tatchell, Peter (1987). 'ANC rejects gay rights.' *Labour Briefing*, 49, October.

Tshwete, Steve (2000). South African Broadcasting Corporation, interview, 11 September.

Van Zyl, Mikki, De Gruchy, Jeanelle, Lapinsky, Sheila, Lewin, Simon and Reid, Graeme (1999). *The aVersion Project: Human Rights Abuses of Gays and Lesbians in the SADF by Health Workers during the Apartheid Era*. Cape Town: Simply Said and Done.

Vimbela, Vera with Olivier, Mike (1994). 'Climbing on her shoulders: an interview with Umtata's first lesbian' in Cameron, Edwin and Gevisser, Mark (eds). *Defiant Desire: Gay and Lesbian Lives in South Africa*. Johannesburg: Ravan Press.

The author would like to acknowledge the insightful comments and support of Dr Alison Bernstein.

210

THE EQUALITY FOUNDATION

P O Box 87722·
Houghton
2041

Telephone: 834 1073
614 7548

The Technical Committee on Fundamental
Rights During the Transition
World Trade Centre
Kempton Park

SUBMISSION TO THE TECHNICAL COMMITTEE ON FUNDAMENTAL RIGHTS DURING THE TRANSITION

Pursuant to publication of the Fifth Progress Report (11 June 1993) of the Technical Committee on Fundamental Rights During the Transition, on behalf of The Equality Foundation we make the following submissions in relation to the proposed formulation of the right to equality before the law (Article 2).

A principal aim of The Equality Foundation is to ensure that the principle of non-discrimination is firmly entrenched in a constitutional state. Race, gender, sexual orientation, ethnic origin, age, colour, disability, religion, creed and conscience are vivid examples of conditions which have given rise to discriminatory practices in the apartheid state. The elimination of discrimination in all its forms, and in particular those mentioned above, is essential to the establishment of a state founded on law.

1.   **Enumeration of protected conditions**

While we appreciate and understand the rationale for the Technical Committee's wish to omit an enumeration of protected conditions, and for giving special recognition to gender and race, there are cogent reasons for dealing specifically with sexual orientation:-

1.1.   in our view, the Technical Committee ought to take note of the great degree of consensus which has already been achieved in the draft bills of rights submitted by certain of the negotiating parties, in particular those of the Government, the ANC, the IFP and the DP.

X   CONCLUSION

I have argued that the debate about non-discrimination against gays and lesbians is a test of our integrity and good faith in the constitution-drafting process. Precisely because neither power nor specific resource allocation are at issue, sexual orientation becomes a moral focus in our constitution-making. There is little cost to the majority if non-discrimination against gays and lesbians is to be entrenched except the disavowal of ignorance and irrational prejudice. Conversely, the claims of the gay and lesbian minority to be protected under law are strong: their history of oppression and their still vulnerable position place them uniquely at the mercy of the majority. Their entitlement to constitutional shielding is therefore strong.

The unifying theme of the last three years in our country, despite the awful carnage that has occurred and what seem to be frequent lapses of good faith, has been our search for transformation. As a nation we are laden with the guilt and shame and inhibitions of the past. In our commitment to creating a common future for ourselves we have at least a chance to embrace new principles of dealing with each other.

In the past we South Africans signalled to each other through our differences - the distinctions of race, sex, colour, creed and religion that separated us. The debate about non-discrimination on the basis of sexual orientation offers an invitation to us deal not in this coinage but in something different.

William Butler Yeats said, 'We make out of the quarrel with others, rhetoric; but of the quarrel with ourselves, poetry.' We have quarrelled with each other enough in this country: we have quarrelled over race and stigma and hatred and separation. Let us quarrel now rather each with ourself in examining our own deepest prejudices. And from that quarrel, may the constitution we produce consist not of rhetoric, but of poetry in action.

WE MUST CLAIM OUR CITIZENSHIP!
REPORT OF THE INTERIM EXECUTIVE COMMITTEE (IEC) OF THE NATIONAL COALITION FOR GAY AND LESBIAN EQUALITY: DECEMBER '94-DECEMBER '95

1 INTRODUCTION

Throughout the world people who have fought for lesbian and gay equality are watching South Africa. We have a tremendous opportunity and responsibility to win equal rights for ourselves and generations to come. Elsewhere, the international lesbian and gay movement has faced a battle for every small legal or social reform. Based on their hard won victories and their defeats, we have the opportunity to win full legal equality. In almost every country, lesbian and gay people have been denied equality under the law. The rights to---education, housing, work, bear and rear children, marry, equal access to social services and justice---remain rights to be won. In addition, the sodomy laws, mainly used against gay men, have produced the belief in society that we are criminals. This affects the visibility of every gay and lesbian person. Not only are lesbian and gay people denied rights and visibility, we are also criminalised.

Under apartheid, the vast majority of our people faced the same oppression. In the same way as African, coloured and Indian people were excluded from *citizenship* rights in South Africa, lesbian and gay people are denied citizenship throughout the world. Recent attacks by Zimbabwe's head of state and his call to arrest gays and lesbians demonstrates the power of those forces opposed to equality.

South Africa's transition to democracy and the inclusion of sexual orientation in the equality clause gave lesbian and gay people full citizenship for the first time in our history. *We must now claim our citizenship*. In the collective memory of lesbian and gay people, the year 1995 will represent a turning point in our history. So far, the campaign of the National Coalition for Gay and Lesbian Equality to retain the sexual orientation clause in the final Constitution has been a tremendous success. In the draft of the final Constitution, sexual orientation remains in the Equality Clause. In May 1996, the final decision to include this clause in its entirety will be voted on in the Constitutional Assembly. However, until the clause is in the final Constitution, and the final Constitution is in our hands, the gay and lesbian community must remain united and mobilised. This is the first step to claim our citizenship.

2 WHERE DID WE START?

In December 1994, 80 lesbians and gay people from across the country formed the National Coalition for Gay and Lesbian Equality (NCGLE). Unlike the Stonewall Group in Britain or the National Gay and Lesbian Task Force in the USA who have many years of experience and organising at a national level, the 1NCGLE had much to learn. We had no national organisation. We had no experience of organising gays and lesbians on a national scale. In fact, the majority of organisations in the NCGLE had no experience of working together. The NCGLE had no money, no office and no staff. At the outset, the NCGLE defined its objectives simply and aimed to unite all organisations and individuals who supported the sexual orientation clause in the constitution. This task appeared to be impossible.

3 WHAT WERE OUR OBJECTIVES?

The NCGLE set itself four major objectives. They included the need to

3.1 Retain sexual orientation in the Equality Clause of the final Constitution;

3.2 Campaign for the decriminalisation of same-sex conduct;

3.3   Commence constitutional litigation challenging discrimination against same-sex relationships.

3.4   Train a representative gay and lesbian leadership on the basis of racial and gender equality; and

Throughout the year, we have focused on the lobbying campaign and fundraising. Discussion on training and legal rights issues are developed in the section on the way forward.

4   WHAT IS THE NATURE OF THE COALITION?

The NCGLE is open to every gay and lesbian organisation which agrees with the above objectives. As a *coalition*, it unites individuals who hold different political and social viewpoints. It unites organisations which have a predominantly black membership with those who have only white members. It includes organisations which have only women members and organisations with a predominantly male membership. It has strong organisations and weak organisations. Members of the coalition include poor unemployed township youth who remain marginalised and invisible, and affluent, visible and dominant individuals within society. The NCGLE has members in almost every province of South Africa. This diversity is the strength of the coalition. And, to ensure that the clause in its entirety remains in the Constitution, this diversity of people and politics is essential.

5   UNDERSTANDING OUR POWER

The inclusion of sexual orientation in the interim Constitution had very little to do with the strength or mobilisation of the lesbian and gay community in South Africa. The Equality Clause is the result of

*   a commitment to human rights and a constitutional order by the ANC

*   the coming out of Simon Nkoli and the creation of GLOW

*   a degree of lobbying at Kempton Park by the Equality Foundation and earlier by a very small group of activists in OLGA

In fact, the lesbian and gay movement is a very weak movement and before the launch of the NCGLE, was completely unco-ordinated, divided and not a political force. The gay and lesbian movement remained predominantly suburban and white. This is still borne out by the key events of the lesbian and gay community. Despite their tremendous success, the Johannesburg Pride Parade and the national Out in Africa Film Festival still attract a predominantly white and middle class gay and lesbian population. Race, class and gender inequalities are the key obstacles to the development of a movement with power. These issues affected the strategic considerations of the lobbying campaign.

6   STRATEGIC CONSIDERATIONS IN THE LOBBYING CAMPAIGN

In developing its strategy to retain sexual orientation, the Interim Executive Committee (IEC) of the NCGLE faced some of the following obstacles:

*   a weak, non-existent lesbian and gay political movement;

*   an urgent set of deadlines determined by the Constitutional Assembly;

*   a vocal, hard-line political opposition in Parliament (ACDP); and

*   lack of infrastructure and finance.

The IEC unanimously decided to focus the equality campaign on a limited intervention, directed solely at lobbying the Constitutional Assembly (CA). We refused to raise the contentious political issues in the media or in the CA. In our view these would undermine the political message which everyone understands: "Equality for All!" In the view of the IEC, issues such as marriage, adoption, gays in the army could divide our weak ranks and unite the opposition against the clause. Undoubtedly, a campaign which focused on these issues would have allowed conservatives in the ANC and the Government of National Unity to abandon their support for the Equality Clause. Further, a campaign of civil disobedience would have been inappropriate *because* the ANC is programmatically committed to lesbian and gay equality. Our campaign had to focus on strengthening the understanding and arguments of our allies in the Constitutional Assembly.

The major political aim of the lobbying campaign was to neutralise or to isolate the African Christian Democratic Party from the other parties. To do this, every political party, including the Freedom Front, was lobbied to ensure that they did not support the reactionary positions of the ACDP.

In the development of the NCGLE strategy, the IEC faced criticism from many individuals and organisations. Criticisms included arguments on how best to win the clause, the tactics and slogans to use, and, the degree of "mass" participation. At that stage, we had only experience to go on. In 1994, the Cape Town Pride March had less than 300 people, the Johannesburg Pride March had 3 000 but less than 10% were people of colour and Durban had less than 100 people at its March. And, of course, we did not know the strength of the opposition. Months later, the debates on whether to mobilise "mass" support and how to do this, whether or not to organise demonstrations and marches, still remain with us.

The Coalition also faced the spectre of mass mobilisation by the religious right. This threat turned into a reality when the ACDP mobilised 10 000 people to march on the Constitutional Assembly against the "secular state" and for a "Christian Bill of Rights". In developing a lobbying campaign, the IEC employed Kevan Botha as the national lobbyist and Clayton Wakeford as the lobbying manager at the Cape Town office. Sheila Lapinsky was mandated by the IEC to co-ordinate the lobbying campaign.

7   THE LOBBYING CAMPAIGN

Lobbying was organised through teams. Initially 42 people attended the lobbying process meetings and many became actively involved in the lobbying process. In addition to IEC members, individuals and members of every Coalition affiliate in Cape Town participated in lobbying members of the Theme Committee on Fundamental Rights and other key political leaders. Of the members of the Theme Committee lobbied, 94% were supportive, with detractors comprised solely of ACDP members.

The Coalition made two researched submissions to the Constitutional Assembly relating to equality. The first submission argued for the inclusion of sexual orientation, referring to the past history of discrimination and legislative exclusion. It focused on the submissions by the ACDP calling for a "biblical" bill of rights. The second submission placed the South African Constitution in an international context, citing the numerous instances of sexual orientation being recognised in international laws and highlighting the interpretations of various international human rights conventions which favoured sexual orientation.

4

8   WHAT HAVE WE ACHIEVED IN THE LOBBYING CAMPAIGNS?

The following is a brief summary of the Coalition's lobbying work and achievements in 1995:

8.1   The Coalition organised lobbying teams to ensure that the politicians making decisions about the Bill of Fundamental Rights were properly briefed and that they had sufficient information on gay and lesbian issues.

8.2   42 Coalition members attended the lobbying process meetings and most became actively involved in the lobbying process. On average, each delegation was made up of 55% African and 26% female members.

8.3   Before the 6 June debate in the Theme Committee on Fundamental Rights, we lobbied 74% of the members either individually or collectivley. Of the Theme Committee members lobbied, 94% agreed to be supportive of the clause, with our detractors consisting solely of members of the fundamentalist African Christian Democratic Party (ACDP). Remarkably, the lobbying team was able to swing the opinion of even the Freedom Front, who ultimately agreed not to oppose the Clause.

8.4   We made two researched submissions to the Constitutional Assembly relating to equality for gay and lesbian people.

8.5   Apart from the lobbying process, we mounted a highly visible campaign in Cape Town for the Equality Debate. Posters supporting equality for all, endorsed by the Black Sash, Lawyers for Human Rights, Women's National Coalition, Cape Mental Health, Human Rights Committee, Women's Health Project, Rape Crisis, AIDS Consortium, Disabled People South Africa and the Coalition have been used nationally, with particularly good effect in Cape Town prior to the Equality Debate.

8.6   In addition, our mobilisation efforts resulted in over 400 supportive letters -- from across the country, from people of every background, in numerous languages -- to the Constitutional Assembly. These are contrasted with the 6 500 petitions and duplicated mantras of the Religious Right who demanded the removal of sexual orientation. The supportive letters make for emotional reading. They make heartfelt appeals for recognition and protection. They tell stories of discrimination and prejudice, and some relate tales of enduring courage and solidarity. These submissions include the voices of prominent South Africans, notably Archbishop Desmond Tutu, Bishop Stanley Magoba and Dr. Mamphele Ramphele. The Constitutional Assembly's Theme Committee recommended the retention of 'sexual orientation' in the equality clause, despite the objection of the ACDP.

8.7   The lobbying and political intervention of the Coalition has affected the major reformulation of government policy in virtually every department. These are some examples of submissions, legislative and policy changes:

          The White Paper on Social Welfare (we submitted comment to the Department of Social Welfare regarding the needs of lesbians and gays, especially lesbian and gay youth)

     *   Position papers by the Independent Broadcasting Authority (we made a submission to the public hearings of the IBA)

     *   The National Truth and Reconciliation Act

     *   Gauteng's Education Bill, including special submissions made by GLOW on this Bill

* The Parliamentary Standing Committee on Defence

* The South African Police Services Act

* Curriculum development for diversity training within the Police Service

8.8 President Nelson Mandela met with a Coalition and Glow delegation of Sir Ian McKellen, Simon Nkoli and Phumi Mtetwa in February and reaffirmed his commitment to equality for all as a fundamental ANC principle.

These represent significant achievements in the first year of the Coalition's existence, of which we can be justifiably proud.

9 LABOUR RELATIONS ACT

One of the most important victories for the Coalition is the inclusion of sexual orientation in the Unfair Labour Practice Schedule of the new Labour Relations Act. For the first time, it is expressly unlawful for employers to discriminate against gay and lesbian people when hiring, promoting, transferring or dismissing an employee in any job.

10 THE ZIMBABWE CAMPAIGN

The Coalition lead the South African opposition to Robert Mugabe and the Zimbabwean government's homophobia. Gays and lesbians picketed the Zimbabwe trade missions in Johannesburg and Cape Town, as well as the arrival of Robert Mugabe for the Southern African Development Community at the World Trade Centre near Johannesburg. This was the most significant political mobilisation of the gay and lesbian community and hundreds of people across the country were involved in the campaign.

Most significantly, national and international political commentators noted that the gay and lesbian lobby placed human rights in Africa on the agenda. The campaign showed that regional coordination among human rights organisations in Southern Africa was essential to developing a human rights culture. The Zimbabwe campaign drew favourable press coverage and every major newspaper supported the Coalition, the Equality Clause and the right of GALZ to organize.

11 TRAINING

The IEC mandate at the December 1994 launch committed the national coalition to 'training'. This mandate was intended to ensure that the lobbying efforts of the coalition were not undertaken by an elite group but involved, as far as possible, the membership of the coalition. Also, it was understood that the momentum provided by a national lobbying campaign could be useful for rebuilding and revitalising some of the coalition's members, and for developing a future majority-African leadership for a national movement of lesbians, gays and bisexuals.

The coalition ran one national training workshop in the course of the year. It proved very difficult to follow-up with effective regional training, and any training activities, taken up a regional level were sporadic and not greatly effective. The national training workshop was, however, an intensely exciting event. Rank and file members of coalition affiliates were able to meet each other and to talk about what could be done nationally to ensure full citizenship for lesbians and gays. Limited success was achieved in the training which accompanied the lobbying visits in the Western Cape, but this did not result in any strengthening of gay and lesbian organisations in the provinces. The absence of a full-time strategic programme

6

based on the needs of affiliate organisations undermined the training. This needs to be remedied in reassessing the development goals of the Coalition.

12   PROVINCIAL COALITIONS

Provincial coalitions were launched in five provinces: Eastern Cape, Free State, Gauteng, Kwazulu-Natal and Western Cape. In Gauteng, more than 400 people attended the provincial launch on 21 March 1995. Provincial co-ordinators were co-opted onto the IEC. Regrettably, provincial coalitions have not mobilised significant support for the clause or the NCGLE. In developing the work for the NCGLE next year, we propose that the following questions be discussed at the provincial conferences.

12.1   How have the provincial coalitions managed to coordinate the work of the coalition?

12.2   Have the provincial coalitions served as a useful forum for coordinating other activities in the province?

12.3   Do the provincial coalitions make local organisations stronger or weaker?

12.4   Do the provincial coalitions make the coalitions stronger or weaker?

12.5   Should we continue the strategy of working through provincial coalitions?

12.6   How should they function and how should they be constituted?

A position on these issues should form a part of mandate of the provincial delegation to the national conference in December.

13   FINANCE AND FUNDRAISING

Lesbian and gay concerns in South Africa, including: human rights, culture, training and development, developing leadership, recreation and unemployment, have never enjoyed significant financial backing from conventional donor sources or by lesbians and gays themselves. The inclusion of 'sexual orientation' in the equality clause and the launch of the Coalition presented a unique opportunity for funding gay and lesbian issues in South Africa. Despite initial scepticism, the prospect of being the first country to include such a clause in its constitution and the advance that this represents for human rights internationally, has enabled the coalition to raise sufficient funds to secure its operations and proceed with the mandate from its founding meeting to secure the clause in the final constitution.

An ad-hoc grouping, affiliated to the coalition and calling itself the Funders Forum, was convened by gay men who worked in development funding for the purposes of coordinating efforts to access money from dedicated education and development funding sources. The members of this group, however, were convinced that sustaining a campaign to raise significant funding in the longer term depended on our ability to demonstrate that ordinary lesbians and gays and straight supporters, inside South Africa, were able to raise substantial funding--through their own efforts! A growing local stream of funding is essential if we are to build a strong funding organisation which will be able to support the activities, both political and social, of lesbians, bisexuals and gay men well into the future. The first part of this strategy has paid off so far as the following breakdown of funds received by 31st October, 1995 illustrates:

217

Interfund - New Initiatives Fund	70,000.00
Liberty Life Foundation	72,171.00
Joseph Rowntree Charitable Trust	132,962.00
Equality Foundation	100,000.00
Equality Foundation (Sir Ian McKellen)	43,343.50
Fundraising - General	16,690.40
Monthly subscriptions and donations	11,382.05
	448,548.95

The fundraising activities, as at 31st October, amount to R 73,415.95. This represents 16.36% of all income generated. However, if the recent R 400 000 grant from the dutch-based HIVOS is taken into account, this percentage shrinks to a far less impressive 8.65% It is the opinion of the Funders Forum and the convenor the IEC, that this represents a superb achievement. However, unless our local, community-based fundraising attempts are taken seriously by all coalition members, we will not make the most of this opportunity which has presented itself. This will seriously limit our financial capacity in the mid to long term.

Of the locally-raised funds, subscriptions and events remain key, while the bulk of was raised from the McKellen visit 7 other events and xx subscribers raised 38% of the total. We are convinced that only these activities realise any real long-term strength, for they represent the support and involvement of ordinary lesbians and gays. This aspect of fundraising needs to be urgently prioritised in the new year. It is particularly regrettable that some members and leading organisations in the coalition do not share this conviction and make no financial contribution to building a strong and lasting national movement.

14   MEDIA

At the outset, the NCGLE maintained that a low media profile in the *lobbying campaign* was essential to set the agenda on the debate. However, the Zimbabwe campaign changed the media profile of the Coalition in the press and electronic media. In addition, the NCGLE has appeared on every major radio and television programme in the country.

Instead of a monthly newsletter, the Coalition has only brought out two editions of *Equality* over nine months. This is partially due to the lack of professional attention to the newsletter and the fact that every IEC member has a full-time job. A professional media campaign should be designed. The IEC has asked Sue Valentine to produce such a plan. The most successful popularising media are the "Scrap Unjust Laws" and the "Equality for ALL" posters produced for the march and the NCGLE t-shirts.

15   ADMINISTRATION

The most remarkable feat of the NCGLE has been the ability to produce an efficient national administration with no managerial support. This included establishing two national offices, minutes for every meeting (and there were hundreds) and financial administration. In this effort, the work of Graeme Reid, Clayton Wakeford, Jill Well-beloved and a range of volunteers and part-time staff has been magnificent. The NCGLE also expresses it appreciation to Douglas and Velcich for their support and meticulous care of the financial administration.

8

16   WHAT IS THE FUTURE OF THE COALITION?

In mapping the road forward for the NCGLE, the IEC considered at least three possibilities:

First, we considered the possibility of closing the NCGLE at the end of this year. This option was unanimously rejected. The political authority gained by the NCGLE at a national political level is key to retaining the Equality Clause in its entirety;

A second option, to continue the NCGLE's current structure was also rejected because the majority of our affiliates are not actively involved in the campaign. In addition, the NCGLE must facilitate the development of a lesbian and gay movement in South Africa which can claim citizenship;

The third option is that the National Coalition establish projects to cater for the development, human rights and lobbying needs of all our affiliates.

The IEC recommends that we take up the third option. The following recommendations are for discussion at the provincial conferences. Provincial conferences are requested to provide a broad, in-principle, mandate for the discussion at the national conference.

17   RECOMMENDATION ON THE FUTURE OF THE NCGLE

The IEC suggests that the NCGLE continues as a national body open to every lesbian, gay, bisexual and trans-gendered organisation which subscribes to the Equality Clause in the Constitution and the four objectives adopted at the Founding Conference in December 1994. The IEC recommends that the functions of the NCGLE should be based on lobbying, networking, co-ordination, as well as development and the promotion of human rights. The NCGLE should retain the political networking, co-ordination and lobbying functions and establish two projects on development and human rights.

17.1   NETWORKING, CO-ORDINATION AND LOBBYING

The newly elected IEC should become the executive of the NCGLE. The executive should be a small, effective body of not more than seven members. From the experience of the last year, the IEC recommends that networking and co-ordination of lobbying efforts should constitute the primary function of the NCGLE national office. The national office will be based in Soweto and employ a full-time national co-ordinator, an administrator and two interns. The Lobbying office in Cape Town should also be retained. Greater and direct contact with all affiliates should be the primary objective of the office. In this way, increased participation in lobbying and advocacy can be facilitated.

17.2   EQUAL RIGHTS PROJECT

The IEC proposes to establish a national equal rights project in 1996 to follow-on from what appears will be its successful lobbying campaign to retain the 'sexual orientation' clause in South Africa's new constitution. While the constitution is expected to be finalised by about June 1996, the NCGLE believes that it is essential to establish--from as early as January 1996--the mechanisms necessary for sustaining a process to scrap the anti-gay laws on South Africa's statute books, and to swing public opinion decisively in favour of equal rights for lesbians, bisexuals and gay men.

219

The IEC proposes that the equal rights project be a professionally based service to all organisations. It will have four main objectives:

17.2.1 To establish a commitment to gay and lesbian equality firmly and broadly within the mainstream human rights movement in South Africa, and specifically, within the professional organisations which are dedicated to human rights;

17.2.2 To develop educational and informational material for gays and lesbians and the broad public on equal rights for gays and lesbians and related issues;

17.2.3 To spearhead the process of litigation and legal reform, both through the courts and at the parliamentary level, to scrap all unjust laws against gays and lesbians, and to campaign for the specific mention of 'non-discrimination on grounds of sexual orientation' in all appropriate instances in official policy and other documents with legal standing;

17.2.4 To graft a component for legal advice and support which is accessible to all gays and lesbians, especially those who live in rural areas and urban townships, on to the existing legal and paralegal service infrastructure and to extend this service where it is practically possible to do so. (This can follow the model of the AIDS Legal Network which is integrating HIV/AIDS issues in the work of organisations such as Legal Resources Centres and Lawyers for Human Rights.)

17.3 DEVELOPMENT PROJECT

One of greatest threats to winning full citizenship for all lesbians and gays, and particularly, our ability to make it permanent, is that most South Africans believe that homosexuality is unAfrican. For as long as the perception persists that most homosexuals are wealthy white men, life will be harder for township lesbians and gays. Furthermore, without the support of the majority of African people for equal rights for lesbians and gays, no one, not even the powerful, can be confident that they will ever live in a society that is free from discrimination.

The majority of lesbians and gays in South Africa are poor. They remain marginalised from the social and economic mainstream and exist separately from the emerging gay and lesbian equal rights movement--which is, in turn, poorer without them.

This understanding underpins the proposal that the National Coalition undertake a development project in 1996.

Development is a massive task. We do not imagine that we can make a fundamental difference to the urgent infrastructural tasks that exists nationally. With some modest and focused work, however, we can achieve the following things:

17.3.1 Develop a majority-African leadership for the lesbian and gay movement;

17.3.2 Assist affiliate organisations to gain access to resources from local, provincial and national government - these resources include access to housing, health-care services, education and training opportunities and so on;

17.3.3 Win greater awareness of lesbians and gays at the community level through our involvement in development work;

17.3.4 use the knowledge gained in development work to the benefit those of us who are poor;

10

The following goals will build a lesbian and gay movement which is as much a home for poor lesbians and gays as it is for those with access to employment and social services. The provincial meetings are requested to discuss the development and human rights projects. Objectives on development needs and priorities need to be agreed on at a provincial level and delegates should be mandated to raise provincial priorities at the national conference.

CONCLUSION

In a year of its existence, the NCGLE has gained tremendous experience. It has also developed a professional political campaign unmatched by any other organisation. The challenge facing the NCGLE and its leadership over the next year remains the objective to actively involve the majority of our affiliates in the tasks we have set ourselves.

221

FROM THE ANGLICAN ARCHBISHOP OF CAPE TOWN

The Most Reverend Desmond M. Tutu, D.D. F.K.C.

BISHOPSCOURT CLAREMONT CAPE 7700

TELEPHONE: (021) 761-2531
FAX: (021) 761-4193

2 June 1995

DRAFT SUBMISSION

Theme Committee Four
Constitutional Assembly
South African Parliament
Parliament Street
8001 CAPE TOWN

Dear Members of the Constitutional Assembly

Re: **The Retention of the Sexual Orientation Clause in the Bill of Rights**

Within the Church of Christ, and indeed amongst adherents of other faiths, there is much debate and difference of opinion on the question of homosexuality. The theological and ethical issues are complex and far from resolved. It is indisputable, however, that people's sexual nature is fundamental to their humanity.

The apartheid regime enacted laws upon the religious convictions of a minority of the country's population, laws which denied gay and lesbian people their basic human rights and reduced them to social outcasts and criminals in their land of birth. These laws are still on the Statute Books awaiting your decision whether or not to include gay and lesbian people in the "Rainbow People" of South Africa. It would be a sad day for South Africa if any individual or group of law-abiding citizens in South Africa were to find that the Final Constitution did not guarantee their fundamental human right to a sexual life, whether heterosexual or homosexual.

I would strongly urge you to include the sexual orientation clause in the Final Constitution.

God bless you

Yours sincerely

222

"Beloved, let us love one another, for love is of God — if there is this love among you, then all will know that you are my disciples."

9. Equality.— (1) Everyone is equal before the law and has the right to equal protection and benefit of the law.

(2) Equality includes the full and equal enjoyment of all rights and freedoms. To promote the achievement of equality, legislative and other measures designed to protect or advance persons, or categories of persons, disadvantaged by unfair discrimination may be taken.

(3) The state may not unfairly discriminate directly or indirectly against anyone on one or more grounds, including race, gender, sex, pregnancy, marital status, ethnic or social origin, colour, sexual orientation, age, disability, religion, conscience, belief, culture, language and birth.

*(4) No person may unfairly discriminate directly or indirectly against anyone on one or more grounds in terms of subsection (3). National legislation must be enacted to prevent or prohibit unfair discrimination.

(5) Discrimination on one or more of the grounds listed in subsection (3) is unfair unless it is established that the discrimination is fair.

ABOVE: Cake commissioned by Bafana Mhlanga for the 'Miss Gay 10 Years of Democracy' beauty pageant. Photographer Sabelo Mlangeni.

BELOW: Bafana Mhlanga addresses a workshop on terminology and etiquette, for the gays and lesbians of Ermelo and nearby rural towns. Wesselton, 13 March 2004.

224

Afterword

There have been gays who are being attacked. Mahlasela was attacked a few weeks ago by people who are hating gays. Toki was stabbed and was assaulted and lost his cell phone, just because he is gay. Jabu was raped and he just arrived at home naked.

You can see how difficult it is to pass through these experiences. But through it all we must celebrate our rights. They are rights and I am stressing we must exercise every right that we believe we deserve. At work don't ever let them discriminate you. At the hospital don't ever let them discriminate you. You are a human being with that dignity which deserves respect. They must not pry in your privacy. If you are gay, you do your job at work. Your private life – that's none of their business.

So today we are celebrating ten years of democracy. As the Rainbow Nation, as a diverse culture.

And don't ever set limits for yourself because you are gay. No. *uNkulunkulu* created you for a purpose. And a nice purpose. You are an apple and don't ever pretend to be a banana, because you will be a second-rate banana.

Happiness starts from you. Be honest always to your parents and to your lover. If you are not honest to your parents, you will never be honest to anyone.

Bafana Mhlanga
Speaking at 'Miss Gay 10 Years of Democracy' beauty pageant, Ermelo
29 August 2004

225

Part 3

Guide to the Gay and Lesbian Archives of South Africa

Introduction

The Collections

Guide to the Resources of the

GAY AND LESBIAN

Archives of South Africa (GALA)

GALA is an independent project of the South African History Archive Trust

GALA

Compiled and edited by Anthony Manion, Graeme Reid and Karen Martin

Gay and Lesbian Archives, Johannesburg, 2004

Introduction

The material included in Part 3 is extracted from the *Guide to the Resources of the Gay and Lesbian Archives of South Africa*, as compiled by Anthony Manion in 2004. We have selected some of the GALA collections which are directly linked to the people, events and issues in *Sex and Politics in South Africa*. Of GALA's total of 158 available collections, 53 are described here.

History of the Gay and Lesbian Archives of South Africa (GALA)

Established in 1997, GALA is an independent project of the South African History Archives (SAHA), which forms part of the Historical Papers collection based at the William Cullen Library at the University of the Witwatersrand (Wits) in Johannesburg. GALA represents a unique resource of material relating to lesbian and gay experience in Southern Africa. It is appropriate that the only lesbian and gay archive on the continent should be located in South Africa, considering that this is the first country in the world to enshrine equality on the basis of sexual orientation in its Constitution. In the light of the constitution-making process and the ensuing legal reforms, South Africa has become a focus for international and local research attention.

Recognising that gay and lesbian communities in South Africa are not homogeneous, GALA strives to reflect that diversity in the collections and by devising appropriate strategies for making the collections more accessible to the public. GALA actively seeks to focus on the histories and experiences of those communities who have been marginalised, not only on the basis of sexual orientation, but also on the grounds of race, class, gender or disability. GALA was established as a community archive that aims to serve the needs of academic research while maintaining its primary function as a repository of community histories and cultural artefacts. This dual function is reflected in GALA's location as a community archive within an academic institution.

We recognise that research is a critical function of a gay and lesbian archive in an African context. The research projects undertaken by GALA emphasise archival collections of life histories, documents, and audio and video recordings of community activities and events. As a national lesbian and gay archive, GALA also strives to collect material from a wide range of geographically dispersed lesbian and gay communities throughout Southern Africa. Our work extends beyond South Africa, and GALA actively promotes organisational linkages and research projects with activists working in other African countries.

Collection

GALA collects a wide range of material, including documents, artefacts and oral material. Like other lesbian and gay archives internationally, GALA pursues an open and flexible acquisition policy, in keeping with the concept of a community archive – this allows individual donors to participate in determining what should be preserved in the archives.

The archives have secured an extensive collection of organisational records, which mark the beginning of the process of establishing the source material for a comprehensive lesbian and gay social history in South Africa. This history sheds light on the broader processes of oppression and social transformation in South Africa and is therefore a useful tool for viewing aspects of South African history from the margins. Contractual arrangements with a number of organisations ensure that future records will be deposited with GALA. The records of the National Coalition for Gay and Lesbian Equality, the Gay and Lesbian Organisation of the Witwatersrand and the Legal Reform Movement (of the late 1960s) are some examples of important organisational collections.

GALA is engaged in an active programme of recovering existing material in other archival repositories. We have identified material in the Library of Parliament and have undertaken a research project focusing on sodomy records in the Cape Town Archives Repository. A recent significant discovery was a series of confidential files detailing police surveillance of homosexuality, which were held in the South African Police Service Archive in Pretoria. Through GALA's intervention these and other confidential files in the series have been transferred to the national archives, where they will be permanently preserved. GALA, in association with SAHA, is currently using new access to information legislation to request hitherto unavailable material on homosexuality from the Military Archives Depot in Pretoria.

Individuals are encouraged to donate personal mementoes, letters, diaries, scrapbooks and photographs to the GALA archives. These contributions, coupled with interviews, provide a unique insight into the experiences of individual lesbians and gay men and form part of the larger tapestry of community history and cultural experience.

Research

The core activity of the organisation concerns its archival collection. Research activities are necessary to consolidate, disseminate and broaden this work.

As a research centre, GALA is well placed for the use of students from South Africa and further afield. International and South African postgraduate students from a range of fields, including social work, journalism, psychology, law, fine art, geography, anthropology, history, literature and cultural studies, have made use of the archives.

Journalists, film makers, television producers, book researchers and human rights activists continue to make use of GALA. As a service to distance users, inventories are sent either via electronic or conventional mailing and copies of relevant documents are supplied to researchers. The web page is also of use to researchers. GALA fields enquiries via email, by telephone, through postal correspondence and during personal visits.

In addition to the general research facility provided by GALA, it also commissions specific research projects. Examples include a research project that focused on the experiences of gay men and lesbians in the South African military; the retrieval of state records on sodomy trials; an investigation of gender identity for African traditional healers involved in same-sex relationships; and an ongoing life history project.

Relationship with the University of the Witwatersrand

The location of GALA within Historical Papers, at Wits, serves to ensure that the collections will be preserved and maintained for posterity. While GALA is an independent project, entirely responsible for its own fundraising and receiving no financial assistance from the university, the close association with Wits means that the collections are accessible to researchers and professionally managed, and ensures the long-term preservation of the collections. GALA's location within the academy also allows GALA to act as a catalyst for the development of lesbian and gay course material at the tertiary level. And GALA has been at the forefront of stimulating new avenues of academic enquiry into sexuality in a South African context.

Contact information

The archives are located in the Historical Papers
Department of the University of the Witwatersrand
(Wits) in Johannesburg. Visitors need to proceed
to the Historical Papers Reading Room, Ground
Floor, William Cullen Library, East Campus. A full-
time GALA archivist is on hand to assist
researchers.

GALA is open to the public on weekdays from
08:30 to 17:00 (except public holidays).
Saturday morning openings can be arranged
by appointment.

Enquiries can be directed by post, telephone, fax
or email.

Postal address: The Director, GALA,
PO Box 31719, Braamfontein, 2017,
South Africa.

Telephone enquiries for the director should
be directed to (011) 717-4239.

Telephone enquiries for the archivist should
be directed to (011) 717-1963.

Fax: (011) 717-1783.
Email: gala@library.wits.ac.za.

Websites
GALA: www.wits.ac.za/gala.
Behind the Mask: www.mask.org.za
SAHA: www.wits.ac.za/saha
Historical Papers: www.wits.ac.za/histp

The Collections

APOSTLES of Civilised Vice
Papers, video recordings, photographs; 1908 to 1999; 4 boxes; inventory available

Brief historical background
Directed by Zackie Achmat and produced by Jack Lewis, the documentary *Apostles of Civilised Vice* (1999) is a social history of homosexuality in South Africa.

Scope and content
The collection is made up of two parts. The first comprises the research material for the documentary, gathered by Zackie Achmat. The second consists of a copy of the film and some production paraphernalia, including scripts.

ASSOCIATION of Bisexuals, Gays and Lesbians (ABIGALE)
Papers; 1992 to 1995; 1 box; inventory available

Brief historical background
ABIGALE was formed in Cape Town in 1992. Its membership comprised mainly urban, working-class African and coloured people. In the predominantly white gay bars and clubs in the city, racism was a major problem, and there were almost no alternatives in the townships or Cape Flats. In the absence of secure places for black and coloured gay and lesbian people to meet and express themselves, ABIGALE met an important social need. Its founding members recognised at the start that this socially supportive work would be a core component of the organisation's mission and saw it as a necessary precursor to more overtly political work. Its members came from a highly politicised background, and many drew inspiration from the experience of ACT-UP, Outrage! and Queer Nation, with their pickets, occupations and anti-assimilationist stance. (For example, successful pickets were held in Greenmarket Square and outside a gay club that discriminated against black and coloured people.) In this, ABIGALE differed from the predominantly white, middle-class organisations that had existed in Cape Town previously.

However, tensions soon developed between members who wanted ABIGALE to develop into a more actively political organisation and those members who saw it primarily as providing a safe space for socialising. This contributed to the collapse of the organisation in 1995, as did accompanying tensions over language and the dominant role played by coloured activists in the running of the organisation.

Scope and content
Organisational records of ABIGALE. Includes newsletters, press clippings, financial records and memorabilia.

AUERBACH, Margaret
Papers; 1979 to 1999; 1 box; inventory available

Scope and content
Organisational records of GLOW, press clippings, photographs and academic papers.

aVERSION Project, The
Papers; 1982 to 2001; 1 box; inventory available

Brief historical background
The aVersion Project was instituted to research stories told to South Africa's Truth and
Reconciliation Commission (TRC) about the abuse of homosexuals by health professionals in
the South African Defence Force (SADF) during the apartheid era. During the period studied,
sodomy was illegal and homosexuals could be punished by the military authorities – although
the authorities sometimes turned a blind eye to homosexuality. 'Medical' treatment was on
occasion offered as an alternative to punishment (which included detention). The project,
though, found that drug, shock and hormonal therapies were sometimes given without the
informed consent of patients, and that some suffered lasting negative effects as a result. This
was a collaborative project between GALA and the Health and Human Rights Project associated with the Department of Community Health at the University of Cape Town. This project was
supported by the Joseph Rowntree Charitable Trust. The research team for the study comprised Mikki van Zyl, Jeanelle de Gruchy, Sheila Lapinsky, Simon Lewin and Graeme Reid.
Since its completion, the findings of this project have been widely disseminated through the
media in South Africa, the UK and Canada.

Scope and content
The collection consists of a research report titled 'The aVersion Project: Human Rights Abuses
of Gays and Lesbians in the South African Defence Force by Health Workers during the
Apartheid Era' (1999) as well as the research material for this report (including interviews –
some embargoed – and background information). The collection also includes the subsequent
coverage of the report and related stories in the South African media.

BOTHA, Kevan
Records; 1986 to 1998; 5 boxes

Biographical note
Born in 1962, Kevan Botha has been active in gay and lesbian politics in South Africa since
the early 1980s, when he was a member of GASA. A lawyer by profession, Botha represented
the Equality Foundation, a trust established to promote legal equality for lesbians and gay
men in South Africa, at the Convention for a Democratic South Africa (CODESA), where he
was responsible for making submissions in the interests of lesbian and gay equality. He then
acted as parliamentary lobbyist for the NCGLE, established in 1994 to protect the inclusion of
'sexual orientation' in the Constitution, and bring legislation in line with the new Constitution.
[Adapted from Aldrich, R and Wotherspoon, G (eds). 2001. *Who's Who in Contemporary Gay
and Lesbian History from World War II to the Present Day*. London: Routledge.]

233

Scope and content

The collection reflects Botha's long involvement in lesbian and gay politics in South Africa, and includes records of GASA and the Johannesburg Gay and Lesbian Pride Parade. Botha's substantial collection of records pertaining to the Equality Foundation and the NCGLE have been transferred to the NCGLE Collection. His collection also contains a large number of legal papers on issues relating to homosexuality and family law, both local and international.

CAMERON, Edwin

Papers; 1968 to 1995; 8 boxes; inventory available

Biographical note

Edwin Cameron (b. 1953) is a respected South African advocate of human rights and labour rights. As professor of law at the University of the Witwatersrand he helped to establish the AIDS Law Project within the Centre for Applied Legal Studies, and was founding convenor of the non-government national AIDS Consortium in 1992 and a leading figure in the national AIDS Convention. He helped draft a charter of rights on HIV/AIDS, and was influential in the drafting of the 1996 South African Constitution's Bill of Rights, as well as the inclusion of sexuality in its Equality Clause. He is also the co-editor, with Mark Gevisser, of *Defiant Desire* (1994), an important study of gay and lesbian lives in South Africa. [Cameron, E and Gevisser, M (eds). 1994. *Defiant Desire: Gay and Lesbian Lives in South Africa.* Johannesburg: Ravan.] Cameron was appointed Judge of the High Court, Witwatersrand Local Division, in 1995. He was elected chair of the Council of the University of the Witwatersrand in 1998. In 1999, prior to his appointment as Acting Justice to the Constitutional Court, Cameron publicly disclosed that he was living with AIDS. In 2000 Cameron was appointed a Judge of Appeal in the Supreme Court of Appeal. [Adapted from Aldrich, R and Wotherspoon, G (eds). 2001. *Who's Who in Contemporary Gay and Lesbian History from World War II to the Present Day.* London: Routledge.]

Scope and content

The collection includes material pertaining to the history of the HIV/AIDS epidemic in South Africa. The material reflects the leading role Cameron played over the years in, amongst others, the AIDS Law Project, the non-government national AIDS Consortium and the national AIDS Convention, as well as in the compilation of a draft charter of rights on HIV/AIDS. The bulk of the material is grouped according to organisation, but in instances where it is not clear to which organisation the material might belong, it has been grouped according to the type of material (press clippings, academic articles, etc.) represented. These are listed alphabetically. The collection also includes documents on the 1985 President's Council enquiry into the Immorality Act and the 1985 GASA National Convention, as well as letters, memoranda, reports and other organisational material. There are two boxes of material on legal issues relating to homosexuality in South Africa. These include the Police Board of Enquiry that found Lt TL van Heerden guilty of conducting herself in a manner 'unbecoming to her rank' because of her lesbian relationship with a subordinate in 1984. It also includes *The State v JDB Lamprecht*, the 1989 prosecution of a well-known actor and radio personality for under-age sex with boys. There are also two boxes of material on *Defiant Desire*. This material includes letters and manuscripts that Cameron received from the individuals who were asked to contribute essays to the volume (see container list for names), his correspondence with his co-editor, letters from Ravan Press and other publishers, publication ephemera, business correspondence and financial reports, reviews of the book, congratulatory letters received after publication, and notes. The letters and manuscripts are arranged alphabetically according to name. A number of the draft manuscripts submitted by contributors are filed with their letters.

The collection also includes correspondence and organisational material documenting Cameron's activities on behalf of gay and lesbian rights in South Africa. The letters in the local and the international correspondence sections, written between 1988 and 1994, and 1992 and 1994 respectively, are arranged alphabetically according to name. Letters on corporate letterheads are filed by the name of the organisation (unless the person is not writing on behalf of the organisation). There are also notes, drafts and complete texts for a number of lectures and speeches given by Cameron on the subject of gay and lesbian and human rights, covering the period 1986 to 1994.

COHEN, Steven
Banners, papers, videos; 1990s; 1 file, 2 banners, 2 videos

Biographical note
Born in Johannesburg in 1962, Cohen was conscripted into the army where he spent much of his time in what he describes as the 'mad house'. He studied arts at the University of the Witwatersrand, and became a collage silk-screen print artist, focusing on controversial images of apartheid, childhood, anatomy and sexuality, his fabrics used in fashion and furnishing. He has had many exhibitions in South Africa, Germany and Luxembourg. From 1996 he became a leading and often controversial performance artist in South Africa, addressing cruelty to animals and hatred of marginalised people: homosexuals, Jews, drug users and 'ugly girls'. In 1998 he won the First National Bank Vita National Art Award, South Africa's leading art prize. Cohen lives with his partner, Elu, a choreographer and dancer, in Troyeville, Johannesburg. [Adapted from Aldrich, R and Wotherspoon, G (eds). 2001. *Who's Who in Contemporary Gay and Lesbian History from World War II to the Present Day*. London: Routledge.]

Scope and content
The collection consists of records of exhibitions and performances, including two videocassette recordings. It also includes two Johannesburg Gay and Lesbian Pride Parade banners.

CONGRESS of Pink Democrats (CPD)
Papers; 1987 to 1988; 1 box; inventory available

Brief historical background
The Congress of Pink Democrats (April 1987 to May 1988) was an alliance of progressive lesbian and gay organisations. It was established at a conference held in Cape Town from 4 to 6 April 1987 under the aegis of LAGO and the RGO. The CDP aligned itself with the struggle for a democratic South Africa. At the time of its establishment the CDP comprised LAGO, RGO, the Guguletu-based AGA and the UCT Gay and Lesbian Association. The founding conference was also attended by representatives of GASA (Johannesburg) and Impact (Johannesburg), but neither organisation decided to join. The CDP did not last long: its second conference, held in Johannesburg in October 1987, was its last, although the CPD continued to exist in name until 1988, when a scheduled conference failed to take place.

Scope and content
Organisational records of the CPD.

235

CONWAY, Daniel
Papers; 2003; 1 file

Scope and content
The collection consists of original research material for Conway's PhD thesis 'Masculinities, citizenship and political objection to compulsory military service in the SADF: 1978–1990'.

Note on the collection
Access to the collection is restricted until completion of Conway's PhD, unless written permission is granted by Conway. Researchers can contact him through GALA.

DAVIDSON, Gerry
Audiocassettes, scrapbook, publications, T-shirts; 1990 to 2003; 1 box, 12 photographs, 37 negatives, 2 audiocassettes, 15 T-shirts

Biographical note
Gerry Davidson has worked in publishing and design for over 30 years, and was the owner and editor of *Exit* from 1990 to 1994. She also briefly published *The Quarterly*, described as a news magazine for gay women.

Scope and content
The collection includes a scrapbook of press clippings relating to *Exit* and gay and lesbian issues, 1990 to 1994, as well as two issues of *The Quarterly* (1992 and 1993), a World AIDS Day poster, fifteen T-shirts and some press clippings. It also includes a life story interview with Gerry Davidson from 2003, by Anthony Manion.

DE PINHO, Helen
Papers; 1990 to 1996; 1 box; inventory available

Scope and content
Organisational records of the NCGLE, Lesbian and Gay Women Empowerment Conference 1995, Sunday's Women, and the University of Natal-Durban Committee on Sexual Orientation. Also articles, papers and policy papers on lesbian health.

EQUALITY Foundation, The
Papers; 1993; 1 box; inventory available

Brief historical background
The Equality Foundation was established in 1993 using funds raised for a prior initiative, the NLRF of 1986. The NLRF was set up in order to facilitate submissions to a proposed President's Council review of existing legislation on homosexuality in the Immorality Act. The President's Council investigation never took place and the funds were transferred to the National Law Reform Charitable Trust. In 1993 these funds (which had accrued significantly) were transferred to the Equality Foundation for use in lobbying for the inclusion of the Equality Clause in South Africa's new Constitution. The Equality Foundation was represented by the lawyer Kevan Botha at CODESA (Convention for a Democratic South Africa). The Equality Foundation also made funds available for the establishment of the NCGLE in 1994.

Scope and content
Papers of the Equality Foundation, including the submission to the Technical Committee on Fundamental Rights during the Transition and its addendum (21 June 1993).

EXIT
Publications, papers; 1985 to 2004; 4 large-format files, 3 boxes; inventory available

Scope and content
This collection consists of a complete set of the South African lesbian and gay newspaper, *Exit*. *Exit* has been South Africa's principal gay and lesbian publication since its establishment in 1985 (when it replaced the newsletter *Link/Skakel*). The publication's content is focused on club round-ups, community news, hunk pictorials and camp humour. It also looks at gay and lesbian liberation, HIV/AIDS, politics and the social issues of the day. The collection is updated on a regular basis. The Gay and Lesbian Library (Johannesburg) donated many of the newspapers in the collection. There are also three boxes consisting of office records, correspondence and paste-ups.

FINE, Derrick
Papers; 1990 to 1993; 1 box

Biographical note
Derrick Fine came to political awareness while studying law at the University of Cape Town in the early 1980s. His involvement in the Detainees' Support Group brought him into contact with Simon Nkoli during the Delmas Treason Trial, and this led to his engagement with gay and lesbian politics. He was subsequently an active member of LAGO and OLGA, and is currently involved in community education and paralegal training.

Scope and content
The material reflects Fine's work in OLGA, and includes records relating to OLGA's involvement in national lobbying for gay and lesbian rights.

GARMESON, Bertram Eugene Joseph ('Joe')
Papers, photographs, scrapbook, audiocassettes; 1948 to 2000; 4 boxes; inventory available

Biographical note
Bertram Eugene Joseph ('Joe') (1928 to 2003) arrived in South Africa as a young immigrant from the UK in 1948 and made the country his home for the next 55 years. After moving from Durban to Johannesburg in 1965, Garmeson became the secretary of the Legal Reform Fund, formed in 1966 to oppose new draconian anti-homosexual legislation in the form of the Immorality Amendment Bill. The fund was established in order to raise the necessary money to secure professional legal representation to the Parliamentary Select Committee established to investigate the proposed Bill. Garmeson played an important role in fundraising and co-ordinating the activities of this fledgling social movement. Based on the committee's recommendations, a revised version of the Bill went through Parliament in 1969.

Scope and content
The collection details the earliest years of the formal gay and lesbian movement in South Africa. It includes the scrupulous records Garmeson kept as secretary of the Legal Reform Fund (initially donated to the Gay Association of South Africa Library and transferred to GALA

237

in 1997). These records include correspondence, minutes, notes, articles and other documents, and offer a glimpse into this singular network of men and women. Other miscellaneous material includes a 1968 radio broadcast on homosexuality on audio tape ('The Broken Link') and Garmeson's scrapbook of newspaper clippings from the 1950s and 1960s. In addition, the photograph albums include some photographs documenting gay life in Durban from 1948 to 1951. The collection also includes Garmeson's donation of hard-to-find gay books (and the GALA archivist has added Garmeson's speech on the donation of his library in 2000).

Note on collection
Please note that the membership lists of the Legal Reform Fund are embargoed.

GAY Association of South Africa (GASA)
Records, press clippings; 1982 to 1988; 10 boxes

Brief historical note
GASA was formed in April 1982 in Johannesburg, and by the end of the year it had established nine branches across the country. In Cape Town it linked up with 6010, a Cape Town initiative which had started at approximately the same time as GASA, and which was thereafter known as GASA-6010. GASA's national office was based in Hillbrow, Johannesburg. In 1984 GASA-6010 opened a community centre in Cape Town, from which it ran a counselling service. GASA held a convention in Johannesburg in 1985 that included speeches on gay rights and explorations of gay life in South Africa, as well as social events.

Scope and content
The collection includes a wide range of organisational and financial records from GASA's national office and regional branches, as well as scrapbooks and press clippings.

GAY Christian Community (GCC), The
Records, T-shirt; 1990 to 2003; 1 box; inventory available

Brief historical background
The Johannesburg-based Gay Christian Community (GCC) provides a spiritual home for lesbian and gay Christians, and has been in existence for the last fifteen years.

Scope and content
The collection consists of GCC newsletters, pamphlets and mail-outs as well as a T-shirt.

GAY and Lesbian Counselling (GLC), The
Papers; 1985 to 1997; 18 boxes; inventory available

Scope and content
Organisational records of Gay and Lesbian Counselling, a Johannesburg support group, and its earlier embodiments, the Gay Advice Bureau and the Gay Switchboard. Access to part of the collection is restricted.

GAY and Lesbian Organisation of Pretoria (GLO-P)

Papers; 1993 to 2003; 8 boxes; inventory available

Brief historical background

The Gay and Lesbian Organisation of Pretoria (GLO-P) was established in 1993. The organisation was modelled on GLOW, and was initially called the Gay and Lesbian Organisation of the Witwatersrand–Pretoria (GLOW-P). The organisation started primarily as a social network. In 1994 GLO-P established the Pretoria Gay and Lesbian Resource Centre, and by 1995 GLO-P outlined its scope of activities to include a telephonic counselling and information service; workshops promoting understanding and identity formation; psychotherapeutic/counselling groups; a resource directory; a gay guide/map to Pretoria and a forum for research on gay-related issues. In 2001 GLO-P changed its name to OUT-LGBT Wellbeing.

Scope and content

The GLO-P/OUT collection consists of newsletters, minutes of meetings, flyers, pamphlets and academic articles as well as six boxes of submissions to the Constitutional Assembly's Theme Committee Four (which included homosexuality and abortion).

GAY and Lesbian Organisation of the Witwatersrand (GLOW)

Papers; 1990 to 1998; 10 boxes; inventory available

Brief historical background

GLOW was formed in Johannesburg in 1988 by a group of black gay and lesbian activists. The person elected to chair the organisation was Simon Tseko Nkoli, who had already gained political prominence as an ANC activist and Delmas treason trialist. At the time GLOW was the only South African gay and lesbian organisation with a predominately black membership. GLOW gained public attention by ensuring a gay and lesbian presence in the 1989 wave of political activism and demonstrations which campaigned for democracy and the unbanning of the liberation movements. In 1990 GLOW was involved in organising South Africa's first Lesbian and Gay Pride March in Johannesburg. GLOW campaigned for gay and lesbian rights in the media, including television and print, and tried to stimulate debate. As part of the democratic movement and under Nkoli's leadership, GLOW condemned the homophobic defence of Winnie Madikizela-Mandela during her trial for murder and kidnapping in 1991. GLOW insisted that liberation from homophobia could not be separated from the broader struggle for liberation in South Africa.

In 1989 GLOW became a member of ILGA. GLOW was involved in the creation of a number of organisations. In 1990, the Township AIDS Project was launched in Soweto, partly by GLOW members, in response to the mounting HIV/AIDS problem. GLOW members were also involved in the formation of the HUMCC in 1994, in response to the need for a church grouping where gay and lesbian Christians could make their voices heard and could oppose the notion that homosexuality was un-Christian or immoral. GLOW was also involved in the formation of the NCGLE and worked closely with that organisation.

239

Scope and content

The bulk of the collection consists of organisational records of GLOW, including GLOW policy documents, proposals, correspondence, minutes and financial records. The collection also contains material from GLOW chapters elsewhere in the Vaal Triangle. In addition, there is some personal material from Peter Mohlahledi, who ran the office from his flat.

GEVISSER, Mark

Papers; 1988 to 1993; 1 box; inventory available

Biographical note

Mark Gevisser is a Johannesburg-based freelance journalist and writer. He wrote mainly for the *Weekly Mail* and was South African correspondent for *The Nation* in New York. He was also formerly a contributor and theatre critic at the *Village Voice* in New York, and his work has appeared in magazines and newspapers in the US, Britain and South Africa. He is the co-editor of *Defiant Desire*, a book on gay and lesbian life in South Africa, published in 1994. He is at present writing a biography of President Thabo Mbeki. [Cameron, E and Gevisser, M (eds). 1994. *Defiant Desire: Gay and Lesbian Lives in South Africa*. Johannesburg: Ravan.]

GOLDSMITH, Adam

Papers; 1982 to 1984; 1 box; inventory available

Scope and content

Adam Goldsmith was a committee member of GASA-Rand, the Rand branch of GASA. His collection consists of records of GASA-Rand, including minutes, details of committee portfolios, proposals, correspondence, financial records, administrative records and some publications. His collection covers the period 1982 to 1984.

HOPE and Unity Metropolitan and Community Church (HUMCC)

Papers, sound and video recordings, photographs; 1995 to 1998; 4 boxes, 99 audiocassettes, 38 video cassettes; inventory available

Scope and content

The collection consists of research material for Graeme Reid's MA thesis on the HUMCC in Johannesburg. Through a detailed ethnographic study of the HUMCC during the period 1995 to 1997, Reid set out to demonstrate how a particular South African church community created the possibility of an integrated cultural identity for gay and lesbian Christians in an African context. His research focuses on healing rituals, the language of church services, gender, gender identity, kinship relations, parents of lesbian and gay church members, proselytising and the significance of the Holy Spirit in the life of the church community. The main research method was participant observation, complemented by household surveys, individual interviews and focus group discussions. The research material includes HUMCC documents (including flyers and posters), periodicals, Reid's research documents and notes, and a large number of sound and video recordings and photographs. There is also a copy of Reid's MA thesis, titled 'Above the Skyline: Integrating African, Christian and Gay or Lesbian Identities in a South African Church Community'.

IMMORALITY Amendment Bill of 1968

Papers, publication; 1968; 2 boxes

Brief historical background

In the 1960s, gay men and lesbians became increasingly visible in South Africa. This heightened public profile led the National Party government to launch a vehement legislative campaign against homosexuality. The trigger for the campaign was a high-profile police raid in

January 1966 on a house in the suburb of Forest Town in Johannesburg, where the police found a homosexual party in progress. The event and the extent of homosexuality in the country were publicised in the media. This sparked off a moral panic that had been fermenting as a result of the increasing visibility of gays and lesbians. The government interested itself in the matter, and in 1967 Peet Pelser, Minister of Justice, announced his intention to introduce drastic anti-homosexual legislation in the form of the proposed Immorality Amendment Bill, saying: 'It is a proven fact that sooner or later homosexual instincts make their effects felt on a community if they are permitted to run riot... Therefore we should be on the alert and do what there is to do lest we be saddled later with a problem which will be the utter ruin of our spiritual and moral fibre.' The Bill outlawed all sexual activity between men, as well as extending the legislation to include women for the first time. The Bill was referred to a parliamentary Select Committee for review, which was to hear the evidence of 'experts' and propose final legislation a year later. The Select Committee called on the public to submit evidence to it and promised confidentiality. In response, a small group of gay and lesbian professionals began organising in the Johannesburg–Pretoria area. The goal of this 'action group' was to raise the R40 000 needed to retain a firm of attorneys to prepare evidence and lead the case against the proposed legislation before the Select Committee. It became formalised as the Homosexual Legal Reform Fund, and was known euphemistically as 'Law Reform'. Law Reform encouraged gays and lesbians to make contributions and to submit evidence through its legal team rather than to the Select Committee directly. This was intended both to protect the identities of those who gave evidence and to allow Law Reform to maintain control over the evidence presented to the Select Committee.

Scope and content
The collection consists of copies of written submissions to the Parliamentary Select Committee on the Immorality Amendment Bill and a copy of the Report of the Select Committee, 1968. Note that the original documents are kept at the Library of Parliament.

KRAAK, Gerald
Papers; 1987 to 2000; 3 boxes; inventory available

Scope and content
This collection reflects Kraak's work as an anti-apartheid activist in exile in the 1970s and 1980s and subsequently as a fundraiser in the development and human rights spheres in South Africa. It includes organisational records, newspaper clippings, magazines, published and draft articles, electronic records, theatre programmes and other papers.

LAPINSKY, Sheila
T-shirts and videos; 1986 to 1993; 12 T-shirts, 6 videos; inventory available

Biographical note
A human rights activist, Sheila Lapinsky has been involved in a number of anti-apartheid and lesbian and gay organisations. The lesbian and gay organisations include GASA-6010, Lilacs, Gender, LAGO, OLGA and the NCGLE. She lives in Cape Town with her partner, Julia Nicol.

Scope and content
The collection consists of 12 T-shirts produced by South African lesbian and gay organisations or commemorating gay and lesbian events, as well as T-shirts in support of the End Conscription Campaign. In addition, there are a few videos.

241

LESBIANS and Gays Against Oppression (LAGO) and the Organisation of Lesbian and Gay Activists (OLGA)

Papers; 1987 to 1994; 5 boxes; inventory available

Brief historical background

Following the failure of GASA-6010 to accommodate those activists in the organisation who wanted to go in a more radical direction, LAGO was formed in Cape Town in 1986. LAGO's membership ranged from about five to twelve people, and was largely composed of visible gay and lesbian activists who had previous experience in the anti-apartheid struggle (for example, Sheila Lapinsky). These activists brought a wealth of insight from their previous involvement and an awareness of the inequalities in South African life. LAGO's significance is partly that it made important links with supportive overseas lesbian and gay organisations. Internal dissent led to the dissolution of the organisation in October 1987, as LAGO's constitution required full consensus for all decisions.

In October 1987 the majority of LAGO's membership reorganised themselves as the Organisation of Lesbian and Gay Activists (OLGA). (This would change to the Organisation of Lesbian and Gay Action in 1992.) This organisation had identical aims and objectives to that of LAGO, but its constitution included procedural mechanisms designed to provide a workable alternative to dissolution in the event of a dissenting minority within the group. OLGA maintained and developed the overseas links established by LAGO. While its core membership varied from between five to twelve people, between 30 and 40 people attended the 'forum' discussion evenings.

Most of the organisation's members were simultaneously involved in other organisations of the United Democratic Front, and in December 1989 OLGA took the decision to apply for affiliation. Their application for affiliation to the UDF was accepted in March 1990. Not everyone in the UDF was happy about OLGA's inclusion – one ex-OLGA member recalling 'a certain amount of twittering behind the scenes'.

In September 1991 OLGA submitted to the ANC Constitutional Committee a proposal for the inclusion of provisions outlawing discrimination on the grounds of sexual orientation in its draft Constitution. These provisions were included in the committee's draft Constitution published in October 1991 and were ratified by the ANC per se in May 1992. In consultation with other lesbian and gay organisations in South Africa, OLGA drafted a Charter of Bisexual, Lesbian and Gay Rights. This was finalised at a national conference held in Cape Town in December 1993. OLGA was dissolved in 1994.

Scope and content

Organisational records, policy papers, correspondence, newsletters, pamphlets and flyers of LAGO and OLGA.

MACHELA, Alfred

Papers; 1986 to 1989; 5 boxes; inventory available

Scope and content

Alfred Machela was the chairperson of the RGO, and his records of the RGO form the core of this collection. The collection also includes his papers from ILGA conferences he attended, and papers from his work with local and international lesbian and gay groups. Please note that the RGO membership lists and some correspondence are embargoed.

MATHOKO'S post box
Metal post box; ca. 1980s to mid-1990s; 1 item

Brief historical background
MaThoko lived at 32 Legodi Street, KwaThema, and died in the early 1990s. Her home was a refuge and meeting place for gays and lesbians. It was also a shebeen (tavern) and the head-quarters of the KwaThema chapter of GLOW. The post box was salvaged from the roof of MaThoko's house after her death and donated to GALA. For many, it is an important symbol of communication and community as it received post for GLOW.

Scope and content
The collection consists of the post box.

McGEARY, Barry
Papers; 1991; 3 boxes; inventory available

Scope and content
Barry McGeary, a Brakpan resident with HIV, was in the news in 1991 over a case against his doctor involving breach of confidentiality. He died of AIDS before the end of his trial and the executors of his estate continued with the case on his behalf. The case is seen as a landmark in AIDS law in South Africa.

The collection consists of material relating to this trial, including trial records, notes, correspondence and press clippings.

MEDIA
Audiovisual material, press clippings; 1983 to 2004; 5 boxes; inventory available

Scope and content
Media coverage on lesbian and gay issues in audio, video and print formats. This collection is updated monthly. Substantial material on: homosexuality and religion; legislation affecting homosexuals; and homosexuality in Africa. The bulk of the collection is for the period 1997 to 2004.

MOKGETHI, Paul
Records; 1992 to 1999; 2 files

Biographical note
Paul Mokgethi is a pastor at the HUMCC as well as a former member of GLOW.

243

Scope and content
The collection includes personal as well as some organisational records.

MOORE, Eliza
Papers; 1990 to 1992; 1 file

Scope and content
The collection consists of miscellaneous papers from the early 1990s, ranging from GLOW to the Johannesburg Gay and Lesbian Pride Parade.

NATIONAL Coalition for Gay and Lesbian Equality (NCGLE)
Records; 1990 to 2000; 70 boxes

Brief historical background
The NCGLE was launched at the end of 1994 with the slogan 'Equality and justice for all'. Its initial purpose was to fight for the retention of sexual orientation in the Equality Clause of the final Constitution of South Africa. The inclusion of sexual orientation in the interim Constitution had opened a window of opportunity for the LGBT community in South Africa. Up until that point there had been little unity or coherence in the community. There had been a few politically motivated LGBT organisations, like GLOW and ABIGALE, and these enjoyed a modest public profile. There had also been individuals like Simon Nkoli or Bev Ditsie, who had made a mark in the political struggle for liberation.

Though the NCGLE was constituted as a representative membership organisation, it was, in reality, set up by a small group of lesbian and gay activists who saw the formation of the coalition as a strategic requirement for strengthening the calls for the retention of the clause. It is generally agreed that the NCGLE succeeded admirably in this objective and that the retention of sexual orientation in the Equality Clause was a consequence of the strategic and focused campaign fought by the NCGLE.

At the NCGLE national conference in 1995, the four major aims of the organisation were defined as follows: to retain the Equality Clause in the final Constitution; to scrap unjust laws; to challenge discrimination through constitutional litigation; and to train representative and effective lesbian and gay leadership.

The work of the NCGLE was grounded in a belief that LGBT rights are linked to issues of human rights. Many of the NCGLE's programmes were aimed at changing the legal and legislative framework, including working for the retention of sexual orientation in the Equality Clause; lobbying government for changes in legislation (examples include the Medical Schemes Bill, the Employment Equity Campaign, the Refugees Act, the Child Care Act, and *Langemaat v Minister of Safety and Security*). The NCGLE was also a member of the Equality Alliance.

The NCGLE has often gone to the Constitutional Court (in conjunction with the Commission on Gender Equality and the Human Rights Commission) to overturn laws dating back to the apartheid period that are in violation of the Constitution. Among these cases are those leading to the decriminalisation of sex between consenting adult men, and the right of foreign partners of South African citizens to gain residency rights. The decisions in these cases are regarded as landmark judgments, and in some instances constitute international precedents.

The NCGLE realised that the law alone was not enough to change societal attitudes, and so made use of other strategies as well. Examples include the Recognise Our Relationships Campaign, the Youth and Religious Lobbying Projects and the programme run during the 1999 elections. It also had a media and communications strategy, which is described in more detail in the scope and content section below.

In 1999 the NCGLE dissolved and the Lesbian and Gay Equality Project was formed in order to continue the legal reform and advocacy work initiated by the NCGLE. The Equality Project operates as a straightforward non-profit organisation (rather than a representative membership organisation) and is governed by a board. It has continued the work of the NCGLE. [Adapted from Nell, M and Shapiro, J. 1999. 'Taking the Struggle Forward', unpublished, internal NCGLE review.]

Scope and content

The records of the NCGLE are divided into two sections: (A) the internal functioning of the organisation and (B) its programmes.

Section A is made up of records documenting the internal structures of the NCGLE; staff or human resources issues; finances and fundraising; and administration. Records include minutes and agendas, correspondence, staff information, staff development and training documents, policy and procedure documents, financial records, funding records and proposals, workshop records, administrative policies and procedures, and database records. The bulk of the records cover the period 1995 to 1999.

Section B is composed of records pertaining to the programme work of the NCGLE, including changing the legislative and legal framework; changing societal attitudes; organising to build a social movement; and the Johannesburg Gay and Lesbian Pride Parade. Important record series within B include records of the Equality Foundation and records documenting the NCGLE's lobbying campaign around the Equality Clause (including submissions, reports, petitions, correspondence and proposals).

Another important record series in B is the NCGLE's Equal Rights Project, which contains records pertaining to the Employment Equity Alliance; the Employment Equity Act; the Basic Conditions of Employment Act; the Code of Good Employment Practice; and *Langemaat v Minister of Safety and Security*. There are also records on the South African National Defence Force; the Medical Schemes Bill; the Refugees Act (asylum); the Marriage Act; the Equality Alliance; and the Child Care Act.

Other important record series include records of two landmark cases around the decriminalisation of sex between consenting adult men, and the right of foreign partners of South African citizens to gain residency rights in the country. There is also documentation from the Gay and Lesbian Legal Advice Centre (GLLAC), the Recognise Our Relationships Campaign, the NCGLE's religious lobbying campaign, and its youth project and election campaign.

Section B also documents the NCGLE's media and communications strategy and thus includes records pertaining to *Equality* (newsletter of the NCGLE); information leaflets, posters, T-shirts and buttons aimed at educating the LGBT community on the work of the NCGLE; and numerous photographs, documents used for radio and television lobbying, press statements and press clippings. The bulk of the records in Section B span the period 1995 to 2000.

Note on the collection

Though the collection contains only one file of embargoed material, as a whole it contains a great deal of private information on staff members and members of the public. Researchers are required to complete a form agreeing to respect the confidential nature of the material.

NICOL, Julia

245

Photographs; late 1980s to early 1990s; inventory available

Biographical note

A librarian by training, Julia Nicol was an active member of the Cape Town-based organisations GASA-6010, Lilacs, Gender, LAGO and OLGA. She is the co-author of the article 'The Lavender Lobby', published in *Defiant Desire* (1994), edited by Edwin Cameron and Mark Gevisser. Since the early 1990s, ongoing health problems have confined Nicol to her home in Cape Town.

Scope and content

The bulk of the collection consists of photographs documenting the activities of the gay and lesbian organisations with which Nicol was involved in Cape Town from 1985 to 1991. The captions to the photographs were written by her. The collection also includes a speech written by Nicol in 1999, and a Gender flyer from 1986.

NICHOLLS, Cambanis and Associates
Papers; 1998; 3 boxes; inventory available

Brief historical note

Nicholls, Cambanis and Associates is a South African law firm that has acted on a number of landmark cases for the NCGLE and the Lesbian and Gay Equality Project.

Scope and content

Records relate to the following court cases in which the law firm acted on behalf of the NCGLE: Polmed; decriminalisation of male-male sex; *Satchwell* v *Minister of Justice*; and *Du Toit* v *Minister of Social Welfare and Population Development*. The collection includes court records, correspondence and related documentation.

NKOLI, Simon Tseko
Papers, photographs; 1977 to 1998; 9 boxes; inventory available

Biographical note

Simon Tseko Nkoli (1957 to 1998) was born in Soweto in a Sesotho-speaking family. He grew up on a farm in the Free State and his family later moved to Sebokeng. Nkoli became a youth activist against apartheid with the Congress of South African Students and with the United Democratic Front. In 1983 he joined the mainly white GASA, and after coming out in an interview with *City Press*, he formed the Saturday Group, the first black gay group in Africa. After speaking at rallies in support of rent boycotters in the Vaal townships, he was arrested in 1984 and faced the death penalty for treason with 21 other political activists in the Delmas Treason Trial. By courageously coming out while a prisoner, he helped change the attitude of the African National Congress towards gay rights. While many gay groups around the world wrote to him and supported his defence, GASA and white-dominated gay organisations in South Africa refused to support someone charged with political crimes. He was acquitted and released from prison in 1988.

Nkoli founded GLOW in 1988, and was later involved in black gay choirs and sports groups. He travelled widely and was given several human rights awards in Europe and North America. He was a member of the ILGA board, representing the African region, and was one of the first gay activists to meet with Nelson Mandela in 1994. As one of the leading person-alities in the NCGLE, he helped in the campaigns to retain protection from discrimination in the Bill of Rights in the 1996 South African Constitution, and for the May 1998 repeal of the sodomy laws. He helped establish Soweto's Township AIDS Project in 1990, and worked there on community education campaigns until 1996. After becoming one of the first publicly HIV-positive African gay men, he initiated the Positive African Men's Project (PAMP), based in central Johannesburg. In the months before his death, supported by his British partner Roderick Sharp, he was writing his memoirs, and was concerned with the anti-homosexual campaigns in neighbouring Zimbabwe, Namibia, Swaziland, Botswana and Zambia. Nkoli died in hospital in Johannesburg on the eve of World AIDS Day, on 30 November 1998. Memorial services were held for him in Sebokeng, and in the Anglican cathedrals in Johannesburg and Cape Town. The September 1999 Pride Parade in Johannesburg was dedicated to his memory, and a downtown street corner was named in his honour. [Adapted from Aldrich, R and Wotherspoon, G (eds). 2001. *Who's Who in Contemporary Gay and Lesbian History from World War II to the Present Day.* London: Routledge.]

Scope and content
The Simon Nkoli dossier covers the most significant period in lesbian and gay political history in South Africa. The highlight of the collection is over 100 letters written during Nkoli's detention at the time of the Delmas Treason Trial. These letters (1985 to 1987) are a testimony to Nkoli's extraordinary courage, and through this personal account give an insight into the day-to-day experience of being in detention.

The collection includes other material relating to the Delmas Treason Trial; copies of letters from the international community in response to an Amnesty International Urgent Action appeal; Nkoli's correspondence with international gay and lesbian organisations; and material which documents the controversy that arose at the 1986 ILGA conference around the continued membership of GASA. Roy Shepherd collected most of the material and stored it before he gave it to GALA. Nkoli also donated some papers and photographs. In 2001, Roderick Sharp donated copies of further letters, as well as some badges.

Since Nkoli's death at the end of 1998, GALA continues to search for additional material for this collection and for other GALA collections which document the life of South Africa's best-known gay leader.

ORAL History Project
Sound and film recordings, papers, photographs; ca 1940s to 2000; inventory available

Brief historical background
GALA's Oral History Project was launched in co-operation with journalist Mark Gevisser to provide background material for Gevisser's film biography of Cecil Williams (*The Man Who Drove with Mandela*). Williams was a well-known theatre director in South Africa in the 1950s. He was also a communist, underground activist and gay.

Scope and content
Gevisser's interviews form the bulk of the collection. However, this is an ongoing project and other oral history interviews unrelated to the documentary continue to be added.

The first part of the collection consists of more than 60 interviews on audiocassette with lesbians and gay men older than 60 at the time of the interview. Some of the interviews have been transcribed, and include some photographs and memorabilia. Researchers interested in South African gay and lesbian life from the Second World War to the 1960s as well as the political milieu in that time will find this collection useful.

The second part of the collection consists of interviews with gay men and lesbians about their lives in South Africa that were not undertaken as part of a specific project.

Note on the collection
Several interviews have restrictions on them and researchers will need either GALA's or the interviewee's permission to use them.

247

PROPERTY of the State
Audiovisual material; 2003; 17 items

Brief historical background
Property of the State: Gay Men in the Apartheid Military (2003) is a documentary film that deals with the experience of gay men in the apartheid military – an environment in which homosexuals sometimes found erotic space, but mostly encountered hostility. It draws on a literary exploration of gay experience in the military in the *grensverhaal* (border story) genre of the 1980s as well as on interviews with conscripts who served in the South African Defence Force and anti-military activists.

The film was scripted and directed by Gerald Kraak and produced by Jill Kruger. It was co-funded by GALA, Out-in-Africa, the National Film and Video Foundation, and the Joseph Rowntree Charitable Trust. It has been screened at local and international film festivals, as well as flighted on SABC 3 (in a shortened version).

Scope and content
The bulk of the collection consists of footage shot for the documentary (in DVCAM and VHS format), as well as two Betacam masters (the full length and shortened versions respectively) and a VHS copy of the finished documentary. In addition, there is a brief interview on audio-cassette with an ex-conscript who had been based at Greefswald, and who contacted the director after the SABC3 screening of the film.

RANDALL, Lee
Papers, images; 1983 to 1993; 1 box, 65 colour photocopies; inventory available

Biographical note
Lee Randall grew up in Johannesburg and her teenage years were strongly influenced by her father's being banned by the apartheid government. She lived in Boston (USA) in her mid-twenties, experiencing at first hand a radical lesbian community; and on her return to South Africa she was a founder member of GLOW and an organising committee member of the first Johannesburg Lesbian and Gay Pride March. During the 1990s she wrote for publications like *Gay Community News*, *Exit* and *The Quarterly*, sometimes under her pseudonym, Dee Radclyffe. Her essay 'Confessions of a Failed Lesbian Separatist' appears in *The Invisible Ghetto* (1993), edited by Mathew Krouse. [Krouse, M. 1993. *The Invisible Ghetto: Lesbian and Gay Writing from South Africa.* Johannesburg: COSAW Publishing.] Currently she runs her own practice as a health professional in Johannesburg, and has been in a committed domestic relationship with her New Zealand partner since late 1997.

Scope and content
The material reflects Lee Randall's involvement in the South African gay and lesbian rights movement during the late 1980s and early 1990s. It includes colour copies of photographs (many of gay and lesbian pride marches in South Africa), local and international publications, transcripts of radio talk shows (on homosexuality in South Africa and gay and lesbian adoption), press clippings, memorabilia and other items.

RUNDLE, Donne
Scrapbook, video; 1990; 2 items

Scope and content

A scrapbook of newspaper clippings, messages of support and other items relating to the first Lesbian and Gay Pride March in 1990, and a video recording of the same march.

SAMPSON, Wayne

Papers; 1986 to 1987; 1 box; inventory available

Biographical note

Wayne Sampson was involved in the Wits Gay Movement while attending the University of the Witwatersrand in the late 1980s.

Scope and content

The collection consists of publications from the Wits Gay Movement, meeting notes and sketches, as well as other Wits publications. It also includes some anti-apartheid and anti-conscription material.

SHEPHERD, Roy

Papers; 1974 to 2002; 15 boxes; inventory available

Scope and content

Roy Shepherd's papers include his notebooks from 1974 to 2003 (including copies of his letters to Simon Nkoli during Nkoli's imprisonment as part of the Delmas Treason Trial) and some material about Christianity and homosexuality.

SIMON and I

Video cassettes, papers; 1998 to 2001; 7 video cassettes, 1 file; inventory available

Brief historical background

Simon and I is a 52-minute documentary directed by Beverly Palesa Ditsie and produced by Nicky Newman, See Thru Media. It recounts the lives of Simon Nkoli and the maker of the documentary, Bev Ditsie, two prominent figures in the South African gay and lesbian liberation movement. The film is described in publicity material as 'a personal statement and a political history', as Bev Ditsie charts her relationship with Simon Nkoli 'through good times and bad against a backdrop of intense political activism and the HIV/AIDS crisis'. The film makes use of a mixed format of interviews and archival footage. The film was commissioned by STEPS (Social Transformation and Empowerment Projects) as part of its Steps for the Future project, a collection of documentaries and short films from Southern Africa.

249

Scope and content

The collection consists of copies of video material filmed or collected for the documentary *Simon and I* (2001), a copy of this film and some production paraphernalia relating to the documentary.

SMITH, Ann

Papers; 1985 to 1998; 6 boxes; inventory available

Brief historical background

Ann Smith has been involved in the gay and lesbian rights movement in South Africa since the 1980s and this involvement is reflected in her substantial collection of records from GASA. GASA – of which Ann Smith was briefly chairperson – was formed in 1982 in Johannesburg, and by the end of the year it had established nine branches across the country.

Scope and content

The collection includes a wide range of organisational records from GASA's national office and regional branches, including minutes, proposals and correspondence. In addition to the GASA records, the collection also includes material about teaching and lesbian identity in South Africa.

SOUTH African Police Services Gay and Lesbian Policing Network
Records; 1990s; 1 box; inventory available

Brief historical background

The South African Police Services Gay and Lesbian Policing Network provide services for LGBT members of the police.

Scope and content

The collection consists of photographs and publicity material documenting their participation in the Johannesburg Gay and Lesbian Pride Parade over the years.

STOBBS, Paul
Records; 1994 to 1997; 3 boxes, inventory available

Biographical note

Paul Stobbs was born in England and came to South Africa as an adult to work for a bank as a trainee officer. He was very involved in LGBT activism as chairperson of the Gay and Lesbian Pride Parade in 1994, 1996 and 1998. He was vice-chair of TOGS and a trustee of the Gay Advice Bureau (GAB) AIDS trust fund.

Scope and content

The bulk of the collection consists of the Pride Committee's organisational records, which include minutes of meetings, policy and planning documents, agreements, financial records, correspondence, promotional material and media coverage.

TATCHELL, Peter
Papers; 1987 to 1999; 1 box; inventory available

Biographical note

A journalist, Peter Tatchell was involved in the anti-apartheid movement in the UK from the late 1960s. He was also actively involved in the London-based queer rights group Outrage!

Scope and content

The collection consists of copies of articles written by or about Tatchell from 1987 to 1990. These focus on developments in lesbian and gay anti-apartheid activism. The collection includes correspondence between Tatchell and leading figures in the anti-apartheid struggle as well as a personal statement by Tatchell. The collection will be of interest to those researching the background to the Equality Clause and the intersection between lesbian and gay and broader liberation politics.

THE ORGANISATION of Gay Sports (TOGS)
Records; 1988 to 1999; 10 boxes; inventory available

Scope and content
Extensive records of The Organisation of Gay Sports (previously known as the Transvaal Organisation of Gay Sport) that include minutes, financial records, correspondence and other organisational records. The collection also contains records of LGBT organisations to which TOGS was affiliated, notably GASA and NCGLE.

TOMS, Ivan
Records; 1982 to 1990; 1 box; inventory available

Biographical note
Toms trained as a medical doctor and worked in the Crossroads shack settlement for eleven years. He was a member of OLGA and the End Conscription Campaign (ECC), and was active in the Anglican Church. He was imprisoned under apartheid for refusing to serve in the SADF.

Scope and content
The material most heavily reflects his involvement in the above organisations. It includes records, original writings and lectures, letters of support during his imprisonment, and memorabilia.

TRENGOVE JONES, Tim
Papers; 1994 to 2000; 1 box

Biographical note
Tim Trengove Jones is a lecturer in the Department of English at the University of the Witwatersrand. He is also a writer who has contributed to a number of publications.

Scope and content
The collection includes the judgment on the registration of the lesbian partner of a member of the South African Police Service on the SAPS medical aid scheme, as well as various newspaper cuttings and reviews.

TRIANGLE Project
Papers, scrapbook, pamphlets; 1982 to 2003; 7 boxes

Brief historical background
The Triangle Project is an organisation that provides health and mental health services to lesbian, gay, bisexual and transgendered people in the Cape Town area. It has been active in its present form since 1994/6, and built on the work of previous LGBT health organisations: GASA-6010 and ASET.

Scope and content

The records include GASA-6010's HIV/AIDS awareness material from the 1980s; correspondence (1982–1983); minutes (1981–1984); newsletters; minutes of the AIDS Action Group; and a scrapbook of newspaper cuttings on HIV/AIDS from 1983 to 1986. There is also a range of ASET literature and Triangle Project paraphernalia. Other material includes photographs of an AIDS memorial and of the opening of the Triangle Project's Guguletu office in 1996.

VELCICH, Alan
Papers; 1988 to 1991; 3 files

Scope and content

The collection consists of records of some South African homosexual and human rights organisations: GLOW; the Johannesburg AIDS Action Group; and the PGLWG.

Acronyms

AAM	Anti-Apartheid Movement
ABIGALE	Association of Bisexuals, Gays and Lesbians
ACDP	African Christian Democratic Party
AGA	African Gay Association
ANC	African National Congress
ASET	AIDS Support and Education Trust
CGE	Commission on Gender Equality
CODESA	Convention for a Democratic South Africa
COSAWR	Committee on South African War Resistance
CPD	Congress of Pink Democrats
ECC	End Conscription Campaign
FedSAW	Federation of South African Women
GALA	Gay and Lesbian Archives of South Africa
GALA	Gay and Lesbian Association
GALZ	Gays and Lesbians of Zimbabwe
GASA	Gay Association of South Africa (later GASA-6010)
GLC	Gay and Lesbian Counselling
GLO-P	(formerly GLOW-P, later OUT-LGBT-Wellbeing) Gay and Lesbian Organisation of Pretoria
GLOW	Gay and Lesbian Organisation of the Witwatersrand
HUMCC	Hope and Unity Metropolitan Community Church
ILGA	International Lesbian and Gay Association (formerly IGA)
LAGO	Lesbians and Gays Against Oppression
LGBT	Lesbian, gay, bisexual and transgender
LILACS	Lesbians in Love and Compromising Situations
NCGLE	National Coalition for Gay and Lesbian Equality (later Lesbian and Gay Equality Project)
NLRF	National Law Reform Fund
NUSAS	National Union of South African Students
OLGA	Organisation of Lesbian and Gay Activists (later Organisation of Lesbian and Gay Action)
OPAS	Organisation of People Against Sexism
PGLWG	Progressive Gay and Lesbian Working Group
RGO	Rand Gay Organisation
SADF	South African Defence Force
SANDF	South African National Defence Force
SHOC	Society for Homosexuals on Campus
SHRG	Scottish Homosexual Rights Group
TOGS	The Organisation for Gay Sports (formerly Transvaal Organisation of Gay Sport)
TRC	Truth and Reconciliation Commission
UDF	United Democratic Front
UWCO	United Women's Congress

Index

Achmat, Zackie 32, 68–9, 111, 118, 176, 199
African Christian Democratic Party (ACDP) 194–5
African Gay Association (AGA) 75, 80
African National Congress (ANC) 16, 20, 30, 42, 48, 81–2, 110, 119–34, 140–7, 148, 174–5, 181–6, 189–90; MK 126–7, 195; Women's League 20
Aliens Act 19
Alternative Service Group (University of the Witwatersrand) 122–3
Anti-Apartheid Movement (AAM) 124, 129, 141
Apostles of Civilised Vice 232
Association of Bisexuals, Gays and Lesbians (ABI-GALE) 83, 103, 232
Auerbach, Margaret 233
aVersion Project 233
Barrett, James 122–4
Berman, Kim 178–80
Black Sash 31, 107, 109, 187
Bosman, Pieter 35
Botha, Kevan 22, 30, 32, 36–48, 50–3, 83, 132–3, 158–63, 166–7, 175, 197, 206, 233–4
Botha, PW 18, 37, 52
Cameron, Edwin 32, 83–4, 94–5, 111, 139, 167, 174–6, 180–7, 195, 234–5
Capital Gay 131–2, 143, 145
Carolus, Cheryl 79
Charter of Gay and Lesbian Rights 83, 147, 178
Child Care Act 196
Christie, Ian 34, 75
Cohen, Steven 235
Commission on Gender Equality (CGE) 111
Committee on South African War Resistance (COSAWR) 121, 122, 127–29, 131
Congress of Pink Democrats (CPD) 42–5, 76, 81, 235
Constitution of South Africa (1996) 14, 20, 48, 81, 111, 133, 136–9, 175, 188–9, 192–208
Convention for a Democratic South Africa (CODESA) 174–5, 210–11
Davidson, Gerry 236
De Beer, Eddie 43
De Klerk, FW 74, 78
Defence Amendment Act 31
Defiant Desire 118
Delmas Treason Trial 20, 22, 29, 51–2, 144, 150–3, 191
De Pinho, Helen 236
Ditsie, Bev 65
Employment Equity Act (1998) 19, 197

End Conscription Campaign (ECC) 31–2, 77–8, 86–7, 102, 176, 187
Equality Clause 15, 19, 20, 21, 110, 112, 126, 136–7, 188–9, 192–8, 200, 205–8, 222
Equality Foundation 50, 133, 174–5, 210–11, 236–7
Exit 32, 37–8, 65, 237
Federation of South African Women (FedSAW) 98–101
Fine, Derrick 73, 118, 147, 237
Forest Town 16
Garmeson, Joe 237–8
Gay Advice Bureau 184
Gay and Lesbian Archives of South Africa (GALA) 136, 188; Oral History Project 247
Gay and Lesbian Association (University of Cape Town) 76, 101
Gay and Lesbian Counselling 238
Gay and Lesbian Organisation of Pretoria (GLO-P) 239
Gay and Lesbian Organisation of the Witwatersrand (GLOW) 18, 30–1, 64–7, 70, 83, 101, 110, 146–7, 174–6, 178, 184–5, 191, 205, 239
Gay and Lesbian Pride March 31, 74, 137, 191, 204–5
Gay Association of South Africa (GASA) 20, 29–30, 34–48, 50, 9–62, 64, 72, 101, 166, 191–2, 238; GASA-6010 (CT) 75, 101
Gay Christian Community 238
Gays and Lesbians of Zimbabwe (GALZ) 203
Gevisser, Mark 118
Ginwala, Frene 47, 119, 147
Greefswald 198
Guardianship Act 196
Heaton-Nicholls, Caroline 22, 30, 38, 41, 51, 158–63, 246
HIV/AIDS 19, 21, 32, 114, 170–1, 183, 197, 208
Hope and Unity Metropolitan Community Church (HUMCC) 31, 64–7, 240
International Gay and Lesbian Association (ILGA) 20, 22, 30, 34–48, 50–3, 75, 166, 192
Immorality Act 193; (1927) 16; (1957) 16, 17; (1969) 17, 240–1; (1988) 18
Judges' Remuneration Act 196, 199
Kraak, Gerald 118–35, 136–9, 241
Labour Relations Act (1995) 196
LAGO News 43
Lapinsky, Sheila 36, 73, 121, 145, 241
Lee's Place, Soweto 64
Lekota, Mosiuoa 'Terror' 29, 130, 150–3
Lesbians and Gays Against Oppression (LAGO) 72–8, 101, 242
Levine, Dr Aubrey 199

Lilacs (Lesbians in Love and Compromising Situations) 100, 112
Luirink, Bart 131
Mabuza, Lindiwe 46–7
Machela, Alfred 30, 36–9, 43–4, 46, 54–7, 76, 82, 242
Malindi, Gcina 41, 150
Mandela, Nelson 47
Mandela, Winnie 174, 178, 205
Matsile, Jerry 46
Mbeki, Thabo 119, 144–5, 149, 190
McGeary, Barry 243
Mhlanga, Bafana 177, 224–5
Mixed Marriages Act 16
Mokgethi, Paul 31, 243
Mokoena, Johnny 41
Mompati, Ruth 30, 132, 142–3, 190
Moore, Eliza 243
Mpe, Phaswane 21
Mugabe, Robert 200–1
National Coalition for Gay and Lesbian Equality v Minister of Justice 138
National Coalition for Gay and Lesbian Equality (NCGLE) 15, 19, 20, 32, 50, 130, 144, 147, 174–6, 192–5, 196–7, 202, 206, 212–21, 244–5
National Defence Act (2001) 19
National Union of South African Students (NUSAS) 120–2, 129
Nhlapo, Paddy 31, 68–70
Nicol, Julia 72–84, 145, 245–6
Nkoli, Simon 20–1, 29, 32, 36–48, 51–3, 64–5, 75, 80, 83, 91, 97, 150–5, 154–7, 164–5, 168–9, 190, 246–7
Nyathi, Cecil 66
Organisation of Lesbian and Gay Activists/Action (OLGA) 17–18, 47, 72–84, 101, 108, 110, 145–7, 178, 186, 242
Organisation of People Against Sexism (OPAS) 74
Pillay, Indres 126
Polmed 19
Prohibition of Mixed Marriages Act 16
Property of the State 248
Randall, Lee 248
Rand Gay Organisation (RGO) 30, 37, 39, 46, 76, 88–9
Rape Crisis 99–100, 108–9
Rapport 32, 170–1
Rundle, Donne 248–9
Sachs, Albie 82, 110, 119, 137, 146–7, 179, 185
Sampson, Wayne 249
Satchwell, Kathy 111

Saturday Group 37, 39, 166; see also GASA
Schiller, Greta 22
Scottish Homosexual Rights Group (SHRG) 34–5, 75–6
Sharpeville massacre (1960) 16
Shelton, Glen 32, 36, 42, 45, 46, 90
Shepherd, Roy 29, 36, 40, 44, 52, 65, 167, 249
Shott, Terry 129
Simon and I 249
Smith, Ann 36, 58–62, 249–50
Smith, Rupert 123, 128
Smith, Solly 30, 132, 143
Society for Homosexuals on Campus (SHOC) (University of the Witwatersrand) 174, 178, 185
South African Defence Force (SADF) 31, 43, 122, 198–9
South African National Defence Force (SANDF) 199
Southern African Liberation Support Committee 129
Soweto 64–5
Soweto Uprising (1976) 106, 127
Special Pension Fund Act 195
Stobbs, Paul 250
Tatchell, Peter 30, 75, 81, 140–7, 148, 190, 200–1
The Organisation of Gay Sports (TOGS) 251
Toms, Dr Ivan 31–2, 73, 77–8, 92–3, 97, 118, 131, 144, 251
Trengove Jones, Tim 251
Triangle Project 251
Truth and Reconciliation Commission (TRC) 22
Tutu, Archbishop Desmond 36, 174, 176–7, 223
United Democratic Front (UDF) 18, 20, 29–30, 42, 78–9, 98, 100, 101, 130, 133, 145, 147, 187, 190–1
United Nations: boycott of SA 40, 46
United Women's Congress (UWCO) 99, 100, 101
University of Cape Town 99, 100
University of the Witwatersrand 59, 65
'Vaal 22' 36–8, 41, 52
Van Zyl, Mikki 98–117
Velcich, Alan 252
Voss, Jon 36–48
Willett-Clarke, James 38
Williams, Cecil 22, 118, 140
Wits Gay Movement 76
Women's Alliance 107
Wotherspoon, Garry 82

255

Acknowledgements

Anthony Manion, archivist for the Gay and Lesbian Archives of South Africa (GALA), brought his expertise and meticulous attention to the book, for which the editors are deeply grateful.

Dennis Altman, professor of politics at Latrobe University, inadvertently sparked the idea for the book when his seminar 'Queer Centres and Peripheries', presented at the Wits Institute for Social and Economic Research in August 2003, provided the opportunity for a very South African discussion on 'how the clause got into the Constitution'.

Rachel Holmes provided wise counsel on the title.

The Wits Institute for Social and Economic Research (WISER) provided invaluable institutional support.

The Gay and Lesbian Archives of South Africa (GALA) opened their holdings to the project, and contributed towards the printing and reproduction costs of the book.

Archive material has been sourced from the Gay and Lesbian Archives of South Africa (GALA); the Department of Historical Papers, University of the Witwatersrand; IHLIA Internationaal homo/lesbisch informatiecentrum en archief, Amsterdam (www.ihlia.nl); *Rapport* newspaper; and Peter Tatchell's personal papers.

The editors acknowledge with thanks the permission given to reproduce the following material in this book:

Jacklyn Cock's 'Engendering Gay and Lesbian Rights: The Equality Clause in the South African Constitution' is reprinted from *Women's Studies International Forum* 26: 1, 2003, pp. 35–45, with permission from Elsevier.

Tim du Plessis, editor of *Rapport*, gave permission to reproduce the cartoon ''n Poefadder het my gepik'.

Photographic credits:

Mike Hutchings (Simon Nkoli and Ivan Toms)
Sabelo Mlangeni (Afterword photographs)